Praise for *Above Quota Sales Management*

"Steve Weinberg has done it again. His previous book provided salespeople with practical advice about B2B buying and the implications for core aspects of selling. *Above Quota Sales Management* takes that a big step further by focusing on sales managers as the key to improving selling performance. The book provides a smart, actionable and research-backed discussion of best practices in hiring, managing and coaching. Read it if you are a sales leader because, as Weinberg reminds us, in a changing world, 'by failing to prepare, you are preparing to fail.'"

—Frank Cespedes, Ph.D., Harvard Business School Professor and author of *Sales Management That Works: How to Sell in a World That Never Stops Changing.*

"WestWave Capital only invests in early start-ups with deep technology in the enterprise market. Many of our Founders come from engineering and deep product backgrounds. I always tell them half of your prospects won't buy from anyone. Steve's book should be read by all executives in the start-up world, not just sales managers. This still rarely happens in our market, where the industry talks about product-led sales. Most large enterprise customers require a technology vendor to understand their business requirements deeply, and they still want a personal relationship with the sales and customer success teams. With today's productivity tools for sales and revenue operations, replay video and *Above Quota Sales Management* will dramatically improve productivity, performance, and profit. Everyone needs to learn how to sell regardless of the role they run in the company they work for."

—Warren Weiss, Forbes Midas List of Technology's Top Investors and one of Business Insider's Top 100 Seed Investors.

"This is a book that should be on every sales leader's desk as an invaluable resource. It contains time-tested sales leadership insights from decades of learning and helping salespeople succeed. The author takes a closer look at the behavior patterns of salespeople with actionable advice on how to manage, lead, support and mentor new and experienced salespeople. The chapter on mental health is a must read. The insights on deploying AI in sales are very timely. A must read for newly promoted sales managers and a terrific success guide for the experienced sales leader."

—Gerhard Gschwandtner, CEO of *Selling Power Magazine.*

"My friend, Steve Weinberg, has published an important contribution to sales management. This book is the missing piece of his first book, *Above Quota Performance*. It is a comprehensive guide designed to help sales teams not just reach, but exceed their sales goals and targets. The book is divided into three major sections: the challenges of sales management, advanced sales techniques, and optimization - a factor often overlooked by sales managers who then struggle to meet quotas.

Steve highlights the fact that 50% of salespeople miss their goals. Recent data suggests that this number is decreasing, but this could be due to sales managers overvaluing pipeline coverage when they should be prioritizing win rates. Some of the issues include a lack of trust, poor leadership, and insufficient prospecting, which poses a real challenge for managers whose senior representatives rely on their existing clients and substantial commissions.

One section explains how to tailor conversations to the buyer's type, a strategy that can be categorized as "knowing your client." This section pairs well with the following one on how to hire and retain the best salespeople. Steve ventures into a tricky area with advice on compensation, a task that can be likened to following an elephant around at the circus—in other words, it's dirty work.

In a time when many salespeople report feeling burnt out, Steve offers help with mental health and wellbeing. This is something managers should pay careful attention to if they want to exceed quotas.

Read and practice what you find here and exceed your quota."

—Anthony Iannarino, bestselling author of five books including *The Only Sales Guide You'll Ever Need*, *The Lost Art of Closing*, *Eat Their Lunch*, *Elite Sales Strategies*, and *Leading Growth*.

"Steve provides an insightful, practical guide to mastering the role of a sales manager. Leveraging the success from his first book *Above Quota Performance*, Steve provides a deep dive into what it takes to be a successful Sales Manager. Sharing personal experience along with delving into several key areas, Steve lays out what a successful sales manager looks like and what those that aspire to be successful sales manager should be mindful of."

—Rick Tkaczak, President of Century Sales Solutions, LLC.

"Steve's breadth and in-depth knowledge of the evolving approaches to sales management is second to none! This book addresses a phenomena never dealt with previously, sales management during a pandemic! Steve tackles what makes sales management different though the same during unprecedented times!

—Jay Ryan, Principal of Executive Sales Playbook Advisors and formerly the Executive Vice President/Head of America's and Global Sales Team for Accuity, Inc, a RELX company.

"*Above Quota Sales Management* is an excellent read for the leadership of today's quickly evolving sales landscape. This informative and easy-to-read book provides practical and well-thought-out approaches to realizing effective management of high-performing sales teams. I was particularly struck by many of the useful insights, such as the 'Theory of Declining Interest' and the impacts of employee turnover. Mr. Weinberg also offers valuable perspectives on the quickly advancing facets of the sales environment, including 'How to Sell to Millennials' and describing what role AI will play in today's selling process. A 'must-read' for today's sales leaders."

—Robert McKay, Global Senior Vice President (Customer Identity and Risk Solutions) at Neustar, Inc., a TransUnion company.

"This is the most pragmatic approach to sales management I've seen and it's chock full of actionable insights. Steve takes the foundation he established in *Above Quota Performance* and provides sales management and leadership with the visibility and techniques needed to overcome today's sales challenges. This book differs from any other I've read on Sales Management in that it takes into consideration the real issues that sales managers must deal with – telecommuting, an incredibly slow return-to-office rate after COVID and the approach to working with different personality types and generational priorities – on both sides of the selling and buying processes. Forget the sales management books written in the past… this is the one you need for today and into the future."

—Steve Maul, Founder, The Semantics Group and Chief Revenue Officer, Innovative Systems, Inc.

"I learned a new word thanks to Steve Weinberg's new book: *firkrimptor*. And I learned a very important new to me statistic: Optimistic sales pros outperform pessimists by 57%. It's why it's so important sales pros must remove the firkrimptors—the sour pusses and negative people—from their lives and their teams. And that's just one of the nuggets in Steve's book. This book is full of them, from personality insights to how hire and how to compensate staff and so much more. A definite 'must-buy' for new and experienced sales leaders."

—Phil Gerbyshak, Chief Happiness Officer and author of *The Happiness Practices*.

"Very thorough and insightful book. It's clear Weinberg has an intrinsic understanding of the world class methodologies available today with a practical touch, based on his wealth of experience, that shows when and where to maximize the benefits. Very refreshing to read."

—Michael Hayes, Vice President, Global Sales, Hubino

"Steve Weinberg has written a book that offers both practical and insightful advice for sales managers to improve the performance of their sales team. Steve's insight into the different personality types of buyers provides sales managers with a fresh perspective on how this important knowledge can help sales representatives alter their presentations to better match the personality of the buyer to increase their closing percentage. Weinberg goes well beyond the typical classifications of extrovert and introvert to explore in surprising detail the 16 different personality types every sales representative will be meeting in the real world. While most sales managers focus on training their sales representatives to learn the corporate sales pitch, Weinberg offers valuable insight to why learning more about the buyer's personality is essential to improving overall sales performance."

—Jenifer Patterson, Creative Director,
The TJB American Business Magazine.

"Steve Weinberg has done it again with *Above Quota Sales Management*. A master salesperson and relationship builder, Steve put all of his wisdom in simple lesson format in this book and it will transform your sales team's skill set to new levels! Steve is a sales Ninja!"

—Tom Markert, FORTUNE 5000 CEO, CMO, CSO and Board Director with Nielsen, Office Depot, IPSOS, True Value.

ABOVE QUOTA
SALES MANAGEMENT

ARMINLEAR

Library of Congress Control Number: 2024930643

ISBN (paperback): 978-1-963271-05-8
ISBN (Ebook): 978-1-963271-06-5

Armin Lear Press, Inc.
215 W Riverside Drive, #4362
Estes Park, CO 80517

ABOVE
QUOTA
SALES MANAGEMENT

**Tips and Techniques to Get the Best
Out of Your Sales Team**

Steve Weinberg

ARMINLEAR

"When a team takes ownership of its problems, the problem gets solved. It is true on the battlefield, it is true in business, and it is true in life."
—John Gretton "Jocko" Willink, former Navy SEAL

This book is dedicated to my grandchildren
Hanna, Lawrence Reed, Stella,
Thijs, Olive, and Holden.

I also dedicate this book to special relatives and
friends that have recently passed:
Timothy M. Berry
Donald H. Breede
Dale M. Friedman
Patricia W. Greene
William L. Goldberger
Marshall K. Hechter
James M. McCormack
Hitesh H. Patel
Patrick A. Potts
Bryan Palm
Merrill G. Stanley
Mark S. Stoyas

CONTENTS

FOREWORD

I have seen many successful enterprise sales pros, and I have unfortunately also seen scores of unsuccessful ones. In my first book, *Above Quota Performance*, the tips and techniques presented were those that had worked for me over the years and were intended to help other sales pros. I was often the top-selling sales pro or the sales manager in my organization, and I became the VP of Sales at several leading companies. While those tips are great for individual sales pros, there is another component to the success of a sales team at any company, and that is the management factor. Many sales managers fail to realize the role they play in their sales pros' success and how to provide them the support and training needed to achieve "above quota performance."

This book builds on the theme of improving sales performance, but its primary purpose is to help the sales manager build winning sales teams that consistently achieve their new sales goals. Within these pages, I will discuss best practices in hiring, managing, and coaching sales pro: how to work in a more collaborative environment with other areas of the company, especially marketing; the role of AI and sales-enablement tools; the importance of utilizing the latest technology to create more opportunities and win more competitive sales; and the importance of supporting your sales force's unique mental health needs. In addition, this book focuses on the sales leadership skills that are needed to compete in the 2020s with the new generation of sales pros and on how to determine the best sales organizational design for your company to achieve and exceed sales goals.

This book is also intended for use by CEOs, entrepreneurs, venture capital investors, and founders of start-ups as a guide on how to establish, build, and optimize a high-performing sales-force and the best practices that will help them avoid some of the typical landmines of building a salesforce. I am confident that sales managers that embrace the tips, techniques, suggestions, and advice that are included in this book will achieve greater sales results immediately.

SECTION 1

Overcoming the
50 Percent Failure Rate

In my previous book, *Above Quota Performance*, I noted that third-party research concluded that the average percentage of sales pros not reaching their sales quota each year is approximately 50 percent. This exceptional failure rate is widely accepted and not often challenged. Corporate CEOs and Chief Revenue Officers (CRO) say they want to fix the problem of such low sales quota attainment. "Exceeding targets continues to be the top goal of sales pros in 2022. In a HubSpot survey, 45% of respondents cited exceeding targets as a top priority."[1] But, if it is such a high priority, why isn't more being done to alter it? The positive financial impact of reducing the failure rate to 35 or even 40 percent would be enormous and could possibly change the profitability of many companies. And it would certainly result in less sales staff turnover, saving hundreds of thousands of dollars for many companies in hiring, training, and termination costs. But I don't see a "moonshot" effort on the part of company executives to fix the problem. Why?

Takeaway 1 – Many CEOs, CROs, and VPs of Sales Accept the 50 Percent Failure Rate

Many company CEOs seem to accept the 50 percent failure rate as an immutable cost of doing business. Like gravity, or the past, it cannot be changed. Some find this sales failure rate intractable, and it is treated as such. Their attention is focused on other priorities, such as bringing new products to market, cost reduction, earnings per share, potential mergers and acquisitions, and causes such as environmental, social and governance (ESG) issues. But changing the lack of success by sales pros isn't like modifying the laws of physics, and I believe it can be challenged and successfully overcome.

But doing so requires a fresh and radical approach, something that most CEOs and VPs of Sales have been unwilling to take the risk to accomplish. They understand the benefits but are reluctant to incur the initial costs or the disruptions of a major change. Or they fear the unknown of making a significant change. The alternative, doing the same things, perhaps with a stronger emphasis on one area or greater micromanagement, may yield an improvement, but will not result in a radical change of results. And the old style of management by intimidation is no longer socially or morally acceptable, especially with the Millennials and Generation Z sales pros. In fact, it is counter-productive and will result in lower morale and poorer results.

In addition, managers responsible for sales teams need to be more confident that they can achieve their team goals. "A whopping 84% of sales leaders today do not actually believe they have the team to make great results and achieve success."[2] Does that mean they don't have properly trained and qualified sales pros, that they have open positions, or that they do not have adequate marketing plans in place to drive new business? The answer is "yes" to all the above.

According to Brainshark and Forbes, "C-level executives in particular know that sales productivity is, in fact, paramount to enabling a company to grow—71% rank it as of critical importance."[3] Increases in sales training and the growth of the sales enablement functions are evidence of the recognition by business executives that corporations must make investments to increase sales productivity. This will be discussed further in Chapter 8.

CHAPTER 1

Identifying the Causes of the Persistent Problem

There is no consensus on how to solve the problem of low sales quota attainment. But there is agreement on what many of the causes are for the failure. In many cases the causes cited for the failure rate depend on who is reporting.

Many sales pros will say it is because quotas are too high. But if 50 percent fail then 50 percent are successful. So, quotas are usually not the problem. Sales pros will also state that they do not receive enough leads. But I have never worked for an organization that provided sales pros with sufficient leads to achieve the sales volume to reach or exceed their quota. In every case, the sales pros had to initiate their own sales programs or prospect for new leads to build an adequate sales pipeline. Not receiving enough leads contributes to failure, but high performers will source their own leads and won't rely on the company to provide them.

Most companies set their quotas, and sales compensation plans, with the assumption that approximately 60 percent of the sales pros will reach their annual sales quota.

My research indicates the following are fifteen key contributors to sales failure, listed in approximate priority order (very difficult since all are important):

1. Not creating trust with the buyer team
2. Lack of compelling value propositions
3. Substandard sales leadership
4. Sales pros not thoroughly qualifying suspects and leads
5. Not receiving a commitment from the buyers to provide adequate time and attention in return for the sales pros' time and effort
6. Limited accessibility of buyers' staff to sellers, resulting in fewer face-to-face meetings
7. Inadequate prospecting, including not targeting the ideal prospects (in the "Sweet Spot")
8. Lack of sales time with the buyers to discuss their issues and your proposed solution
9. Insufficient contact or meetings with the economic buyer/key decision-maker
10. Selling based on price and not on value
11. Deficient communication and confusing messaging to prospects and poor follow-up
12. Insufficient sales team onboarding efforts and time allowance before going on quota
13. Recent trend of not bringing suppliers in early and resultant shorter sales cycles
14. Not enough differentiation from competition
15. Too much time wasted on internal meetings and tasks

None of the above reasons are recent developments, nor are they the result of changes in the marketplace. Most are the result of not executing the basics of good salesmanship. For example, I have seen excessive amounts of time wasted on prospects that were not properly qualified or were way outside of the sellers "Sweet Spot." The sales pros either were lazy, not properly trained, or had "happy ears," meaning they only heard what they wanted to hear from the buyers. They also did not understand the fundamentals of the mathematics of the funnel.

Sales pros also have a difficult time extracting themselves from prospects once they determine they are not going to buy in the current sales period, perhaps because they have built a friendship with them or because they do not understand that the time they are wasting could be better applied to more qualified prospects. Sometimes this is the result of investing so much time on an account that sales pros believe that they should continue calling on the prospect with the hope that they will close soon. But it doesn't happen. And the result is that they have wasted a lot of their precious time on a prospect that will not buy from them. It is an emotional response, not a logical one, and has been termed the "sunken cost fallacy," which is defined as investing time, effort, or money into endeavors, regardless of whether the benefits exceed the costs.

There are also varying degrees of competencies of sales management. Mostly I have seen sales managers simply monitor sales forecasts and pipelines from the comfort of their office. Many do not go out with the sales pros on in-person calls to offer invaluable hands-on "one on one" coaching and call debriefs (which will be discussed in more detail later), but rather offer advice on closing deals from afar. This is inadequate sales leadership and needs to be addressed to improve results.

A logical cure for the low sales closing rate would be a re-emphasis of simple sales basics. Most sales teams have annual (or quarterly) sales training or sales refresher sessions. But this is not enough. Sales pros attend the sessions and then return to their habitual sales practices. The reality is that many experienced sales pros, who have been properly trained, often consciously choose to ignore the basics, believing that their sales craftmanship is above average. And by ignoring the basics, sales pros fail more than those that pay more attention to doing a better job of qualifying their prospects: for example, sales managers, who are often strug-gling to staff and train their teams, frequently do not hold their team members accountable for their deficient actions and results. And the time managers spent on sales training is often wasted.

Complicating matters, it is much more difficult for sales pros to be successful now than it has been in the past, even as recently as two or three years ago. Competition amongst sellers is tougher and, in many cases, sales pros need to compete against low-cost providers. Most decisions are now made by committees consisting of many functional areas within a company, rather than a small group of one to three people. It is often more difficult to gain access to all the key people involved in the decision.

So, we have had a perfect storm: sellers are not executing sales basics; they have less access to the buyers; buyers have become more educated; competition is tougher—and then the coronavirus happened in 2020.

The Effects of the Coronavirus on Selling

When the world encountered the coronavirus pandemic in early 2020, employees no longer went into their offices and instead telecommuted. Sellers were not allowed to physically visit their prospects. Video applications such as Zoom and Skype became the de facto standards for sales meetings. In addition, the coronavirus pandemic completely turned selling upside-down and altered the accessibility of buyers to sellers, and the travel policies of most companies prohibited visits as well.

The whole sales paradigm changed on the spot in 2020, without any warning; everybody—sellers and buyers—were caught unprepared.

Sellers had to quickly make the following eight adjustments due to the coronavirus:

1. Both sellers and buyers had to adapt to the new paradigm of limited access and fewer opportunities to meet in person. Sales pros had to adapt their sales cycles and methodologies to the newly changed environment. In addition, buyers were also not as available as they once were to all suppliers, even virtually. And buying teams had to learn to collaborate on a videoconference rather than in person.

2. The marketplace became more digital. Social media is now where most buyers (especially millennials) are doing buying research.

3. Buyers tended to be far more educated on what is available in the marketplace now.

4. Sales pros needed to provide more compelling value propositions to gain the attention of the buying team.

5. Sales pros had to become masters at using videoconferencing technologies. This required understanding how to optimize the video experience, including lighting and sound, but also etiquette. (I saw a lot of time wasted by people that were unfamiliar with how to launch and manage a teleconference.)

6. Companies needed to make drastic changes to their websites and marketing collateral to recognize the change in the digital marketplace. Printed material is no longer as important as how the company presents itself on its websites and social media.

7. Sales managers had to do a much better job at onboarding and coaching in this new virtual environment.

8. Socially conscious purchasing has become more important in the post-pandemic area. Sellers needed to communicate what their company was doing to make the world a better place.

But, except in unusual cases, sales quotas for 2020 were not reduced and sales pros were held to the same levels of achievement under a completely different, and indeed hostile, environment.

This change is permanent; selling is not going back to the way it was before the pandemic. CFOs at the selling companies have adjusted their financial budgets to reflect the reduction in travel and entertainment expenses, and increases in profitability, and they have seen that the company can continue to operate in this manner. Both sellers and buyers have adjusted to the "new normal" and it is unlikely that a return to the pre-2020 sales and buying practices will occur. Those that do not accept this are doomed to fail in 2023 and beyond.

To best transition to this new style of selling, the sales pro needs to consider these seven suggestions:

1. Schedule more telephone or video conversations with the buying team *before* the sales presentation than previously. Build stronger relationships with the buyers, in the absence of a personal visit, and learn more about what they are trying to accomplish. The sales pro needs to stress the mutual benefit of these calls. Don't abuse their time—keep the calls short and to the point.

2. Construction of a well-prepared meeting agenda, before the meeting, is critical. It should cover all the areas that are important to the buyer and should be agreed upon with the prospect in advance. Also, the content needs to be able to be covered comfortably within the timeframe. It is important that the meeting does not end prematurely, without a close, because you have run out of time.

3. Almost every videoconference I have attended has begun with technical or audio difficulties. The sales pro should contact each attendee in advance to familiarize them with the video software and ask everybody to access the meeting at least ten minutes before the beginning to work out any issues.

4. Videoconferences can be recorded for those that cannot attend the meeting. This is a sub-optimal substitute for attending it live, but it offers the salesperson the opportunity to reach any absent person.

5. If the presenter is not the sales pro, there should be complete agreement within the selling company on the outline of the meeting and the roles of each person. The sales pro should be very active during the meeting, with interruptions to check-point whether there are any questions, a desire to go into an area not on the agenda, or if the agenda needs to be altered because of time constraints.

6. Videoconferencing frees up the time many sales pros have spent traveling and will allow time to contact more prospects. This should increase sales productivity and results, even considering the probable decrease in the win/close ratio due to the lack of in-person contact.

7. Since there are no in-person introductions and handshaking at the beginning of the meeting, the sales pro must create more effective meeting introductions than in the past. This should consist of greater discussion of the buyer's roles and function in the company, the project background and timeline, as well as a greater explanation of the goals of this meeting.

In addition to the changes due to the pandemic, the recession of 2022 added challenges to the sales environment as well. Companies typically cut back on non-essential purchases and hold off on filling open staff positions during recessions. But companies still need to fix broken systems, such as a supply chain issue, and obey compliance issues and federal and state regulations.

An effect of recession on sales cycles is that larger expenditures may require additional justification. Sales pros need to work with the buying team, and perhaps their finance staff, in computing a positive return on investment (ROI) that is substantially beyond a break-even.

Buyers are far more educated and discerning in the digital marketplace. This has already resulted in sellers experiencing shorter sales cycles. (Actually, sales cycles take about the same amount of time as they always have, but sellers are often not brought in at the beginning of the cycle, so it feels shorter.) Sellers should be able to find more qualified prospects because only the more serious buyers will provide them with any time to discuss their needs and review proposals. There will be fewer "tire-kickers." Sellers also can use the latest technology to emphasize how they can provide value to the buyer.

On the Positive Side

We have entered a new marketplace with tremendous opportunities for sales managers and sales pros who adapt to the changes to prosper. They must be nimble to take advantage of the changes in the post-pandemic, digital marketplace. They must recognize and properly react to the changes. Sales managers must prepare their sales pros by discarding their previous sales methodologies and practices. This requires immediate, unique approaches to prospecting and business development practices, new value propositions, updated marketing collateral, and follow-up techniques that sales managers must lead. In addition, sales and marketing managers need to better understand how to take advantage of the tremendous potential of utilizing social media, especially with Millennials. The sales pros' 50 percent failure rate in achieving their annual sales quotas has continued to endure for the reasons listed above. This failure rate is not immutable, and though not easy, it can be changed to a smaller percentage. Suggestions on how to achieve this will be discussed in the next chapter.

The enterprise selling paradigm changed dramatically in the 2020s. This is due to technology, the ages of the audience (more Millennials in the workforce), and the coronavirus pandemic that closed many corporate offices for most of 2020, all of 2021, and into 2022. Accessibility of buyers in person became impossible. Sales meetings and presentations shifted to video platforms such as Zoom, Vimeo, and Microsoft Team. As we enter the post-pandemic period, sales pros have found that they are not returning to the pre-pandemic practices. The sales paradigm has shifted: CEOs and CFOs are very happy with the reduction in the cost of sales and will resist resuming the old practices.

The coronavirus pandemic is not just impacting the style of B2B sales, it also is transforming other commercial enterprises, such as real-estate, insurance, vehicle purchases, consumer goods, and financial advisor/wealth management practices. Also, much of our secondary and university level education has been shifted to video instruction as well.

Like the dinosaur and woolly mammoth, those who fail to adapt will become extinct.

CHAPTER 2

Solutions for the Sales Manager to Fix the 50 Percent Failure Rate

The sales manager has a significant role in altering the 50 percent failure rate of sales pros achieving their annual sales quota. It requires changes in managing style and a paradigm shift in the management of the sales pros' sales cycles. Sales managers must be more involved in the onboarding and training of sales pros, as well as day-to-day coaching sales pros to improve their sales skills and follow-up techniques. Sales managers need to be more hands-on than they have been in the past and must do more than just manage pipeline reports and forecasts. It is not easy changing how one has managed a sales team, but it is mandatory to achieve consistent success in the post-pandemic digital marketplace.

How does a sales manager achieve this? It's no easy task. Here are a few suggestions:

- **Be patient:** The change will not happen overnight. It is not unlike changing a company's go-to-market strategy. Your company must be willing to change from being short-term profit-oriented to looking at an investment that will yield greater results in the long term.

- **Re-emphasize sales basics:** Pay special attention to understanding your target market and Sweet Spot, increasing prospecting efforts, better qualification of leads, utilizing questioning techniques, using superior listening skills, building rapport and trust, selling based on value not price, attentive follow-up, and closing at the proper time.

- **Motivate your team:** Sales management must properly manage and motivate their team members. They must hold them accountable for reaching their sales targets.

- **Re-examine your hiring process:** What is the profile of a good sales pro? Are you trying to hire younger, more inexperienced sales pros and then develop them, or older, more experienced, and probably more expensive, sales pros that may be more set in their ways. What is your current interviewing process?

- **Set achievable goals:** Are your sales quotas reasonable and achievable? How do you know? Have they been validated recently? How many people achieved their quota last year? (60 – 70 percent of the total number of sales pros should be able to do so.) Have the quotas been set from top-down revenue planning? The sales manager's quota should not be the sum of the individual quotas of the sales pros reporting to them.

- **Retain your high-performing sales pros:** Retaining your high-performing sales pros and reducing turnover are key to reducing the failure rate. Have you conducted exit interviews? There will be valuable information gained from them. Did they receive enough sales and product training? Did they feel they were mistreated? If so, how? What were their expectations? Where did the company fail? We'll look into this more later in Chapter 10.

Takeaway 2 – Retention of High-Performers is Key to Reducing the Sales Pro Failure Rate

- Invest in an onboarding program and sales enablement function to promote sales quota success. This would include a dedicated sales enablement person assigned to this task. Bigtincan noted that CSO Insights reported, "The percentage of salespeople achieving quota at organizations with a formal sales enablement charter stands at 73.6%. The average quota attainment across the study was 57.7% and this represents 27.6% improvement."[4]
- Have the new sales pros shadow high performers by attending sales calls with them.
- Examine how sales pros spend their time. Often, they waste time chasing unqualified prospects and on non-sales tasks, such as entering and updating data in the CRM system, working on RFPs, attending internal

meetings, and on customer satisfaction issues. These activities take as much as 30 percent of a sales pro's work time. Updating CRM should be completed before 9:00 a.m. or after 5:00 p.m. each day. And the CRM should work for the sales pro, not the other way around.

- New hires should visit existing customers to learn more about the value they are receiving from your company's products or services. Or ask some of your customers to come to your office and address your new hires. I am reminded of a very insightful quote from sales trainer Jon Selig: "Most reps sell solutions they've never used, to people whose jobs they've never had, in industries they've never worked in"[5] Sales pros should try to learn about their products and services from customers (not the marketing or product marketing staff), learn about their day-to-day jobs, and immerse themselves in the industry so that they become familiar with key trends and jargon.

- Enforce whichever training program your company chooses. During my career, I attended at least twenty sales training meetings. They ranged from good to outstanding, but 100 percent of the time sales management did not follow through on the sales trainer's ideas and recommendations. And this was not unique to the companies I worked for. "According to a recent survey, 84% of all sales training is lost after 90 days."[6]

- The blunt instruments of sales edicts and executive and sales management ultimatums will not improve the long-term results.

- Recognize that sales managers are key to improving sales pros' performances. The managers should receive separate sales training from their teams on different topics, such as how to provide timely coaching to their teams, hiring tips, and how to help underperformers.
- Measure your success or lack of success with each change and adapt accordingly.
- Follow up with sales pros regularly to assure that they use the training they've received and to reinforce its principles.

Absent the changes such as those proposed above, I do not see the 50 percent failure rate changing very much in the future. Sales managers need to make the proper investments to see a reduction in the failure rate and a positive return on their investment. Despite the popular myth, Albert Einstein did not say, "Insanity is doing the same thing over and over again and expecting different results," but, nonetheless, this surely applies to not making changes to your sales staffing, onboarding, and training practices and expecting an improvement in results.[7]

The Number One Mistake That Sales Pros Make!

I have often been asked by sales managers what I considered to be the number one mistake many sales pros make. I can think of a top ten very easily, but just one? There are so many to consider. So here are my top ten in no specific order, (much as I would like to rank them, I just can't seem to do it!):

1. Failing to put in place an effective personal prospecting program

2. Failing to properly qualify prospects
3. Failing to properly explain your value proposition
4. Failing to call on the real decision maker
5. Failing to understand their "real why" for purchasing
6. Failing to ask trial close questions at appropriate times
7. Failing to welcome all objections
8. Failing to understand the prospect's buying process
9. Failing to build a sufficient pipeline to reach the sales quota
10. Failing to prepare a compelling business case to inspire the prospect to decide to change from the status quo

The Easiest to Fix

There is one overarching theme to the issues above, and high-performing sales managers have a role in fixing it—that many sales pros do not *listen*. Listening is paying attention to *and* effectively interpreting what other people are saying. It completely focuses on what the prospect tells you—*listening* is not just *hearing*. Hearing is the recognition of noise. Listening is an active exercise that "requires training, persistence, effort, and most importantly, the intention to become a good listener."[8] Make no mistake, listening is a skill that needs to be developed and enhanced, perhaps like playing a musical instrument. And listening needs to be practiced extensively to excel at it, indeed, even to be proficient.

Takeaway 3 – Sales Pros (and Sales Managers, too) Need to Listen, Not Just Hear

Do you remember playing the game "telephone" when you were young? The participants would sit in a circle, and one person would whisper a secret to the person seated next to her. Then that person whispered the secret to the next person with one additional bit of information, and so on. The last person in the circle then said the secret out loud. Often the secret was changed in both words and meaning. How does this happen? I suggest it is simply because of poor listening skills.

Here are some top examples of sales pros exhibiting poor listening skills. These can all be observed and corrected by sales managers:

1. The sales pro needs to listen better during the qualification of a lead. Some sales pros tend to have "happy ears" and hear what they want to hear. They didn't pay attention when the prospect said she was not committed to making a change this year, or that she has not run her idea by the executive sponsor. This results in time wasted on an unqualified or unmotivated prospect.

2. The sales pro does an inadequate job of learning the prospect's needs because they are more interested in selling their product or solution than listening to the prospect. They jump into a selling mode quickly after the introduction. These sales pros are not concerned with what it means for the prospect, but only for their own goals.

3. Talking over the buyers or interrupting them. I saw this all the time. The sales pro didn't wait for the prospect to finish talking before they interrupted.

4. Getting ready to speak while the other is speaking. Instead of listening to what the prospect says and then

contemplating a response, they start thinking of their response while the prospect is still speaking.

5. When discussing objections, some sales pros get defensive and try to counter them as they are spoken, or written, without taking the time to drill down and understand the real reason or issue for the objection.

Sales Managers Can Help Sales Pros Improve Their Listening Skills

Sales managers should work with sales pros to improve their listening skills. There are many ways to do this. One of my recommended methods is to hold exercises at team meetings and individual training where a sales pro can practice gaining better listening skills. For example, ask a sales pro to speak about any subject for four to six minutes and challenge the other sales pros to:

1. Not interrupt
2. Maintain silence and eye contact
3. Pay attention to any nonverbal language by the speaker
4. Not check their smartphone or emails
5. Raise one's hand when requesting to speak
6. Ask clarifying questions at the conclusion.

Afterward, ask sales pros to summarize what they heard and repeat back as much of the story as possible to the speaker or the group. Ask the person speaking to evaluate how well you listened to them. You can also make each succeeding story more difficult by adding details, such as where it occurred, how people were dressed, emotions, etc. Do this exercise several times a year until your team has mastered listening. These team exercises can be fun, and there are many other listening exercises that you can try.

When coaching an individual sales pro, the sales manager's first step to improve listening is to ask the sales pro to put away his smartphone and turn and face the person speaking to him. Advise him to lean forward physically (but not get too close!) rather than sit relaxed to let the speaker know he is paying complete attention, and focus on the content and any expressions, volume, and body language of the prospect. Remind him that these signals can help him understand how the person he speaks with perceives him—as a friend or foe. Like any skill, listening proficiency and comprehension will improve as your sales pros practice it.

Takeaway 4 – Sales Pros Should Ask Open-Ended Questions to Solicit More Feedback from Buyers.

Sales pros can also improve their listening proficiency by asking open-ended questions (those not answered with a "yes" or "no") and focusing on listening to their responses. They should not interrupt when others are speaking.

Also, they should commit to only responding to a question or comment once they completely understand what the prospect has said or written. If a sales pro is having trouble with this, the next time they have a conversation with their prospect, advise them to mentally count to ten before responding and reflect on what they just heard and its effect on their pitch and value proposition. The prospect will believe that your sales pro has listened to their concerns before you respond, which will improve the conversation's success. Sales pros may then need to change their sales strategies. Improving listening skills will have the greatest impact on changing your sales team's results.

"When we shift from 'listening to respond' to 'listening to understand,' we can move mountains."[9] Fixing the 50 percent failure rate is not hopeless, but reducing the rate does require consequential adjustments. The likelihood is that your organization assumes that it is unchangeable, so if you can reduce competitive losses, and increase your team's win rate, you would be making a significant positive contribution to the bottom line of the company. In addition, your sales pros will benefit from greater satisfaction, higher earnings, better self-esteem, and a longer career at your company.

Teaching your sales pros to listen better will not only help them in their sales careers but will also benefit them throughout all aspects of their lives. And becoming better listeners will positively impact their win rate. They will understand their prospect's issues better, which will increase their credibility. And, by encouraging them to wait before responding to questions, they will be greatly appreciated by all people with whom they converse.

CHAPTER 3
Aligning Sales and Marketing in Your Company

I have been employed by several technology companies where the goals and strategies of the sales and marketing departments were not aligned and, in some cases, conflicted. If they were aligned, both areas (and the company) would have benefitted from the synergy. I believe this is common in many corporations, regardless of the size. Some sales enablement solutions attempt to solve the misalignment between sales and marketing. Still, the misalignment cannot be solved with a technology solution but rather through executive management and communication.

The Benefits of Sales and Marketing Alignment

A *Brainshark and Forbes* survey found that "the fact that companies with strong alignment between the marketing and sales departments come out on the top of the sales productivity scale.

Three-quarters (74 percent) of top-performing companies report good alignment between their sales and marketing departments, compared with just half (49%) of other firms. In fact, most companies (87%) that are below their revenue plan report poor alignment between sales and marketing teams."

The symbiotic relationship between sales and marketing is critical for sales to function effectively. Sales can exist without marketing, but it is like a person swimming using only one arm. You may be able to get where you're going, but it will be much more difficult.

"Arguably, the relationship between sales and marketing is the most important one within a company when it comes to driving sales productivity. Half (52%) of top performers say that working closely with marketing to better support value selling with content is the top way that sales support (sales operations) can drive sales productivity, compared with 32% for other firms. Next in importance for top performers is working closely with marketing to define and create more relevant content. This is also the top method identified by the rest of the companies."[10]

Takeaway 5 – The Marketing/Sales Problem Begins with the Budget

The divergence between marketing and sales usually begins with the annual budgeting process. The CEO and finance staff develop the budget with their goals for the next year. The Chief Marketing Officer (CMO) is rarely given enough budget money to adequately complete the goals of the company, which now include maintaining a superior website, advertising, branding, marketing collateral, public and investor relations, and participation in trade shows. Marketing usually asks for additional staff to accomplish the goals. But when the budget requests are accumulated the CEO goes back and tells marketing they can add one or two people, but they still must accomplish the goals given to them with a minimal increase in their budget. So, the CMO goes back to her staff and tells them they must work extra hard to accomplish the goals and they do not have any time to take on any other projects. In addition, the marketing department is forced to reduce the advertising and trade show budgets, which are often the first casualties of a tight budget. That is where the problem begins.

The Vice President of Sales is also given a new revenue goal, which is an (often ambitious) increase in sales over the prior year. But the VP of Sales is often able to add staff to reach the goal. At various points throughout the year, sales pros will go to the marketing department and ask for assistance. It could be to update a PowerPoint presentation, or to help format a Request for Proposal, or a specific marketing collateral request. Since marketing does not have the resources available to respond to the request there is a "disconnect." Marketing will either tell the sales pro they will get to the project when and if they have time, or they decline to help. The sales pro goes to her manager and the conflict may be escalated. Hopefully, the two managers of sales and marketing are friendly and can work out some compromise, which usually results in marketing personnel working overtime. But sometimes they cannot work it out, resulting in acrimony between the two groups.

Chief Marketing Officers "rank demand generation as the top way that marketing can add unique value to organizational strategy, but many organizations struggle to convert top-of-funnel lead generation performance to later-stage commercial outcomes."[11] Yet, I have not worked for a company, *or ever heard of one,* where the marketing department generated sufficient (or even 50 percent of sufficient) quality leads to supply the sales pipeline.

There are other disconnects: Often, the goals of the two groups are not compatible. For example, marketing may be working on new branding or on helping to bring a new product to market while sales may have a priority to enter the Asian and African markets by staffing in those areas. And, in many companies, there is minimal, if any, communication between the members of the marketing and sales departments. They are also often located separately in the company so informal contact between the two groups is minimal.

Now a Solution

An optimum situation is one in which the CMO and VP of Sales are given joint goals that must be accomplished by both. That means that the marketing and sales departments both own the revenue goals as well as the new branding or new market goals of the company. The CMO receives a bonus if the revenue goal is reached, and the VP of Sales is given a bonus if specific marketing goals are accomplished. (It is amazing what happens when a bonus is involved.)

If advertising and trade shows need to be cut back, then the sales department needs to prioritize the costs of those versus costs included in their budgets, such as for additional sales pros, pre-sales pros, travel and expenses, expenditures on applications such as CRM, and even new laptops. If the sales department feels that advertising and trade shows are priorities for lead generation, they can help fund the expenditure.

To increase communication between the two departments there are scheduled meetings where specified staff meet and discuss all outstanding issues that have carried over from the prior meeting or are new for this period. In addition, I suggest that informal lunches or after-hour gatherings are held where members of both departments are encouraged to meet each other, socialize, and discuss any personal issues that any may have with the other group.

Why Marketing Messages are Often Ineffective

According to Highspot, a leading sales enablement company, "70% of (marketing) content goes unused."[12] That is a startling statistic and indicates to me that many marketing departments are very busy producing material that nobody wants to use.

The marketing professionals I have met or worked with have had good intentions and wanted to help the company promote its image and products, build brand loyalty, write copy, create effective marketing programs, handle essential publicity, build an impressive website, place the company in relevant trade shows, and create sales leads. The effort is usually there—but as one of my managers told me, "Don't confuse activity with results."

However, I have found that many marketing messages are ineffective and often confusing. Perhaps the marketing staff was focusing on being unique and creative, rather than on the objective: promoting the company, the product, or its benefits. The messages most often do not answer the key question that most prospects are interested in: "What's in it for me if I buy your product or service?"

Takeaway 6 – Sales Pros Need to Review the Content of Your Company's Marketing Messages

But the marketing messages are often full of clichés, superfluous jargon, or artsy images that the marketing professionals believe will attract viewers. But what do these tell you about the company, the products, or most importantly, how the buyer will benefit from doing business with your company? Isn't the objective to get the buyer interested enough to seek more information? Or perhaps it is to impress buyers with the company's talent?

I have found current customers and prospects to be an incredible resource for knowledge of current trends. In addition, they have helped me understand the value they received from our products and services. I have attended many executive meetings, as VP of Sales, and have often repeated requests from customers and prospects and was told that they, or I, didn't know what they were talking about. (This happened a lot when I worked for a large marketing research company.) The reality is that the customers and prospects knew more than our product marketing teams did. This was because they were currently encountering many of the issues and needed immediate solutions. The marketing department was usually six months to two years behind due to their focus on projects that they had committed to completing during the current period, often more than one year ago.

One time I was so frustrated with my management team's rejection of the input I was providing that I asked a customer's marketing research executive to come in and directly address our executive team at our regularly scheduled staff meeting, which he willingly did at his company's expense. Afterward, I was told by my peers that this person did not know what he was doing. And, unfortunately, they ignored his input.

A simple answer is that your company's marketing and product management staff needs to visit customers and prospects regularly to solicit information. Surveys are not adequate—it needs to be a person-to-person conversation. And they need to listen to the customer or prospect—not come in with their own assumptions that they try to validate!

To summarize, many companies have not solved the critical alignment of their sales and marketing functions. It seems to be a "no brainer" that these two functional areas would work well together, but that is often not the case, for the reasons I cited above.

Marketing's function used to be centered around improving brand awareness, advertising, trade shows, public relations, producing materials and collateral, and campaign management. In recent years the responsibility of building and maintaining a website and handling social media has usually been added to the marketing function. The importance of having an impressive, "world-class," website and a strong presence on social media cannot be overstated. The result, given these new responsibilities and usually accompanied by a less than generous budget, has been stress between the marketing and sales functions. And the latter often complain that they do not receive enough leads.

I have suggested that the goals and objectives of both the sales and marketing executives be aligned and shared. Standard weekly, bi-weekly, or monthly conversations between the sales and marketing executives and their subordinates need to be initiated to promote cohesion, a stronger partnership, and greater cooperation.

The sales function needs to participate in assuring that the marketing messages resonate better with their buyers and the marketing department needs to get out of the building and visit customers and prospects regularly.

SECTION 2

Advanced Sales Techniques

This is the section that many sales managers will turn to immediately after purchasing this book: how can I help my team increase their closed sales—*this year?* My previous book, *Above Quota Performance*, was written to assist sales pros in building more robust pipelines and closing more sales. It contains hundreds of tips and techniques that have worked for me and will work for your sales pros, but the onus is on the individual sales pro to utilize the tips. Here, we will focus on the best practices for the sales manager to directly help the sales pros close more sales through better leadership, communicating company goals and individual expectations, improved performance management and staffing, superior coaching, building compensation plans with the proper incentives, choosing the best sales model for your company, removing internal obstacles, holding sales pros accountable, and active deal management.

Some sales pros, especially high performers, will say that the best sales managers are those that leave them alone to work their opportunities independently. Although they may voice this wish, especially to their peers, most sales pros would welcome assistance that helps them close more sales. And the sales manager is not doing her job if she does not actively engage with all sales pros on her team, including the prima donnas. However, while support is necessary, micromanagement does not work well in enterprise sales management. Sales pros resent managers who tell them what to do every step of the way. It will also stall their development as competent sales pros—if they stay with the company. Good management is about striking the balance between support and micromanagement.

Most sales pros desire the sales manager to simplify, not over-complicate, their sales processes, especially those that relate to internal procedures, such as reducing the administrative burden of the Customer Relationship Management (CRM) system and contract negotiation. This will result in providing the sales pros with more time to sell—and a better state of mind.

According to a Forbes 2018 study "nearly two-thirds (64.8%) of reps' time, on average, is spent in non-revenue-generating activities, leaving only 35.2% for functions related to selling."[13] Sales pros spent approximately 17.9 percent of their time updating their opportunities and processing orders in their CRM system.[14] In my last sales position, spending one to two hours entering each sales order into our cumbersome, modified CRM system was not unusual. Sales management leaders expect their sales pros to achieve their sales quotas despite having two days less of productive time available to them each week. And surprisingly, more than 33 percent of their time is spent on reading and responding to emails.[15] I believe this has gotten even worse in the last five years; the reduction in selling time has negatively impacted selling success. It is suboptimal—and must be changed!

CHAPTER 4

Preparing Your Team for Deal Pursuits

Having your sales pros prepare formal sales plans, tracking their progress against them, and having sales pros alter it when needed are very important to sales success. Many sales pros do not like to complete forms, whether on paper or online, nor do they like the idea of somebody else, specifically their managers, tracking their progress. But those sales pros are missing the benefits of sales planning and tracking.

Sales managers and sales pros will receive a greater return for their efforts by utilizing a formal sales methodology. The benefits of being fully engaged in this process are:

- Easier tracking and monitoring of your opportunities in the funnel (rather than on slips of paper, Excel, or in one's head)
- A proven methodology that has worked for hundreds of organizations
- The usage of common terminology that everybody in the company utilizes and understands (for example, "economic buyer")
- A tool to be used for account reviews

- Identifies the roles of each person for the prospect and key company relationships
- Will help ascertain where you need assistance and by whom
- Should increase win percentages by enforcing best practices at each stage
- Identifies and schedules the next steps
- Records conversations and saves documents
- Provides insight to the sales management and marketing team of all opportunities in their various stages
- Can be used for later win/loss and metric analysis

Takeaway 7 – Sales Pros Must Prepare a Sales Plan for All Key Opportunities

A formal sales plan does not need to be completed for each qualified prospect. Still, I recommend they be completed by the sales pro for all medium to larger revenue potential opportunities or more complex or competitive situations, as they will help the sales manager and sales pro organize the proper tactics and strategies needed to win sales. I prefer to put this plan in writing, either electronically or on paper. It needs to be continually updated as the sales pro progresses through the sales cycle, preferably daily, as every sales cycle is dynamic. Recording all interactions and updating forecasts are disciplines that the sales manager must enforce to maximize sales efficiency.

The sales plan will define how the sales pro plans to sell this opportunity to a specific prospect. It takes a holistic view of what needs to be done to close this specific sales opportunity, in the current time frame, and is not a plan for all sales efforts to this company or enterprise (which is usually termed an "account plan.")

The sales plan should include a summary of the sales opportunity (remember it should have already been qualified by the sales pro and is in the funnel.) It should also include the single sales objective (not the overall account strategy), the dollar amount of revenue forecasted, and the expected close date. An assessment of the current position will provide a truthful view of how sales pros feel they are doing compared to the competition, which are listed and includes "no change/status quo." The assessment will include the perceived strength and weaknesses against the competition—from what the sales pro believes is the buyer's point of view. It is beneficial to compare this prospect to your company's Sweet Spot or Ideal Customer Profile to give you a measurement of how close this prospect compares to the norm of the best customers to pursue. This results in a focus on the higher probability prospects. There will be times when the sales pro may want to seek customers outside of this profile, but the decision of whether to do so needs to be challenged by the sales manager.

The prospect's staff that the sales pro believes will be involved in the sales process need to be identified and any contact with them categorized as having a favorable or unfavorable reception. If they have not been met, it is a red flag. If the contact reception has been unfavorable, what specific actions will the sales pro utilize to reverse it, and when are future meetings scheduled?

An overall *honest* assessment of your sales pro's current position today needs to be completed by the sales pro for each sales opportunity, including what possible actions will be taken to improve things. All ideas must be considered. The assessment should consider emotional responses including feeling comfortable, uncomfortable, fearful, insecure, or any other condition. The assessment must also include all decision makers and especially the sales manager; it doesn't help a sales pro win a sale or gain assistance if the sales manager isn't kept informed of progress details.

Takeaway 8 – The Sales Plan Must Be Continually Updated by the Sales Pro

The sales plan for each opportunity should be reviewed and updated daily by the sales pro in the CRM system throughout the sales cycle, and should be discussed, in a detailed conversation with the sales manager at least once every two weeks, at minimum, ideally during an account review. That includes the forecasted close date. The sales process is dynamic, not static, and all information needs to be continually updated. Very few data points will stay constant throughout the process and all assumptions must be revisited and red flags be accounted for.

I have always appreciated the quote attributed to World War II General Dwight D. Eisenhower: "Plans are worthless, but planning is everything."[16] That is because planning is momentary and doesn't consider the circumstances that change once the task or opportunity commences that are unknown at the initial preparatory stage. It is the same with sales. Nothing ever stays the same. If one does not quickly adapt to change, the sales opportunity will be lost.

Takeaway 9 – Be Sure to Have Your Sales Pros Identify All Red Flags for the Opportunity

One of the common mistakes I have observed in sales is that sometimes sales pros are so close to their opportunity that they miss some obvious, or perhaps not, clues. Perhaps they are so engaged with one or two people that they are not aware of other dynamics that may be occurring. One of the benefits of using a sales methodology is that when the sales pro updates his sales plan, either manually or electronically, you can identify and review the "red flags" or areas that have not been properly addressed. This could be an outstanding objection, a technical buyer whose questions have not been answered, or an economic buyer who was not met. I have also seen some very competent sales pros become overconfident about an opportunity to the point where they assume they will be the chosen supplier. When the buyer chooses another supplier, they are shocked and assume that something nefarious has happened or that the buyer was stupid. Most often, neither was true, but they missed something important to the buyer. The usage of a sales planning tool by sales managers and sales pros will help cure (but not eliminate) overconfidence, which is a "deadly sin" in sales, one step above incompetence. It will also provide you with a tool to begin your discussions with sales pros about their pipeline and active opportunities.

Also, by utilizing a sales planning tool the sales manager can provide guidance to the sales pros on preparing to approach and sell each opportunity. Preparation includes planning, under-standing your value propositions and being able to articulate them simply to an audience unfamiliar with your company, researching the targeted companies and their vertical markets or industry, role-playing your company's "pitch," understanding how to position your solution, confirming that everybody on the sales team has defined roles and are on the "same page," having proper resources and marketing collateral, accumulating a collection of similar company references where your solution brought value/positive results to the customer and executing a perfect sales process. Working with sales pros to properly prepare will help them win before the sales call is ever initiated. Failure to plan will often result in a lost opportunity.

Sounds simple, but it isn't. Being an expert on your offerings and knowledge of the competitors will result in a competitive advantage or "the edge." Calling on a prospect without the preparation I have described above is like crossing a stormy sea in a rowboat. You may be able to arrive at your destination, but your success is enhanced with proper planning and resources.

If you and your sales pros know the strengths and weaknesses of competitors (and you should), the sales pros can emphasize your product's strengths versus their product's weaknesses and subtly capitalize on that. I found that some competitors' sales presentations were often very predictable, and I was able to use this against them. I once even gave one of my competitor's sales presentations, using their sales material, to a client who wanted me to differentiate our solutions.

It is often said (and often attributed to Benjamin Franklin) that "By failing to prepare, you are preparing to fail."[17] I have seen several instances where poorly prepared, over-confident, sales pros tried to improvise a presentation to prospects and customers and the results were often very disastrous. They did not know the company, their audience, their needs, the background for the meeting (the why), and what they wanted to accomplish during the meeting. They did not discuss and reach an agreement on the agenda with the buyer's key people in advance. They delivered a scripted presentation, often consisting of thirty or more slides. This is incompetence and a recipe for disaster. The buyer sees a sales pro who did not respect them and their time and did not want to invest enough effort to prepare in advance for the meeting. The meeting will probably be shortened, and the decision-makers may walk out of the room. The sales pro then wonders what went wrong. Often, they report back to you that your price is too high when it was not actually a major factor in the decision. It is on you, as their sales manager, to prevent this from happening by enforcing proper preparation for each sales opportunity.

Takeaway 10 – By Failing to Prepare, You Are Preparing to Fail

The role of each person in the sales presentation needs to also be determined in advance of the meeting, and I recommend conducting a walk-through, or role-play, a few days before the meeting with a follow-up the evening before or the morning of the meeting to assure that everybody knows what is expected of them.

Takeaway 11 – The Sales Pro Owns Their Success or Failure—Nobody Else. But the Sales Manager Owns the Success or Failure of the Sales Team.

I have heard sales pros blame many others for a poor presentation, but it is always their great salesmanship if it goes well. On my sales teams, I always stressed that the sales pro owns the success or failure of the presentation and the sale closing. If it does not go well, it is the sales pro's fault for not preparing properly. It is the sales pro's responsibility to make sure that each person knows their role and is completely prepared to discuss their material or topic. The team should always discuss these before the day of the presentation. The sales pro is the "captain of the ship" and is responsible for everything that occurs, good or bad.

That being said, my responsibility as the manager was to make sure my sales team, and each sales pro, had the resources, training, and support they needed to properly prepare. While sales pros must take accountability for their presentations, sales managers must take responsibility for their teams. If your team is underperforming or has lost a big sale, it is your responsibility to find out what happened and how to help your team move forward and do better the next time. Sales managers have their form of preparation that is equally important and must not be neglected.

Perhaps it is possible to build an equation that indicates that for every hour devoted to preparation for the meeting, the odds of being chosen by the buyer will increase by 5 – 10 percent incrementally. It is almost impossible to over-prepare for a call or opportunity. The famous inventor Thomas Edison noted: "Unfortunately, there seems to be far more opportunity out there than ability . . . We should remember that good fortune often happens when opportunity meets with preparation."[18]

Although it rarely happens, it is very important that sales and marketing be aligned in your company and the executives of both areas placed on similar compensation and annual objective/evaluation plans. Then, their interests will be better aligned.

If I were to begin with a start-up organization in an executive sales capacity tomorrow, my first task would be to define a sales methodology to follow and to change it as I gain new information. Then, I would define the target market and ideal customer. This is a very process-driven approach. I believe that repeatable processes need to be implemented by the sales manager for the team to be successful. I don't believe in depending on unique instances of sales success. (I call those "meteors.") Every sales pro should follow an established methodology, utilize an account plan that is continually updated, and deploy a common language to describe where they are in the sales process, as well as the people they are working with at a prospect's organization. Many companies use a 5-10 step pipeline so that sales pros describe where they believe they are in the sales pipeline. This makes planning, account reviews, and sales forecasting more effective,

I strongly encourage the use of commercial sales methodologies and that it is interfaced to a CRM system. There are many excellent methodologies available in the marketplace today. Whichever methodology is chosen, it must be thoroughly utilized throughout the organization. I have seen many companies implement sales methodologies and then ignore them. If that is the case, the sales managers are unable to conduct account reviews properly or do reasonably accurate sales forecasts, two of the most critical functions. And the company will have wasted a lot of money.

CHAPTER 5

Tips and Techniques to Help Your Team Win More Sales

As a sales manager, there is a lot you can do to help train and prepare your team to achieve success. Below are several tips and techniques that you can utilize to train your sales pros.

Refine Your Approach

> ## Takeaway 12 – The "Best" Product Does Not Always Win!

When I first became a sales pro, after being an accounting manager, I was acquainted with all the fixed asset software packages on the market. I considered the McCormack & Dodge system, which I was selling, to be the best on the market. I defined "best" as the solution having the most features ("bells and whistles"), functionality, ease of use, and telephone support.

But how do we really define "the best?" Is it the product that had the most customers, the most features, the most time on the market, the least amount of "bugs," the one that has the best post-sales service record, the one that has the most recommendations by independent third parties, the most references, the most effective sales pitch, the prettiest or most handsome sales pro, or the one with the nicest brochures? What I believe is the best is probably not what many others think is the best. It is a subjective judgment. Some people like abstract art, such as those created by Jackson Pollock. While I like the varied colors, I would rather look at landscapes and portraits. Baskin Robbins has 31 flavors because consumers have different tastes. But this was at the beginning of my sales career, and I was naïve. I was also very loyal to my employer. I had been a dissatisfied customer of my competitors' software packages. I had also recently surveyed the market as a buyer, so I was convinced my offering was the most ideal for any potential customer. Why would a company choose a lesser solution? I was very energetic and emotional about this. When I did a presentation on the features and benefits to a prospect, I was able to articulate the reasons why the solution I was offering was the one they should choose. And this worked well for me for about two years. I did not lose one competitive sale that year, sold twice as many units as the next highest sales pro in the company, sold the greatest dollar amount deal, and became a sales star.

Shortly afterward, new products with more features and functionality entered the market. When I reported back to the company that we needed to add features to be more competitive, I was informed that there was a formal development schedule and the next two releases had been defined, so it would be at least one year before that would occur. This caused a change in my original assumption. For me to continue to be an over-achieving sales pro, I could no longer rely on the belief that our product had superior functionality to win a competitive sale. I had no formal sales training at that point, so I had to rely on developing better sales skills to close sales. This was a real "eye-opener" for me and resulted in me changing from a naïve person who was very good at explaining how my company's solution works (a product expert) to a professional sales pro. I had to transition from the paradigm of "the best product always wins" to "the most effective sales pro usually wins." This also meant I had to lessen my long-standing practice of emphasizing product features and functions to prospects.

I learned that the sales process and building trust with buyers were more important than the product's features and functions. The "how" and the "why" were far more important. This transition later helped me manage Nielsen Marketing Research's sales force when it was confronted with its first real competitor in fifty years—one that offered a new, highly flexible solution with superior technology. When I joined them, Nielsen's sales force had not conducted a formal sales training program or even an annual sales meeting in more than twenty years. They had viewed sales pros as "account managers" who were highly trained in discussing sales movement in different geographies with their customers. The notion of having a competitor in the marketplace was never considered. They were essentially a monopoly for market research in the consumer-packaged goods research market. The question was not whether their customers purchased services from them but how much they would spend. The goal was to encourage them to spend more by providing greater value. But the new technology was highly attractive and was available at a lower cost.

The solution was quickly training my sales force on winning in a highly competitive marketplace. I brought in a professional sales trainer, role-playing, and introduced the rest of the team to many of the techniques I had personally developed.

I realized that to be successful in sales, sales pros need to continue to develop and continually update their skills, especially staying up to date on the latest technological developments. Sales pros do not reach a certain level of competence; just like a journeyman tradesperson, they need an occasional refresher. It requires continual training and practice. I knew that when I did not conduct a sales presentation for a few days, I would become rusty, and my delivery would not be as smooth. If that was true for me, surely my team was the same. If one does not continually train and practice, one will often fail.

Your sales pros must understand how their products or solutions compare to competitors, not just features and functions, but the whole company, including customer service, as that is often a differentiator. This means you must have your team research your competitors' offerings and discuss them with customers who use the competitor's products or have recently evaluated them. Also, have sales pros look at competitors' advertisements and the material they give out at trade shows. I have often asked buyers what they liked or did not like about competitors' solutions—without ever challenging or commenting on it. If I knew the competitor had a nice feature or function, I would tell the buyer that I found the feature interesting or valuable for some people but unnecessary for everyone. (I would also urge our developers to incorporate that feature or a better one as soon as possible!)

Takeaway 13 – The Time Gap That Competitors Announce New (Superior) Features Is Now in Days, Not Months

Buyers approach purchasing more holistically now and are interested in the entirety of the solution. They currently do not care as much about specific features and functions, and the relationship with the selling company has become preeminent. Also, the lag time between when a seller adds a "cool" feature to its solution and when its competitors also have it, or one even better, has diminished from years or months to a few weeks or days now. Products and solutions look more alike now than they did years ago, and differentiating products is more difficult for both buyers and sellers. Buyers are also more educated, discerning, and able to control the purchasing cycle more than ever.

Sales pros can no longer show up at a buyer's location, perform a demonstration, and then follow up on open questions before closing the order. They must navigate through the ups and downs of a complex sales cycle. Competition has become more intense as the internet has provided more information to both the buyers and all potential suppliers. Fewer companies are now competing for the buyers' purchases. Great service is now expected from suppliers and is rarely a differentiator.

Defining the "best" product on the market is now very difficult and is indeed different for each buyer. And if there were a market leader, it could still change in a matter of weeks. Think about the Kodak film cameras, Blockbuster video stores, the Blackberry smartphone, or the Motorola and Nokia cellphones. Therefore, having the best product does not assure sales anymore.

Work With the Supreme Blocker

There are fewer executive or administrative assistants in large and medium-sized corporations today. Many have extraordinary discretion regarding whether the executive they work for is made available for a meeting, telephone call, or email, how much time is allocated to your meeting, who else attends it, and how much information will be provided to you before the meeting. In that sense, they are gatekeepers or blockers, but unlike others, their purpose is to protect the time and interests of the executive. Let us assume that these assistants are very important people, and your sales pro's relationship with them can positively or negatively affect the outcome of your sale.

Some sales trainers and sales managers have devised various schemes to work around or trick the executive assistant, and they spend a lot of time planning how to do this and hoping that their cunning idea works. My view is the opposite. I train my sales pros to work *with* the executive assistant and gain their cooperation. It makes reaching the business executive much easier; when they do, they will not have to apologize for their deceitful conduct.

Takeaway 14 – The Sales Pro Must Always Have a Business Reason When Calling a C-Level Executive

A couple of rules should be emphasized when training your sales team in this technique. My first rule about working with executive assistants is that sales pros should always have a valid business reason for calling the C-level executive. She will likely ask why you are calling the executive, and you must have a ready answer. It could be that the sales pro wishes to discuss the value proposition or to provide current industry information to the executive. The sales pro can explain to the executive assistant that she is calling Ms. Benson, the CEO because she wants to discuss an idea that will increase revenues, decrease costs, improve operational efficiencies, or help the company achieve its published strategic short or long-term goals. She is not calling to chat. Do not encourage a sales pro, under any circumstances, to go into a sales pitch with the executive assistant—or with the executive—at that time. The initial goal is to gain access to the CEO, not to try to sell her. This is an important point when training your team.

Secondly, your sales pro should have scheduled the call with the executive or executive assistant and followed up with an Outlook or Google Calendar invitation confirming the call to get on their calendar. Then, when the sales pro calls on them, they can say, "I have previously scheduled this call with Ms. Benson at 10:00 a.m. today." The call will almost certainly be forwarded to the executive once the assistant confirms it has been scheduled.

Takeaway 15 – The Sales Pro Must Never Try to Go Around or Mislead the Executive Assistant

Thirdly, never have your sales pros try to go around the assistant to the executive. Some sales books offer tips on how to get around the executive assistant or gatekeeper, but this is a huge mistake and may make an enemy who can create problems later during the sales cycle. Sales pros should want the executive assistant to be their ally, not an enemy. If they call Ms. Benson, the CEO, and the executive assistant answers the telephone, be polite to the extreme. She is as important as any executive to successfully concluding a sale.

Here are a few tips on working with an executive assistant that you can use to train your team:

1. *Always* be respectful of the executive assistant's time and position. If the executive assistant is preventing you from speaking to the executive, she is just doing her job; it is not personal. Do not talk down to her or adopt a condescending tone. The executive assistant is in that position because she has demonstrated better-than-average skills in helping the executive with administrative tasks, such as identifying and screening out sales calls. She did not achieve that position because she was lucky—she earned it. And she probably has the executive's trust. She also has almost complete control of the executive's calendar.

2. *Never* ask an executive assistant to break a confidence with the CEO. For example, "Can you please tell me what Ms. Benson thought of my proposal?" is asking the executive assistant to betray confidential information. I would assume they would find that request insulting and dismiss it, and they would probably report the conversation to the executive.

3. *Never* mislead the executive assistant about why you are calling or want to set up a meeting. Did I say one never? *Make that ten nevers!* Answer all her questions completely and truthfully. It is, however, appropriate to ask the executive assistant for help. For example, "Can you please tell me if Ms. Benson prefers to be contacted via email or telephone?" is an acceptable question.

If the executive assistant gives you advice, guidance, or suggestions, then follow it exactly. For example, "Please call Ms. Benson at 5:15 p.m. two weeks from Wednesday," or "Please do not call Ms. Benson again."

4. Please let her know if you have met or interacted with the executive assistant's boss. Examples of what to say are, "I had the pleasure of meeting Ms. Benson at last year's trade conference," or "Please remind Ms. Benson that we met last year when she approved our previous proposal."

Let me tell you a great story that exemplifies how a good relationship with an executive assistant can make all the difference: Hale Irwin is a famous professional golfer who won the prestigious US Open tournament three times. Shortly after his last win, our parent company, Dun & Bradstreet (D&B) booked him for a golf event with key customers in the Chicago area. I was contacted by the D&B executive in charge of the event three days before, and he informed me that he had a cancellation and an opening. He asked if I wanted to invite one of our customers. I confirmed that I did.

One of my sales pros was calling on a large consumer packaged goods company. The CIO, Jerry, loved golfing and had an office filled with golf memorabilia. The sales pro, Mike, and I decided to invite him. When we called him, we received a message that he was away and to call his executive assistant, Eleanor, if something was important. We called Eleanor and asked her to contact Jerry to invite him to golf, which was the following Monday—in three days. She informed us that he was presently in Hawaii on a golf vacation, and she would not interrupt him. There was also a five-hour time difference between Wisconsin and Hawaii, and she could not try to reach him for several hours. She also said his schedule for Monday, his first day back after his vacation, was full. After some coaxing, I assured her that Jerry would probably want to golf with Hale Irwin. She finally said she would call him very late on Friday. Sure enough, Jerry accepted our invitation. Eleanor called us back and seemed upset that she had to cancel his Monday meetings. When he arrived at the country club on Monday morning, he confirmed that Eleanor was upset, but he was delighted to be there to golf with Hale Irwin. Later, Mike was able to close a very large sale with this company. We sent flowers to Eleanor.

It is sometimes appropriate to send a gift basket, flowers, or candy to an executive assistant after they do you a favor, such as rearranging the boss's schedule to accommodate your request for a meeting at a specific time. This should not be a normal practice, as some would see it as bribery. But it can show your appreciation for accommodating you. I would send something small and tasteful, not something elaborate and attention-grabbing.

Establishing a good working relationship with the executive assistant is essential to helping the sales pro gain access to key executives and to build trusting relationships with the executive, all of which are necessary to close the sale effectively.

Identify the Buyer's Personality
This chapter is unique amongst all sales books I have read. Its purpose is to introduce a new concept that, used effectively, can help sales pros close more sales. The notion is that a single message

will resonate differently with buyers based on their personality and that a message that is adjusted to fit the buyer's personality is more effective.

Sales pros, unfortunately, often treat buyers as one monolithic group and tend to prepare marketing material and messages that are often undistinguishable and impersonal, only varying them by vertical market or season. But buyers are not all the same. They work at different companies and have various other goals, objectives, and reasons for speaking with you.

Also, each buyer has a unique personality and different personal needs and wants. They also may plan to use your product or solution differently in their company. But, more importantly, their motivation or "why?" is unique to them and their circumstances. Therefore the "one size fits all approach" of marketing and sales messages should be sent to the sales training junkyard.

Assessing the Buyer Beforehand

Personality information is a valuable data point or tool for sales pros to understand their buyers, and it is instrumental to sales success. It will help the sales pro in his conversations with the buyer when it is crucial to relate to their needs, motives, and goals. And, importantly, it will give the sales pro an edge over their competitors.

Have you ever noticed that some people have simple offices, while others are well decorated, perhaps with many photographs of their family or last vacation, their diplomas, or company awards? We can learn about a person's personality by observing their behavior, as well as how they set up their office or workspace. Observant sales pros can use this information to initiate a conversation and build rapport with a prospect. In addition, it will help to recognize the different personalities of the people you are calling on and adapt your sales pitch accordingly.

Takeaway 16 – It Is Important for the Sales Pro to Tailor Their Message to the Buyer's Personality

One way for the sales pro to increase his chances of closing the sale he is currently working on is to better understand his buyer's personality. For example, a well-prepared message considered too aggressive by one buyer may be perfectly acceptable to another. It will help you to know how to approach them best.

I suggest that sales pros prepare personalized messages to approach your buyers and explain your proposition value based on their perceived personality type rather than using the standard material produced by your product marketing department. The messages should be utilized throughout the sales cycle, not just at the beginning.

Think of two very different buyers and how they will receive this message:

"We have a new product being released next month. I can only provide a little detail on it, but we are confident that it will handle your needs and is better than anything else on the market. It utilizes the latest and greatest artificial intelligence technology."

Buyer 1, Tony, an extrovert, is very impulsive and wants to find a solution as soon as possible. He is not concerned with how it will work or any difficulties in deploying it in his company. However, he does want something reliable that will make him look good to his manager.

Buyer 2, Marie, an introvert, is very cautious and methodical. She wants to dig into the details of your product and understand the engineering specifications. She is also very concerned with the issues resulting from transitioning from their current environment.

Which buyer do you think will be most interested in our new product? Tony will want to move forward now, and Marie will not.

What Are the "Tells" that Sales Pros Can Use as Clues

Learning how to read people similarly to playing poker can help increase your skills and improve your selling skills. I may be among the world's worst poker players, probably why I get invited to many poker parties! Unfortunately, I cannot keep a passive expression that hides my feelings, regardless of the cards I am dealt in a poker game. I am very easily read visually—gamblers call these "tells," or unconscious or careless behavior that may reveal deceptions, intentions, thoughts, or emotions. For some people, it could be as simple as involuntarily scratching an itch or even a long stare. When I have a poor card hand, I am visually disappointed and usually fold my calls early, rarely bluffing—because I lose a lot of money whenever I do. When the dealer gives me a good hand, such as a pair or three of a kind, I am happy, sit up, pay more attention, and stay in the bidding longer. I am not surprised when the other guys fold their hands and leave when I stay in.

My actions give away the contents of my hand and make it a lot easier for my opponents. I know I am giving away valuable information to an opponent, but I cannot help it. I do not have what is called a "poker face" or a blank, emotionless expression.

Seven Selling Tells

Sales managers can help prepare sales pros to recognize common tells during sales situations. This will assist them in determining their next course of action. For example, if the prospect appears disinterested, the sales pros should not continue with their present course of action, but should pivot to another that is more effective. Or, if the prospect appears excited with the sales pro's pitch or proposal, rather than continuing with their planned sales pitch and risking the introduction of an objection, perhaps they need to proceed to the solutioning step in the sales process. I have found short role-playing exercises (five to ten minutes each), either with the team or individually, to be very effective in preparing the sales pro to recognize and take advantage of the sales tells. Below are eight tells that your sales pro may encounter when selling and what he can expect from them:

1. The procurement or strategic sourcing person enters the sales cycle. You have been working with the prospect's evaluation team for months, and suddenly, a procurement professional has joined the meetings. This person has also started asking probing questions about pricing, warranties, delivery availability, and contractual conditions. Guess what? This is a tell that the prospect has decided on your solution—or at least you are one of the finalists. The bad news is that the procurement person usually holds the aces and will add stress to the sales process by insisting on a better price or other conditions that have not been previously discussed with the prospect. The good news is that you are closer to a sale.

2. The prospect begins planning implementation steps, asking your sales pro about post-contract issues such as "When can we schedule the training?" "How can we introduce the product or service into the company with the least amount of disruption?" "When will your technical resources be available to us?" And so on. When this happens, it is a good sales tell that informs your sales pro that you are winning—or may have already won the decision.

3. The decision has occurred, and your company has lost. The person or persons your sales pro has been calling on and found accessible are no longer so. Instead, they start "ghosting" your sales pro, or avoiding his calls and emails. If your sales pro reaches them, they keep the conversations brief—but do not inform your sales pro that he has lost. But he has, and they are just delaying telling him. Perhaps they have not announced the winner yet and want to keep your company as a second or third option. Or, like many people, they are avoiding unpleasant conversations. Silence may be golden to some, but to sales pros, we would rather hear the truth. Your sales pro can ask them what they can share and what he needs to do better in the future.

4. "You did a great job for us." Sometimes, your contact starts a conversation with the sales pro by complimenting him on what a good job he did for them. This is a tell that your sales pro lost. They are trying to make your sales pro feel better by letting him know they liked him and how he handled them—but he still lost. I call this the "but" conversation.

5. The prospect uses a personal nickname. Warren Weiss is a highly respected friend who is the managing partner of a leading technology venture capital firm. He has an unusual nickname, Bunny, that originated in childhood as a term of endearment and is commonly used by many friends and family. He always introduced himself as Warren when he was out on sales calls. He knew he had won the deal when the prospect started calling him Bunny. Why? By using his childhood nickname, the buyer has indicated that she trusts him and is comfortable referring to him by his nickname.

6. Interpreting body language can also help determine how well the prospect responds to the sales pro. For example, hands on the hips or standing with one hand on a hip is body language that indicates confidence. This stance is typically linked with authority and power. The person is telling your sales pro they are in charge, not your sales pro, and he needs to understand that. On the other hand, if the prospect stands with their hand in a pocket, that indicates a casual and carefree attitude. That could mean they are very comfortable with your sales pro—or do not take your sales pro seriously.

Does the prospect mirror or unconsciously copy the sales pro's body movements? Human behavior expert Maryann Karinch explains, "Mirroring is natural when two people feel a connection. It can also be a tool to engender connection if used carefully. For example, the sales pro should do the same if the prospect goes from crossed arms to a more invitational posture. You're essentially returning an invite into that person's space with an invite into your space—even without moving toward one another."[19] Also, the sales pro should never purposely attempt to physically mimic the prospect in body language or even how the prospect speaks. This can seem contrived and insulting, and will most likely cause subliminal discomfort with the prospect. That can result in killing the deal.

7. Request for an immediate price or discount. Your sales pro has had minimal contact with the prospect, and she asks you for your "best" price or a discount before you have had any discussions about their needs and whether you can add value to the company. Some may think this is a sign of interest from the prospect, but it is not. It may be the opposite! They may want to know your company's price to eliminate you from further consideration, or they are just window shopping. Therefore, your sales pro must delay the price conversation without being too evasive.

Reading the Room

Sales tells can happen with groups, not just individuals. For example, if your sales pro is presenting to a group that needs more information or feedback, yet they have the expressionless "zombie look" and are not agreeing or disagreeing with your sales pro during the meeting, that is a big tell. What does this mean? And what should your sales pro do about it?

It may be indicative of any of the following:

- Your sales pro lost them. The group is not interested and not paying attention. But they want to be polite, not just stand and walk out.
- The prospect has already made their decision to purchase another product. But they thought seeing what else is out in the marketplace might be helpful. Unless the sales pro comes up with something that shakes them up or changes the status quo, they will send the sales pro a nice "thank you" after the meeting.
- They need to comprehend better the material your sales pro is presenting. Unfortunately, that happens more often than we realize. Sometimes, this is due to an agenda that does not meet their needs or through the usage of jargon or acronyms that they need help understanding.
- They are not "qualified" prospects. If so, your sales pro is wasting his time.
- They don't like you or your product or service and are there because somebody (perhaps an executive) has insisted.

If this happens, the sales pro must try to re-engage the audience. He should stop the meeting and ask them why they seem disinterested. Then he can respond by correcting the problem, which can be as simple as adjusting the agenda "on the fly" or give up and go home if he is wasting his time and energy. It may be as simple as holding a spontaneous coffee or restroom break. Your sales pro may ask the audience provocative questions to get their attention, such as, "How is your company handling the transition to electric vehicles," or "What has been your experience with deploying artificial intelligence at your company?" Sometimes it will help if your sales pro tells them a story or shares an experience that they can relate to and that adds value to the discussion, such as "I met with a company last year that was in a similar situation as yours. They experienced inventory outages and supply chain problems. We worked with them for several months to arrive at a solution." Get creative; don't be ordinary. What do you have to lose?

A good poker player plays bad hands well, not just the good ones. It is the same with exceptional sales pros. When the sales process doesn't go as planned, adapt to the circumstances.

Sales pros need to understand the "best product" does not always win. In fact, it has nothing to do with whether you win or lose. Selling is not about demonstrating product features and functions, partly because it now takes a rival company days, not months, to incorporate new features or functions. Sales is all about building trust and solving the prospect's problems. Most prospects will not tell your sales pro directly where his proposal stands, so some detective work needs to be done, including better listening and better observation of body language signals.

CHAPTER 6

Who Is Your Sales Pro Selling To?

To understand how to customize sales pitches, a sales pro needs the means to identify buyers' personalities to build a message that resonates with them. Unfortunately, finding such a tool is a complex problem I have struggled with throughout my sales career.

Early in my sales career, I was told that it was imperative to become an expert on our product to be successful in sales—know its features and functions and be able to explain them to prospects briefly. That involved extensive training with product managers, who described the product to me, including how they thought the prospect would benefit. I received a standard sales script and was told to memorize and be able to recite it, word-for-word, at sales presentations that were sometimes hours long. I did both and became very successful. I assumed that standard messages worked well. However, the reality was that I succeeded despite the erroneous advice I received.

When speaking with buyers, I often found that some were more interested in various features, functions, and perhaps the latest technology, some were more than willing to chat with me for long periods, while others were abrupt and wanted to get down to their needs immediately. I became good friends with some, and others kept me at a distance. So, of course, I adapted and tried to work with them as they preferred.

At a company training session, I was introduced to the Myers-Briggs (MBTI) personality test. The mother-and-daughter team of Katherine Briggs and Isabel Myers developed a personality type indicator in the 1960s based on the teachings of early twentieth-century Swiss psychiatrist Carl Jung. Myers and Briggs defined eight personality preferences: People will either be an Introvert (I) or Extrovert (E); Sensor (S) or Intuitive (N); Thinker (T) or Feeler (F); Judger (J) or Perceiver (P). There is no superior or inferior type, and each person has some traits of the other types. They are not value judgments, just indicators of one's personality. The eight preferences can be described as follows:

- **Extrovert (E) or Introvert (I)** – How does the person process information? Extroverts are concerned with what happens in the outer world of actions, objects, and persons. Extroverts get their "energy from stimuli from the outside world."[20] Introverts are concerned with the inner world of their concepts and ideas. They get their energy from "staying within their own world."[21]

- **Thinker (T) or Feeler (F)** – How does the person make judgments or decisions? Thinkers tend to be more objective, impersonally considering the causes and effects of decisions. Feelers prefer to make decisions that take other people's feelings and how they will affect them into account.

- **Sensor (S) or Intuitive (N) –** How does the person organize her life? How does she make decisions? Sensors tend to value the immediate, empirical facts of experience. Intuitives are more tuned into relationships.
- **Judger (J) or Perceiver (P) –** How do most people prefer to live their lives? Judgers want to live in a well-planned and orderly manner. Perceivers are much more flexible and want to be spontaneous and adaptive.

Takeaway 17 – There Are 16 Different Myers-Briggs (MBTI) Personality Types

Each of the eight classifications are further broken into sixteen personality types. So for example, some people can be an ETSJ, and others can be an IFNP or any of the sixteen combinations of E, I, T, F, S, N, J, or P.

Interested persons can take a short (twenty to thirty minute) assessment to determine their MBTI personality classification. The result will be one of sixteen combinations of preferences, such as ISTP, ESFJ, or ENTP. So for example, one personality classification ISTP represents a person that is an introvert (I), a sensor (S), a thinker (T), and a perceiver (P). Of course, no personality type is better or preferable to another. It simply represents your attributes. You can learn more about MBTI at https://www.the-myersbriggs.com/en-US/Products-and-Services/Myers-Briggs. Other popular personality preference indicator tests are DISC and Enneagram. However, MBTI was the easiest for me to relate to, and it is designed for use by non-psychologists.

Many psychiatrists and psychologists dismiss the MBTI as

being unscientific, saying that it uses artificial binaries, can be inaccurate and arbitrary, many traits are on a single spectrum and that the results are too stereotypical. Their criticism is focused on the psychological validity of the test. People are not just extroverts or introverts; many are ambiverts. But MBTI has existed for over seventy-five years and is still very popular. "Today, the MBTI assessment is used in 115 countries, is available in twenty-nine languages, has been used by eighty-eight of the Fortune 100 within the past five years, and is taken by millions of people worldwide."[22] And, according to Forbes magazine "the MBTI remains one of the most widely recognized personality tests globally for its simplicity, ease of use and longstanding history as a workplace tool . . . The test has been used as a tool for teambuilding, conflict prevention and leadership development purposes. The MBTI may also help people determine how compatible they are with one another, romantically or platonically, says Vitelli."[23] I am suggesting that it can also assist you in helping close sales.

Though not a social scientist, I have found the information helpful in learning how to customize messages to buyers. MBTI is not "pop psychology" or "psycho-speak," nor is it part of any trend or cult. It is not like a horoscope because one takes a test to determine what the personality is. The MBTI should be considered indicative but not definitive of one's personality. It does not measure or predict job performance or predict future behavior. The results of personal assessments should be discussed with a person that is a qualified psychologist, psychiatrist, or certified in the methodology by Myers-Briggs.

Recognizing the Personality Types

While it might be useful to hire a MBTI professional to come in to train your team on this topic, this chapter will serve as a good basic tutorial to get you and your team started. You do not need a psychology degree to recognize and understand the sixteen MBTI personality types. You can use your observation skills to pick up on the clues before you. You can confirm your suspicions by asking your sales pro (and they can ask the buyer) questions about their likes and dislikes to help discern their personality type. As the late baseball Hall of Famer Lawrence P. (Yogi) Berra once said: "You can observe a lot by watching."[24]

To get started, as the manager, I'd recommend you try to determine your sales team's individual types through observation. If they elect to take the test, or you hire a professional to come in for training, you can verify your observations. But this is good training for you and will help you train your team in the same skill. This skill will help them in many aspects of the sales cycle.

First, your sales pro's oral and written messages must address areas of concern to the buyers or offer interesting industry facts or updates on technology. The buyer must believe that the sales pro's conversation or message is bringing value to them, and not just pitching a product. Many of my sales pros have asked me how they can find out what the buyer's needs are. I have addressed this, at length, in *Above Quota Performance*. That is one resource to recommend to your team. But the simplest way is to advise them to ask their buyer directly what their needs are.

In addition to speaking to the buyer's needs, messages will be best received when they are oriented toward the buyer's personality. This is where MBTI training will help. Sales pros need to make intuitive guesses to identify who their buyer may be. Fortunately, some clues will help disclose their type immediately: visually, by conversation, by how they interact with others, their plans, how they make decisions, and even how they organize their workspace. You will notice that extroverts and introverts behave differently in meetings and your interactions with them. "Extroverts are more likely to say what they think and talk through their thought processes, while introverts take in the information and sort through it in their own heads."[25]

Unfortunately, identification has become more difficult because of limited in-person interaction with buyers, but obtaining some of this information through videoconferencing and questioning is still possible.

I am not suggesting that sales pros ask buyers to take a personality assessment quiz and then, depending upon the result, adapt to a style, like a chameleon, they think is most compatible with them. The point here is to be familiar with the different personality types and to listen to your buyers to frame the best strategy to secure a sale.

Below are general descriptions of the eight classifications of personality types:

- **The extrovert types, (ESTP, ESFP, ENFP, ENTP, ESTJ, ESFJ, ENFJ and ENTJ) are social people.** They like variety and action and meeting and conversing with others. They are talkers more than listeners and are likely to dominate a conversation. They like working in teams or groups rather than alone. They have many

friends and are good at meeting new people, which
is great for prospecting and setting up meetings with
prospects. They are usually approachable, welcome
telephone calls, and are willing to hear your ideas. They
will meet with you for lunch or possibly a drink after
work. Extroverts enjoy being the center of attention.
They often have a lot of energy. On the negative side,
extroverts often act too quickly, sometimes without
thinking about the consequences—talk first, think later.
And extroverts can be boastful and argumentative,
so one should not argue with them if one wants to
establish a good relationship. They can be impatient.
They also dislike following complicated procedures.
They will try to avoid reading instruction manuals.

- **The introvert types, (ISTJ, ISFJ, INFJ, INTJ,
  ISTP, ISFP, INFP, and INTP), on the contrary,
  like the peace and quiet of being by themselves.**
  They are uncomfortable in groups and teams and like to
  work alone. They are deep thinkers and prefer quiet to
  concentrate. Introverts are usually very reflective. They
  are listeners more than talkers. They are careful with
  details, usually analytical, and will likely want to think
  things over before deciding. They may be perfectionists
  to a fault. Introverts dislike interruptions, so they will
  try to avoid prospecting calls.
- **The sensing types (ESTP, ESTJ, ESFP, ESFJ,
  ISTJ, ISFJ, ISTP, and ISFP) are very pragmatic
  and confident.** They like to have procedures or an
  established way of doing things. Sensors dislike new

problems unless they can be solved with established procedures. They normally reach conclusions step-by-step and like to concentrate on their work, are patient with details, and are very comfortable with precise work. Sensors are usually very results oriented. These people will excel in the analytical part of the evaluation and will be helpful in computing the return on investment. Their negatives are that they usually dislike change without a low-risk way to implement it. They want you to have a detailed proposal with realistic projections rather than idealistic forecasts. Sensors may be arrogant and lack trust in other team members.

- **The intuitive types (INFJ, INTJ, INFP, INTP, ENFP, ENTP, ENFJ, and ENTJ), on the other hand, like to solve new problems where they can create their own procedures.** They can multi-task and think about several things at the same time. They are original and very imaginative. Intuitives are often charismatic and idealistic. They enjoy learning new skills and dislike repetitive tasks. They are usually quick to reach conclusions and often make errors of fact or precision. They can be absent-minded. One needs to double-check their work.

- **The thinking types (ISTJ, INTJ, ISTP, INTP, ESTP, ENTP, ESTJ, and ENTJ) are good communicators.** They normally do not show their emotions and enjoy analyses and putting facts into order. Thinkers can remain calm when others get upset. They tend to make impersonal, deliberate, objective decisions. They would rather be right than liked. On the negative side, they tend to be more firm-minded than gentle-hearted and may hurt people's feelings without knowing it. They often make decisions without paying sufficient attention to other people's wishes. They are usually not very approachable in sales situations and can be over-cautious.

- **The feeling types (ISFJ, INFJ, ISFP, INFP, ESFP, ENFP, ESFJ, and ENFJ) are very sympathetic and all decisions must consider other people's feeling.** Feelers are very aware of how they affect others. They enjoy pleasing people, even on minor matters. Feelers also can be persuasive and manipulative. They rely on their own instincts, not objective analyses. Since they do not like upsetting people, they avoid delivering bad news. They may not stand up for their own beliefs and will let others make decisions if they believe their idea may not be accepted by others.

- **The judging types (ISTJ, ISFJ. INFJ. INTJ, ESTJ, ESFJ, ENFJ, and ENTJ) like to plan their work and follow the plans have built.** They like to make and use lists, are thorough, and like to finish the tasks they start. They may be impatient and oblivious that new tasks need to be completed. They don't like to be kept waiting. And they do not like surprises. On the negative side, the judgers dislike being interrupted and may make premature decisions. They can be dogmatic and inflexible.

- **The perceiving types (ISTP, ISFP, INTP, INFP, ESTP, ESFP, ENFP, and ENTP)** are usually flexible and adapt well to changes. They are curious, like to explore the unknown, interested in meeting new people, working on new problems or finding new situations. Perceivers are usually well-liked and do not complain. On the negative side, they can easily be distracted, are often indecisive and tend to postpone unpleasant jobs. They may be inflexible and are most comfortable operating inside of a system.

AI Apps Can Search the Internet to Determine Personality Types

AI (artificial intelligence) chatbot applications (such as ChatGPT, Findem, Seekout, JOBVITE, Arya, and HireVue,) can now scour the internet to help determine a person's personality type by reviewing their online activity, such as their LinkedIn.com profile, their Facebook, Twitter, and Instagram postings, any articles they have posted, news articles, court proceedings, and property records, and all of their social media posts. The information gained may help potential employers determine whether the applicant fits the company and position well. How can we determine the personality of the buyer's team members and then customize our message? It may be easier than it seems.

The Sixteen MBTI Types and How Sales Pros Can Sell to Them[26]

ISTJ – "The Responsible Realist"

ISTJs are loyal, practical, dependable, independent, hard-working, focused, and responsible. They are superb managers driven by accountability, productivity, and bottom-line profitability, not emotions or empathy. ISTJs are normally quiet and careful leaders. Their priorities are work first, then family and community. They like to create order in their personal and professional lives and do what needs to be done. They are "workaholics" and often bring work home. They thrive on being highly organized and like to follow prescribed routines. ISTJs can get caught up in the details of problems. They also can struggle with tactfulness and empathy. These are the people that the customer wants to scrutinize contracts.

Their office will be neat, efficient, very plain, with a place for everything. The furniture would be sturdy, reliable, and functional, nothing modern. They probably will not have photographs or awards on the wall. This profile comprises the population's largest segment (about 16 percent, and normally more men than women).[27]

Billionaire investor Warren Buffett and Amazon founder Jeff Bezos are typical ISTJs. Former Secretary of State Condoleeza Rice is as well. Actors Robert De Niro, Matt Damon, and Denzel Washington are also probably ISTJs.

How your sales pro should sell to an ISTJ: They are problem solvers, so your sales pro should help them solve one more. They are not change agents and may be risk-averse, so the presentation and proposal should be well prepared, thorough, and filled with facts (they respect facts), especially how they can derive a significant ROI from your solution. The sales pro should sell the dependability and functionality of your product but avoid selling them on social benefits—they don't care.

ISTP – "The Logical Pragmatist"

ISTPs are action-oriented, adaptable, tactical leaders who like to try new ways of doing things. They tend to be pragmatic, intuitive, perceptive, and spontaneous and may not be good planners. They detest routines and schedules set by others. ISTPs are analytical, like to solve problems, and are normally perfectionists. They like to figure out how things work. They understand things more than people. Telling them that "we have never done it this way" will annoy them and invites them to make a change. ISTPs are self-sufficient, observant, like working independently, very open-minded, do not like routines, and can be impatient. They enjoy issuing and grading requests for proposals (RFPs). They are often quiet amongst other people and like to observe others without interacting with them. ISTPs are very calm and do not panic during a crisis. They are natural risk-takers who would want to skydive, race, or ride motorcycles. You might see a photograph of them rock climbing or doing something independently, not in groups.

ISTPs' (and INTPs') offices may appear cluttered, but these types are efficient, well-organized, and know where everything is. They appreciate beauty and prefer minimalism with sufficient storage to meet their needs. If given their choice, their office would be in a private area, perhaps a basement.

James Bond, the fictional British secret agent created by Ian Fleming, would be a typical ISTP. Russian President Vladimir Putin is also an ISTP, along with actor/director Clint Eastwood and NBA superstar Michael Jordan.

How your sales pro should sell to an ISTP: They are normally reserved and cautious, often difficult to read, which makes them challenging to sell. They will try to make the most objective, pragmatic, impersonal, and analytic decisions. ISTPs are not normally very diplomatic or emotional. They want to buy new and interesting things. Your sales pro should explain how your product is innovative, how it works, and how they will be ahead of their competitors by buying it. They like to review facts, so provide them with relevant information in a well-designed, logical format. Product guarantees are not important to them. Your sales pro will want to take advantage of their inclination for action. ISTPs do not always consider the long-term vision, so point out the long-term benefits. Even though they like to write and issue RFPs, your sales pro should not encourage (or discourage) them to do so.

ISFJ – "Practical Helper"

ISFJs are usually optimistic, warm-hearted, compassionate, empathetic, generous, loyal, committed, conscientious, and people-oriented leaders. Their personal values drive them, easily perceive the needs and emotions of others, and enjoy caring for people. They are detail-oriented, methodical, and accurate workers. ISFJs are usually well-grounded and content to work by themselves behind the scenes. They may be adventurous. These are the people who excel at organizing the office picnic. They are the least assertive of the 16 MBTI types.[28] On the negative side, they can be perfectionists.

Their office would be very welcoming since harmony, order, and efficiency are important to them. It would be very clean, neat, and orderly. They might exhibit their sentimental items and community service accomplishments. ISFJs, like ISTJs, prefer a lot of storage at their office. They are the second largest segment of the population.[29]

Book and movie characters Forrest Gump and Sherlock Holmes' fictional partner John Watson would be typical ISFJs. In addition, former President Jimmy Carter and the late Mother Teresa (who devoted her life to people in need) are ISFJs. The DC Comic character Clark Kent, a.k.a. Superman, and the Disney character Cinderella are ISFJs. The fictional droid character C-3PO, a loyal member and servant to his team in *Star Wars*, would also seem to be a typical ISFJ.

How your sales pro should sell to an ISFJ: They will be very considerate to you, so your sales pro should reciprocate thoughtfully to their needs and schedule. It is important to the ISFJ that the job is well done, so the sales pro should emphasize your company's outstanding track record of satisfying its customers. It is important to them that the solution positively impacts people, so the sales pro should sell the social benefits of your product. Engage them in discussions on what they are doing to serve their community. They will protect their company, its culture, and its traditions, so emphasize the overall benefits that their company will derive from your solution. ISFJs will normally avoid confrontation, so it may be difficult for the sales pro to determine a proposal's status. They will also not engage with your sales pro if they perceive your company's values are different from theirs. They are well-organized and thorough, so your sales pro's proposals should be detailed, well-written, grammatically correct, and in perfect order.

ISFP - "Versatile Supporter"

ISFPs are aware of their environment and live in the "here and now."They are creative, appreciate beauty, and imaginative. ISFPs are the most artistic of the 16 MBTI types. ISFPs are usually very introverted, sensitive, quiet, and easygoing. They are deeply empathetic and like to observe others from the sidelines. They are not natural leaders, are people of few words, and do not need to influence others. They believe in "live and let live." But they are team players. ISFPs don't like having their time planned for them or dealing with deadlines and many rules.They are normally kind, sensitive, and unassuming, with strong communication skills. "ISFPs also tend to have fragile egos and react badly to criticism—however well-intentioned, and it is difficult for them not to take it personally."[30]

Their office (and the INFPs) would be decorated nicely, with many of the most modern and tasteful amenities and decorations, as they love beautiful things. They are very detail-oriented, and disdain clutter and furniture that have clashing styles.They would also prefer window offices to take in the outside beauty.

Musical artists Brittney Spears, Christina Aguilera, and Paul McCartney are typical ISFPs. Also, fictional characters Harry Potter from the *Harry Potter* books and movies, Jon Snow and Daenerys Stormborn Targaryen from *Game of Thrones*, and Rocky Balboa from the *Rocky* movies are ISFPs.

How your sales pro should sell to an ISFP: They are one of the most difficult types to sell to as they do not share much information and often struggle coming to closure. Your sales pro should use extra efforts to build trust with the ISFP buyer and should emphasize any artistic or creature features in your product. They also like practical solutions to explore new ideas. The sales pro should stress your company's compatibility with their company's current practices. The proposal needs to be presented logically, allowing them time to think it over. ISFPs are not usually very good planners. They will not respond well to hard closes, so don't ever think of trying.

INFJ – "Insightful Visionary"

INFJs are passionate idealists and value-driven humanitarians who seek harmony in their lives and workplaces. They are naturally empathetic, champions of the less fortunate, inspirational to others, and interested in the betterment of the world. INFJs are quiet, reflective, contemplative people who are normally very compassionate, sensitive, conscientious, and creative. They are also big-picture thinkers. INFJs are insightful in others' emotions and situations. INFJs believe "developing warm and meaningful connections with others is one of the most satisfying things in life. While yes, INFJs are introverts, they also deeply crave purposeful relationships. They enjoy empathically connecting with others and then making time to recharge on their own in a quiet place."[31] INFJ is one of the rarest personality types.[32]

INFJs like personal privacy, so they may want to meet in a conference room. They strive for perfection and prefer neatness and order, so you would expect their office to be tidy and uncluttered, with no stacks of papers on their desk. They would display diplomas and awards on their office walls, as they are proud of their achievements.

Music superstars Alanis Morrissette and Lady Gaga, Harry Potter author J.K. Rowling, Princess Leia Organa from George Lucas' *Star Wars,* and Jay Gatsby from the F. Scott Fitzgerald novel *The Great Gatsby* are typical INFJs. The lead character of the *Godfather* movies, Vito Corleone, would also seem to be an INFJ.

How your sales pro should sell to an INFJ: They seek meaningful relationships, so be sure to establish trust. Ask them to share their thoughts. They want to better themselves and others, so your sales pros should explain how they will help them achieve that goal. Stress the visionary aspects of your product that differentiate it from others. Your sales pro should explain that you seek a long-term business arrangement with their company. Discuss how your executives are thought leaders in the industry. INFJs are very caring people, so the sales pro should explain the social benefits of your company and its products. They avoid conflict, so it may not be easy to get them to explain your proposal's status. Your sales pro needs to explain how your product or solution will benefit the buyer's company's workers—the human aspects-rather than emphasize technology. They are also perfectionists and workaholics, so the sales pro must be sure to submit a well-prepared proposal to them in a timely manner. They do not care for negative feedback, so the sales pro should not be critical of their work.

INFP – "Thoughtful Idealist"
INFPs are very easy-going, empathetic, flexible, and adaptive. They are humanitarians, dreamers, imaginative idealists, contemplative, very private people who seek peace and tranquility. They

care about people and do not want to hurt their feelings. They value uniqueness, authenticity, self-expression and may practice Zen. "INFPs believe that each person must find their own path."[33]

The INFP's office would likely have stacks of incomplete projects on their desk, preferably away from the hustle and bustle. Their office would normally reflect their emphasis on creativity and humanism.

Luke Skywalker, the complicated lead character from the *Star Wars* motion pictures and Peter Parker, the Marvel character *Spiderman*, would seem to be typical INFPs. So would the Muppets' Kermit the Frog; Charlie Brown, the Peanuts cartoon character; Barry Allen "The Flash;" and the tin woodman from *The Wizard of Oz*. And, from the real world, the late John Lennon and singer Alicia Keys are INFPs.

How your sales pro should sell to an INFP: INFPs are excellent listeners. They will probably not share their thoughts, so your sales pro must ask many probing questions to get information. The sales pro should focus on fulfilling their dreams and possibilities. Since they make decisions subjectively, they can be challenging to sell unless your sales pro creates trust. Because they care about people, they may avoid telling your sales pro the truth, especially if it is bad news or a serious objection. Your sales pro must do much digging to determine the opportunity's status. INFPs are passionate about their pursuits—if your sales pro can link her proposal to their goals, she will close the deal! They also have excellent written communication skills. Instead of putting them on the spot in a meeting or a telephone call, the sales pro should ask them for the status of your proposal in an email or text. Also, they should ask the INFP (and other Ps) to prepare an informal meeting agenda in advance and adhere to it. But also anticipate that the meeting will run over the allotted time. INFPs are also very contemplative and will not make decisions quickly and easily, so you must be patient and empathetic. Their decision must align with their values and morals—the sales pro must determine what those are.

INTJ – "Conceptual Planner"

They are innovative, logical, intellectual, and decisive and can be analytical and skeptical. INTJs like to innovate, are independent, and prefer to do things their way. They have a calm demeanor and are confident in their abilities. They are usually very determined and reach decisions after preparing a detailed analysis. They seek harmony, are intuitive-dominant, believe in self-improvement, and want to improve themselves and others. INTJs are very "tuned in" and can easily read other people's emotions. They prefer to be by themselves to recharge. On the negative side, they can be cold and unsympathetic, which leads some people to believe they are arrogant. INTJs are often uncomfortable in social settings and may prefer to observe rather than engage. This type is the rarest in our population; only about 2 percent of Americans are INTJs.[34]

I expect their office to be clean and well-organized as they disdain chaos in their life. They may also have inspirational posters and similar books on their shelves. INFJs and INTJs like quiet areas and new gadgets at the office.

Facebook co-founder Mark Zuckerberg, scientist and movie character J. Robert Oppenheimer, and former Secretary of State Hillary Clinton are likely INJTs. The fictional character *Sherlock Holmes*, created by British author Sir Arthur Conan Doyle, would be a typical INTJ. Also, the Wicked Witch of the West from *The Wizard of Oz*, and the fictional character Stephen Strange from *Dr. Strange* are INTJs.

How your sales pro should sell to an INTJ: INTJs are independent and hard to read. They are confident, logical thinkers who are more comfortable with concepts than facts. They also like to seek perfection and solve problems. And they are driven by their original ideas to achieve improvements. The sales pro should present well-organized value propositions to INTJs. They are willing to look at a proposal from another perspective, so if your initial proposal doesn't resonate with them try another angle. They also can overlook the fine details of a proposal, so the sales pro should offer to help them build their detailed analysis. Since they can be skeptical, the sales pro should be prepared to provide proof of value and perhaps references of similar companies that have benefitted from your product or solution. They also place a high priority on social issues. The sales pro needs to be sure to adhere to the agreed-upon agenda and meeting timeframe. Promptness and staying on task are important to the INTJ.

INTP – "Objective Analyst"

INTPs are the dreamers that are often engaged in their own thoughts. They are curious, analytical, highly energetic, independent thinkers and are often intellectually challenging. They "approach life with skepticism and curiosity, rigorously analyzing anything that interests them. And while INTPs are known for their love of logic and understanding, they are less known for their empathy. They consider themselves detached observers, seeking clarity and understanding more than anything else."[35]

INTPs have new ideas and theories and are not burdened by the current practices. They are willing to challenge others, express their opinions openly, and say what is on their mind, even though they are introverts. They are not normally deadline oriented. They are not self-focused and may also be socially cautious and awkward. They are not "tuned in" and often oblivious to the world around them. They normally do not micro-manage and welcome all opinions. "INTPs are free-spirited idea mills and absentminded professors, which makes them fun to be around, easily diverted, and a plethora of unending creativity."[36] They like to work autonomously and do not like operating in a bureaucracy with a lot of rules.

Their office may reflect their creative, easy-going nature and appear to need more organization, with papers that are strewn about and half-completed projects apparent. Tidiness and cleanliness are not that important to them. They may have photographs and posters on the floor instead of hanging on the wall. And the office may have their favorite books on the shelves or on a credenza.

Yoda, the fictional Jedi master character from *Star Wars*; Alice, the fictional character of Lewis Carroll's novel *Alice's Adventures in Wonderland* and Disney animation character; Greek philosopher Plato; Dutch artist Vincent Van Gogh; English novelist George Orwell; the late Steve Jobs, the co-founder of Apple; billionaire entrepreneur Elon Musk; and Albert Einstein, the famous scientist, would be typical INTPs.

How to sell to an INTP: These people will not naturally engage with others, so establishing rapport will be difficult. And they may be unpredictable. It may even be difficult to schedule a meeting, so your sales pro may need to send them more information via email than you would with most people. It is best to schedule the appointment at least two weeks in advance—and "one-on-one" to achieve the best results. INTPs are logical, like solving problems, and will respond positively to a well-thought-out value proposition. They enjoy sharing their theories, so your sales pro needs to listen to them. They will likely challenge your sales pro's facts and assumptions, but they will not force their ideas on you.

ESTP – "Energetic Problem Solver"

ESTPs are outgoing, charismatic, energetic, fact-based, straight-shooting, action-oriented, confident, and "live-for-the-moment" individuals who can quickly look at a situation and improvise. They enjoy conversations and being around others. ESTPs are fun-loving optimists and tend to be the most spontaneous, impatient, and impulsive personality types. They do not like routine and predictable tasks. ESTPs prefer freedom, dislike having their time scheduled, and disdain rules. They prefer to solve problems, are good trouble-shooters, and want to get things done. Now. They are usually supportive of others. ESTPs have been multi-tasking most of their life. They are also perceptive and can easily read others' emotions and body language. Read manuals? No way. ESTPs don't need manuals. They are for other people.

An ESTP's office will appear disorganized (except to them) and may reflect their risk-taking by containing unusual furniture and bold colors. Their office will be clean, not cluttery. They will likely display photographs of their close family and have plaques of their accomplishments, diplomas, or company awards on the wall.

Some famous ESTPs are showman P.T. Barnum, former British Prime Minister Winston Churchill, and Presidents George W. Bush and Donald Trump. Scarlett O'Hara, the lead female character from the movie and book *Gone with the Wind*, is a resilient survivor who wants to live for today and is also a typical ESTP. Lt. Pete "Maverick" Mitchell, the lead character in *Top Gun* and *Top Gun: Maverick*, acted by Tom Cruise, would be an ESTP. Also, actor Dwayne "The Rock" Johnson and NBA basketball star Stephen Curry are ESTPs. This author is also an ESTP.

How your sales pro should sell to an ESTP: It should be easy to schedule a meeting as they are very social and will normally take calls. They are impulsive, emotional, quick decision-makers, and like to seize opportunities. ESTPs may also be very assertive and want to take charge of interactions. They like socializing but will quickly get down to business when you meet them. Since they want to solve problems using logic, your sales pro should explain (emphasize the "pros and cons") how your company's solution will help fix the issues that bother them. Please provide the facts to help them build their internal business case. Be real! ESTPs don't care about abstracts or theories, so the sales pro needs to stick to the facts. They will say what is on their mind, so don't worry about them hiding facts from you. And they will take risks. Don't worry about social causes; they are not important to them. They are also nonconformists, so they do not care about the latest trends. The sales pro should not delay getting your proposal to them. ESTPs are often very skilled negotiators, so the sales pro should be ready to discuss your proposal. Don't push them to make decisions; it is not necessary. They will quickly decide by themselves.

ESTJ – "Efficient Organizer"

ESTJs are often in leadership positions due to their take-charge personality and versatility. They are very outspoken and dependable. ESTJs make "objective, non-personal, analytical decisions."[37] They thrive on orderliness, efficiency, fairness, and continuity, enjoy sorting out chaos, and implementing new procedures to fix problems. "If you want a job done, a regulation established, or an ongoing program evaluated, call on an ESTJ to manage it."[38] They are usually outspoken and direct. ESTJs love to share their opinions, as well as their expertise. They are confident in their abilities and like to have a high degree of control over situations. They may use their domineering personality to assert their ideas over others without care for offending other people. And they may tend to be micro-managers. They are normally not very empathetic. "They often show they care by troubleshooting, offering advice, or helping out with a tangible need. Often, an ESTJ is the first to line up a meal plan for someone who is sick or to offer to drive someone to a doctor's appointment. And as always, ESTJs can learn and practice empathy just as anyone can."[39]

I would expect that the ESTJs fingernails would be trim and immaculate. And they would have very smart and coiffed hair styles. They would probably not have any body tattoos showing.

Their office would be clean, tidy, and well-organized. They would be upset if it was otherwise. It might also display that they are in charge by showing company recognition photos and awards. The ESTJ might have a company organization chart on the wall.

Former President Harry S. Truman would seem to be a typical ESTJ—"The buck stops here." Syndicated television Judge Judy Scheindlin is also an ESTJ. Fictional *Harry Potter* character

Hermione Granger and Disney characters Minnie Mouse and *Toy Story's* Woody would also be ESTJs.

How your sales pro should sell to an ESTJ: ESTJs are assertive, direct, and have a clear idea of what they desire. As such, they are likely to provide your sales pros with current information on the status of their proposals. They like responsibility and making decisions. They are also biased toward prior procedures and solutions that worked well for them. The sales pro should stress how your solution is pragmatic and will help them bring greater efficiency and order to their company. They will want to have control over the buying process. Accommodate this and refrain from fighting them on it. They will also be disappointed if you do not agree with their well-thought-out proposal or analysis, and they may be unyielding, so be prepared to handle this situation in a delicate, non-confrontational manner.

ESFP – "Enthusiastic Improviser"

This personality trait is very sociable, spontaneous, fun-loving, and adaptive. ESFPs prefer freedom. They disdain structure and order, and live in the moment. They are generous, value relationships, are team players, love conversations, and are easily recognized because of their desire to entertain. They experience life to its fullest extent. ESFPs have high energy and like to improvise, juggle multiple projects simultaneously, or multi-task while meeting deadlines. They can easily read other people's emotions and body language. ESFPs love surprises.

Office? The ESFP may not have one. If they did, it would appear disorganized but not messy and cluttered. And it would be a nice office, with artwork and plants.

Former President Bill Clinton and tennis superstar Serena Williams are ESFPs. Also, Sean Penn's Jeff Spicoli surfer dude character in the *Fast Times at Ridgemont High* movie is a typical ESFP. Daisy Buchanan, the character in F. Scott Fitzgerald's *The Great Gatsby*, who desires to live life to the fullest, and the fictional character Ron Weasley from the Harry Potter books and movie, as well as the cowardly lion from *The Wizard of Oz*, would also be ESFPs. Disney characters Donald Duck and Lucy van Pelt, the *Peanuts* cartoon character, are ESFPs. Entertainers Jimmy Buffett, Dolly Parton, and Katy Perry are also ESFPs.

How to sell to an ESFP: These individuals are among the best types to sell to, as they are very cooperative and should agree to meet with you. Your sales pro should engage in small talk to build rapport. ESFPs are imaginative and adaptive and will be willing to listen to your proposal. However, they usually dislike abstract theory and written explanations, preferring concrete value propositions. They want to be helpful and resourceful, so they will happily work with your sales pro on building a business case. Do not worry about preparing them before the meeting. They will make decisions based on their own criteria.

ESFJ – "Supportive Contributor"

ESFJs are charismatic leaders who enjoy harmony and a sense of stability in their lives. As extroverts ("the life of the party") and as "feelers," they easily perceive other people's feelings and needs, not wanting others to be unhappy. They are generous and like to connect with and enjoy serving others, especially those that are like-minded. ESFJs are also concerned about their appearance (how they are groomed and dressed) and will notice and compare their appearance with others. They like to be the host or hostess. ESFJs like to create a sense of order, rather than chaos. They will always put the team's needs ahead of their own. Their home and home life are the centers of their focus. They are creative, problem solvers, decisive, and loyal. They are empathetic, diplomatic, and are the most harmonizing of the 16 personality types.[40] They are usually gracious, thoughtful, and have good interpersonal skills.

ESFJs do not thrive working alone. Their office would be well-organized, utilitarian, warm, inviting, and spacious. They would probably exhibit photographs of themself in groups, perhaps on a church retreat or trip. Both the ESFJ and ENFJ like to personalize their offices.

Dorothy, the fictional character from Frank Baum's *The Wizard of Oz*, would be an ESFJ. Disney characters Snow White and Mary Poppins are ESFJs. Warner Bros movie character Barbie is an ESFJ. In real life, Pope Francis is an ESFJ, as are music superstars Taylor Swift and Ariana Grande, actors Jennifer Garner, Hugh Jackman, and President Joe Biden are ESFJs.

How your sales pro should sell to ESFJs: ESFJs are very pleasant to sell to because they are trusting, approachable, cooperative, and friendly. They are productive and want to be in charge, so your sales pro should not challenge their leadership. They often overlook the long-term aspects of plans, so your sales pro should point out the longer-term benefits of your proposal. ESFJs values are very important to them, so the sales pro should try to connect your proposal to their personal values. They will decide if your sales pro convinced them that your proposal is realistic and practical. They like to be helpful and will be cooperative. Do not expect ESFJs to create a solution independently; draw them into the solution your team designs. They will reject your sales pro and her proposal if it creates friction amongst their evaluation team.

ENFP – "Imaginative Motivator"

These are the "glass half full," optimistic, upbeat, inspiring, outgoing, enthusiastic people who try to be helpful to others. They encourage freedom and independence and are not obsessive about control of a situation. They have good interpersonal skills, want to be liked by others, and are self-expressive, thoughtful, empathetic, and socially gracious. They like to go to work, are resourceful, innovative, and agents of change. They are likely to rebel against established routines. ENFPs want to make the world a better place.

They are bored by details. ENFPs (and ENTPs) would thrive in shared offices. If they had their own office, it would probably be filled with décors representing their joy with the world, such as bright flowers or colors. And it would probably appear untidy and disorganized.

Mr. Rogers from the public television show of the same name would be a typical ENFP, as would the Greek philosopher Socrates. The wizard from *The Wizard of Oz,* Disney characters Mickey Mouse, Pinocchio, Peter Pan, and Aladdin, and the Tyron Lannister character from *Game of Thrones* would also be ENFPs. Actor Jim Carrey and the late actor/comedian Robin Williams are both ENFPs. The fictional character Carrie from the television series *Sex in the City* would also be an ENFP.[41]

How your sales pro should sell to ENFPs: ENFPs will be willing to meet with your sales pros and are not threatened if they invite others. Since they may have trouble staying focused and finishing projects, your sales pro may need to keep bringing them back to the subject matter or your proposal. ENFPs are open to ideas, so it is good to brainstorm with them. They usually like change, so take advantage of their willingness to explore other possibilities. Your sales pro will enjoy meeting them and should engage their imagination and spontaneity by showing them a solution that will immediately benefit their company. Your sales pro should be sure to thank them for meeting with them.

ENFJ – "Compassionate Facilitator"

ENFJs are optimistic, charismatic leaders, that excel at encouraging and motivating their teams. They are natural extroverts and usually have many friends. They are humanitarians and care for the well-being of other people. Empathy comes very easily to them. "Enthusiastic and warm, ENFJs are driven by a desire to help others and impact meaningful change in the world. As idealists, they have an innate desire to be imaginative, creative, and find meaning and purpose. They are often seen as insightful and emotionally conscious."[42]

ENFJs prefer their lives to be structured, scheduled, and organized. They are easy to converse with, have excellent communication skills, are very persuasive, and tend to inspire others. They are very self-disciplined and focused. ENFJs are natural sales pros and are "team players."

Their office would have a large conference table to allow discussions and collaboration. It would be clean and neat. They may demonstrate their enthusiasm for life and people with personal photographs on the wall.

Television personality and actress Oprah Winfrey is an ENFJ. Also, actresses Viola Davis and Meryl Streep, musician Bono, the late Rev. Martin Luther King, Jr, and the late Nelson Mandela are or were ENFJs. Also, the fictional character Albus Dumbledore from the *Harry Potter* books and movies is an ENFJ.

How your sales pro should sell to an ENFJ: It is vitally important for your sales pro to build trust with an ENFJ. Feelings and values are important to them so that they will empathize with a well-thought-out proposal. They dislike criticism and may procrastinate to avoid those situations. ENFJs are friendly, excellent communicators, and should be willing to discuss the pros and cons of purchasing from your company. Your sales pro should be sure to explain the benefits their company will derive from your product or solution in order of importance. ENFJs are very persuasive and will want you to see the situation their way. But they are prone to making hasty decisions. Try to withhold criticism of their handling of the evaluation. They will also reject your sales pro or the proposal if you create disharmony amongst their team.

ENTP – "Enterprising Explorer"

ENTPs are spontaneous, high-energy, curious, resourceful individuals. "They are energized by working with others, focused on understanding people and problems, creative and systematic thinkers, and comfortable with frequent, fast-paced change."[43] ENTPs are natural innovators, creative problem solvers, and love challenges. They are usually analytical. They embody "If at first you don't succeed, drop it and try something else."[44] ENTPs are naturally friendly and like to work in groups, but can also be incredibly competitive. They like to brainstorm new ideas and expect them to be taken seriously. Their schedules are flexible, they disdain routine tasks and repetition, and they are often not committed to meeting deadlines. They excel at troubleshooting and are idea people who willingly contribute their thoughts. ENTPs like to multi-task and test idea limits. They may be involved in many community or social functions. Their office would change frequently, and it may appear disorganized when you visit. They prefer to hang out in a coffee shop.

Tony Stark, the *Ironman* Marvel comic character, and the talkative and the inquisitive droid R2-D2 character from *Star Wars* seem to be typical ENTPs. Another would be one of my favorite television characters, Ralph Cramden, from *The Honeymooners*, who always tried to devise a "get rich" scheme that always failed. The scarecrow from *The Wizard of Oz*, the *Peanuts* cartoon character Snoopy, President Barack Obama, actor Tom Hanks, Walt Disney, and the Cosmo Kramer character from the television show *Seinfeld* are also ENTPs.

How your sales pro should sell to an ENTP: ENTPs are inventive, like new ideas, and will not resist change, never saying, "We have always done it this way." Your sales pro should leverage their interest in problem-solving and challenges by presenting innovative, logical proposals. ENTPs naturally tend to be outspoken and speak their mind, so take advantage of that by asking "open-ended" questions. They are also argumentative, love to debate, and to procrastinate, so expect some pushback on your proposal.

ENTJ – "Decisive Strategist"

ENTJs are natural leaders and usually very energetic people. They are strong-willed, honest, and intelligent. They are driven by a need to accomplish goals and are long-term planners with the vision to see the big picture of a situation and think strategically. As extroverts and leaders, they are direct and forthright. They are the most assertive of the sixteen MBTI types and will usually speak their mind.[45] ENTJs are always willing to be decisive, take charge, and efficiently organize other people and resources to see a project to completion. Because of this, they are excellent CEOs. They are original thinkers, enjoy challenges, are pragmatic problem solvers, like to accomplish tasks, are unafraid to make decisions, are skilled at understanding others, and love negotiating. ENTJs can be argumentative like ENTPs. They are very perceptive and can usually read the emotions of others. But "ENTJs feel that emotions are mere roadblocks to productivity and clear thinking."[46] They can be impatient with people that are resistant to their ideas or are negative.

Their office would be very inviting and conducive for discussions. It might have a large desk and plush leather chairs. ENTJs are very efficient, and everything will be in its place.

Microsoft co-founder Bill Gates, television personality Simon Cowell, presidential candidate and technologist Vivek Ramaswamy, and actor Harrison Ford are ENTJs. Also, The Muppets' Miss Piggy character, Disney *Toy Story* character Buzz Lightyear, Bruce Wayne, a.k.a. Batman, and fictional *Harry Potter* character Hermione Granger would also be typical ENTJs. Napoleon Bonaparte, Julius Caesar, Alexander Hamilton, and possibly even Aristotle were ENTJs.

How your sales pro should sell to an ENTJ: ENTJs are usually honest and straightforward, even blunt, so it should be easy to ascertain your competitive position. As an extrovert, they are very willing to meet with your sales pro, who needs to emphasize the strategic aspects of your proposal, for example, how it helps the buyer's company grow organically, expand operations, increase time to market, or cut costs. They are decisive, motivated by change, and like to get things done quickly, so provide them with the necessary information to move forward quickly. The sales pro should avoid getting drawn into an argument because ENTJs can be blunt, argumentative, and like to negotiate.

Last Thoughts

Understandably, a sales pro might have difficulty recognizing the various MBTI types, especially with limited in-person access. This table indicates how the various MBTI types would probably dress for work, so it can aid sales pros in recognizing them, as personal appearance and one's office are the easiest and most apparent clues.[47]

PERSONALITY TYPE	FASHION
INFJ, ENFJ	Creative; classic romantic, striking outfits, accent something important to them
INTP, ENTP	Prefer comfort, loose fitting; will dress sharp when necessary
INTJ, ENTJ	Professional, minimalistic, mix and match, hate mediocrity, individualistic

ISFP, ESFP	Individualistic, perfectly coordinated, very stylish, comfortable
ISTP, ESTP	Practicality and comfort, coordinated, matched to the situation, like aesthetics
ISFJ, ESFJ	Classic time-tested, comfortable, coordinated, important to look good, not trendy
ISTJ, ESTJ	Dressing right is a priority, function & effectiveness, no-nonsense, traditional
INFP, ENFP	Drawn to fashions that are somewhat romantic, personalized, and unusual

With this information, you can begin to recognize the buyer's personality so that the sales pro can craft individualistic messages that will best resonate with them, rather than providing the same corporate-crafted marketing message to all. Here are four charts that show the different attributes of the various MBTI that will be useful in crafting your strategies and messages and guiding you on how to best approach the individuals.

	ESTP	ISTP	ESTJ	ISTJ
Conversational	Y	N	Y	N
Change Agents	Y	Y	N	N
Examine Details	N	Y	Y	Y
Want to impact	Y	Y	Y	Y
Social Good	N	Y	N	N
Decisive	Y	Y	Y	Y

	ENFJ	INFJ	ENTJ	ISFJ
Conversational	Y	N	Y	Y
Change Agents	Y	Y	Y	Y
Examine Details	N	Y	Y	Y
Want to impact	Y	Y	Y	Y
Social Good	Y	Y	N	N
Decisive	Y	N	Y	Y

	ENFP	INFP	ENTP	INTP
Conversational	Y	Y	Y	N
Change Agents	Y	N	Y	Y
Examine Details	N	Y	Y	Y
Want to impact	Y	Y	Y	N
Social Good	Y	Y	N	N
Decisive	Y	N	Y	N

	ESFJ	INTJ	ESFP	ISFP
Conversational	Y	Y	Y	Y
Change Agents	N	N	Y	N
Examine Details	Y	Y	N	N
Want to impact	Y	Y	Y	Y
Social Good	Y	Y	N	Y
Decisive	Y	N	Y	N

If there are many people are on the buying team, it is essential to customize your messages to each person. To do so, it is prudent to try to determine the personalities of the key decision makers, including the economic buyer, and for the sales pros to prepare their messaging in a manner they will best receive.

By recognizing buyers' different personalities and applying this information, the sales pro can gain an advantage in closing the sale by approaching each in a more tailored, compatible manner. Using personality type methodologies such as MBTI to recognize each type and improve your messaging could be the edge that your sales pro needs to close the sale.

CHAPTER 8
Selling to Millennials

It is presumptuous to generalize the characteristics of a whole generation of Americans and project those observed characteristics of the entire group to each person. Given the many non-homogeneous people in each generation, how can someone generalize how to sell to any group? There are tens of millions of people in each category, and each person is very different from the others in most respects, including personality, background, financial circumstances, aspirations, physical characteristics, preferences, behaviors, and skills. Is grouping people according to birth years a media creation that is baseless for analysis? Isn't the categorization and naming of a generation another form of a "pop psychology" myth? Perhaps. However, the media, reporters, psychologists, and sales pros, including me, have been able to study the commonalities of the groups and have noticed many key similarities within each group. There is value in understanding the contrasts and preferences of each generation to determine how your sales pros can best approach each generation in a sales situation.

The Greatest Generation, Baby Boomers, and Generation X

For the first time in American history, five different generations could be working side-by-side at the same company. The eldest generation has been nicknamed the "Silent Generation," consisting of individuals born between 1928 and 1945. They are also called "traditionalists" or "the Greatest Generation" because of the Tom Brokaw book of the same name. Most of the members of this generation have retired or died, but there are still a few million born in the 1940s in the workforce and they comprise about 0.2 percent of the total population.[48] This generation was very loyal to their employers and usually worked at one or two jobs during their life.

The next eldest generation is the remainder of the over 77 million American "Baby Boomers" born between 1946 and 1964. Currently, they are the second largest generation in the US, comprising over 21 percent, but many have retired from the workforce, and most will likely be retired by 2030.[49] At work, the Baby Boomers "played by the rules" and were generally self-sufficient.[50] They worked hard for promotions and pay increases. They are often characterized as intelligent, honest, hard-working individuals with high morals and values.

Baby Boomers typically worked for three or four, or more, employers throughout their careers, sometimes changing jobs involuntarily because they were the victims of downsizing due to the changing economy, mergers and acquisitions, globalization, ageism, and creative destruction. They grew up "making phone calls and writing letters, solidifying strong interpersonal skills."[51] The widespread use of computers came into use during their working career. Baby Boomers viewed the new technologies as productivity tools rather than a way of staying connected with the news and their friends. Their strong work ethic, respectfulness, and high morals and values often characterize them.

Generation X or "Gen X" are Americans born between 1965 and 1980. They currently comprise a substantial amount of the corporate workforce. Gen Xers are the bridge between Baby Boomers and Millennials in many ways and are sometimes termed "the sandwich generation" or the "MTV generation." These people have used technology, such as desktop and laptop computers, throughout their careers. Many people from this generation are now in management positions at corporations. Gen Xers are sometimes called "latchkey" kids because they typically came from families where either both parents worked, or they came from a single parent household; when they came home from school, there were no parents present so they used a key to enter their house. They "prefer to work independently with minimal supervision. They also value opportunities to grow, make choices, and have relationships with mentors. They also believe that promotions should be based on competence, not rank, age, or seniority."[52] Gen Xers are often characterized by their use of technology, work ethic, and desire for a work/life balance.

The Millennials

Millennials are the generation of Americans born from the early 1980s through 1999, and are sometimes referred to as "Generation Y." They came of age during the economic recession of 2006 – 2008, which still affects their life and attitudes. There are now over 83 million Millennials in the US,[53] and over 1.8

billion Millennials in the world, which is 23 percent of the population, surpassing the number of Baby Boomers.[54] Millennials now outnumber the other generations in the workforce, and it is expected that they will make up 75 percent of the American workforce by 2025.[55]

Because they are such a large percentage of the workforce, it is vitally important to understand their unique characteristics and why selling to them requires a different style than to other generations, rather than a "one size fits all" approach.

Takeaway 18 – Millennials Now Comprise the Majority of Today's Workforce

Millennials have been characterized in many ways. They are better educated, in general, than the generations that came before them, according to Pew Research.[56] They have delayed marriage and many still live at home with their parents.[57] "On the negative side, they've been described as lazy, narcissistic and prone to jump from job to job. The 2008 book *Trophy Kids* by Ron Alsop discusses how many young people have been rewarded for minimal accomplishments (such as mere participation) in competitive sports and have unrealistic expectations of working life."[58] Everybody received a trophy for participating, not just the child or team that finished first. Growing up, they were taught that competing in a game or contest was good enough and that teamwork was more important than individual achievement.

On the positive side, Millennials "are generally regarded as more open-minded . . . Other positive adjectives to describe them include confident, self-expressive, liberal, upbeat, and receptive to new ideas and ways of living."[59] I have found many of them to be more open and honest than prior generations. They are also very concerned with wellness and physical fitness. And they are always busy, including early in the morning and late at night.

Dr. Ralph Ryback noted in *Psychology Today* that "This blog-savvy generation was raised by parents who were not authoritative, but rather saw themselves as partners. Millennials grew up making the rules rather than having their parents tell them what is right. Their lives are now run by their smart gadgets, their third appendage."[60]

Millennials and Technology

Millennials are often characterized by their ubiquitous use of technology, their keen interest in music and pop culture, their liberalism and tolerance, and their casual dress codes. Many have never worn a business suit to work. More than nine out of ten Millennials own smartphones, much more than any other generation.[61] The internet and mobile telephones have always been available, and they use social media extensively. They are plugged into the internet 24/7. Many receive daily news from social media, preferring posts from their friends and people they follow on X (formerly Twitter) rather than television or print newspapers. Millennials are much more likely to use streaming services like Netflix, Apple TV, or Amazon Prime, for entertainment than television or going to a movie theatre. They usually do not use their smartphone to communicate via voice but prefer texting to emails or telephone calls. Millennials are more apt to purchase online than going to brick and mortar stores. They are leading this trend, and others are following their steps. They have used automated teller machines, or ATMs, all their life, and many have never written a bank check or draft.

Some in the media have referred to Millennials as a "Peter Pan" or "boomerang generation" because many have had to move back in with their parents or siblings due to economic constraints. "Forty-five percent of Millennials (ages 23 to 38) cite the cost of living as holding them back from buying a home, compared with just 38 percent of Gen Xers (ages 39 to 54) and 31 percent of Baby Boomers (ages 55 to 73)," per a study by Bankrate.com.[62]

As a workforce group, Millennials are much more diverse than their predecessors. There are more women, more minorities, more foreign-born and non-native English speakers, which comprise about 15 percent of the Millennial workforce, and more openly gay people in the workforce than previous generations.[63] They are also much more educated than their predecessors in some areas, such as familiarity with technology, but less educated in others, such as grammar, spelling, geography, finance, history, and economics. They are more connected to their friends than older generations. They are very adept at multi-tasking.

A story in *Time* magazine said polls show that Millennials "want flexible work schedules, more 'me time' on the job, and nearly nonstop feedback and career advice from managers."[64] But they also want to receive raises and promotions without giving up flexibility. A recent Deloitte study found that Millennials want to balance workplace flexibility and job stability. Millennials tend to stay in their jobs longer than Gen Xers and about as long as Baby Boomers.[65] My experience is that well-educated Millennials expect quick job promotions and will look elsewhere if that does not happen. They also seek a positive job culture with more meaning, defined as a job where they can help others and live their desired quality of life.

Another *Time* story titled "The Me Me Me Generation" begins with this polemic description of Millennials: "They're narcissistic. They're lazy. They're coddled. They're even a bit delusional. Those aren't just unfounded negative stereotypes about 80 million Americans born roughly between 1980 and 2000. They're backed up by a decade of sociological research."[66] The *Time* article also points out that Millennials adapt quickly to a rapidly changing world.

Millennials value work-life balance more than their predecessors, providing greater satisfaction in their social lives, and improved physical, emotional, and mental well-being. "This generation is not as willing to sacrifice their personal lives to advance their careers. Millennials like to 'work hard, play hard' and appreciate a company that values this balance."[67] They also may want and expect instant gratification. "Millennials value *experiences, personalization, authenticity, and transparency*. They appreciate socially and environmentally conscious companies, and value flexibility, communication, and collaboration."[68] They care deeply about social issues like climate change, affordable healthcare, and diversity. In addition, "Millennials are passionate about issues such as sustainability, social justice, and economic equality. They are also passionate about technology and staying up to date with the latest trends, as well as being actively involved in their communities and finding ways to give back."[69]

Millennials prefer learning online to attending lectures and are more apt to go to Google search or the internet for advice. They spend a lot of time browsing for all information, from news to recipes to music to navigation. They also tend to believe much of what they read on social media (good, bad, or otherwise.) It is not unusual to see Millennials sitting in the same room, texting each other instead of talking. They also use social media apps extensively. Most post messages and photos from their smartphones daily. Many settle their group restaurant checks by using the Venmo app.

These characteristics do not apply to everybody, but they provide a basis for understanding the generation. Given this generation's size, you likely have sales pros and prospects that fall into this category.

Assuming that many of your sales pros are Millennials, the changes you need to make as a manager are:

- Recognize that they are motivated differently than previous generations. For example, they are less motivated by earnings and commissions. They also value their leisure time more than others. And they will want enough time to exercise or do their yoga exercises.
- Millennials loathe ultimatums, which will only annoy them, and they will likely resign and go to work elsewhere. They also disdain conflict, so your conversations with them must not be aggressive.
- Values matter a lot to them, as do social causes such as diversity, equality, and inclusion (DEI). They may care more about saving the earth than closing another deal.
- They like honest and timely feedback but do not want to be lectured. They want coaching and mentoring. They need to feel that you are interested in their careers, not just in achieving your sales or revenue goals.

- Lead by example. Demonstrate how it is done.
- Encourage Millennials to ask questions to clarify any issues.
- Your language needs to be adapted to their needs. They want you to speak with them as an equal, not as a manager. Get used to hearing "dude," "so," "basically," and "like."
- Don't expect them to call you on the telephone. They will text you.
- They desire flexibility in most aspects of their life. They need time to take their dog to be groomed.
- They like an enjoyable work environment. Billiard and foosball tables are standard in many companies.
- They will be dressed more casually than others. You will probably need to remind them not to wear blue jeans, khakis, and Birkenstock shoes on sales calls (unless they are calling on other Millennials.)
- They do not understand why you do not use CashApp, Venmo, or Apple Pay to pay bills or are not on TikTok and other social media apps.
- Ironically, Millennials do not like to be called "Millennials" or have someone categorize them as such. They also seem to review the next age group, Generation Z, disdainfully.

Millennials and Learning

Millennials (and Gen Zers) prefer to learn differently than their predecessors. The previous generations learned from studying independently in schools and universities and listening to others, but primarily by doing "on-the-job" training and repetition. Millennials, however, have learned mainly through internet browsing, online research (either in formal education or on their own), and social media. They also have shorter attention spans. Millennials (and Gen Zers) value face-to-face interaction and group or team collaboration. This must be taken into consideration when selling to Millennials.

Thought leadership is also very important to Millennials. People with recognized expertise highly influence them. These are the people that the Millennials recognize from social media, such as Elon Musk, Bill Gates, Richard Branson, Oprah Winfrey, Brené Brown, Cristiano Rinaldo, the late Steve Jobs, and some highly read influencers on YouTube and TikTok, such as Evan Edinger, Steven Bartlett, and Hazel Hayes. And in my experience, they do not understand why paperwork needs to be completed to memorialize agreements. They also believe they should be adding value for their customers.

Roles of Millennials in Purchasing Decisions

It is essential to understand Millennials' typical roles in corporate buying decisions. Although few Millennials have ascended to "C" Level roles in corporations (other than their startups) at this point, some have already entered positions in companies where they can either influence or have the authority to make a buying decision, as there are 87 million global Millennials (almost 40 percent of the total) on LinkedIn.com with 11 million global Millennials in decision-making positions.[70] About 13 percent are decision-makers, and 17 percent are project managers, but the most significant portion of the buying team is the researchers.[71]

They can utilize their proficiency in reaching the internet to provide information to the team. Your company's marketing material, user testimonials, and reviews must be updated so that when people do research, your company will be included in evaluations.

In addition, more Millennials are now working in the corporate procurement function, which is increasing in size at US corporations. "In the (UPS) 2019 survey, 38% of the respondents were Millennials, up from 28% in the 2017 edition of the survey."[72] Sales pros need to understand how to work best with them to close sales better.

Takeaway 19 – Millennials Are More Involved in Purchasing Decisions Now

How to Sell to Millennials

I have described some differences between Millennials and other generations and explained how their company purchasing habits differ greatly from their predecessors. Now that I have discussed their background, likes and dislikes, and greater involvement in purchasing decisions, *how do you help your sales pro sell to them?*

First, we need to look at their needs and motivations—those characteristics we reviewed above. Millennials' hierarchy of needs is very different from that of other generations. Your sales pros must recognize when selling to a mostly Millennial audience and then adapt their selling styles to recognize the difference in typical Millennial personalities and styles. Otherwise, the competitor's sales pro will be cashing the commission check.

Here are twenty tips on how your sales pros need to sell to Millennials:

1. Understand that the most significant purchasing influence on Millennials (and, to a slightly lesser extent, Gen Xers) are third-party, unbiased reviews. Friends and family would be the next most important.[73]

2. Assess what information they have and their perception of it. Millennials will do a substantial amount of research before contacting a potential vendor. As noted above, they are habitual internet browsers. When they contact your sales pro, they are already farther along in their buying process than your sales pro may realize. They will rely on information gained from reviews and vendors' websites.

3. Build trusted relationships with decision team members. Trust is critical to Millennials (as with other generations, but even more so with Millennials.)

4. Focus on results and demonstrate the value derived by other customers. Explain what they can expect to happen if they purchase your solution, and what the experience of other companies has been.

5. Emphasize showing Millennials that their ideas and opinions are valued.

6. Be straightforward and exceedingly clear. Communication will often be an issue. This generation has relied primarily on texting each other, even in the same room. Sales pros of other generations may need to adapt their oral and written communications when

dealing with Millennials. Your sales pros may send a message, question, or request via email or voicemail that you believe is straightforward and receive an inadequate response, such as "okay."

7. Become comfortable with online pitching. Zoom, FaceTime, Skype, and other video apps are usually acceptable to Millennials and may be the only way to meet with them face-to-face until your sales pro has gained their trust.

8. Promote the Brand. Millennials are typically loyal to well-known brands like Nike, Coca-Cola, Amazon, and Google. Your sales pro needs to think about how he can position your company's solution like a brand. Millennials value brands that enhance their lives and the lives of others.

9. Highlight the technical aspects of your product/solution. Your team needs to take advantage of the Millennials' natural curiosity, as they seem more inquisitive than other generations. Millennials want to know *who, what, where, and when.* They want to *get under the hood* and learn more about your product or solution.

10. Be authentic and sincere, direct, and factual. The sales pro needs to lead the Millennials to internet sources, such as websites, Google reviews, LinkedIn.com postings, or news and industry sources, where they can research. Millennials enjoy doing this, and the results of their fact-finding will give them greater credibility. Help your team prepare a list of the research sources that can be provided to Millennial prospects.

11. Promote your company's causes to them. Millennials
    are normally very concerned about the environment and
    sustainability, much more so than prior generations. If
    applicable, your sales pro should show how your product
    is environmentally friendly and socially conscious. "75%
    of Millennials say it's essential that a company gives back
    to society instead of just making a profit."[74]

12. Customize presentations to Millennials and minimize
    any industry jargon. Sales pros should use simple,
    concise, and non-ambiguous language that is easily
    understood by all. No niche acronyms, please.

13. Value diversity. As a sales manager, assemble a qualified,
    diverse team with a variety of perspectives and
    backgrounds, and your sales pros will then naturally
    follow suit when selecting their team for each pitch.

14. Emphasize simplicity. Millennials prefer "all in one"
    solutions versus "best of breed" or solutions from
    multiple vendors. Your sales pro should show them how
    your *simple* solution will solve many of their issues or
    problems. Reducing emotional stress is important to
    Millennials, so emphasize how your company's solution
    will ease their stresses, not add to them.

15. Your sales pro should highlight any "smart" features
    in your product or Wi-Fi connectivity upfront
    in your presentation to gain their interest. He
    should demonstrate this in his meetings with the
    Millennial prospect.

16. Avoid the hard close. Your sales pro should not attempt
    any sales tricks, such as "the price is going up tomorrow;

you need to buy now." This tactic will certainly turn them off.

17. Connect with your prospects. This is especially true if your sales pro is not a Millennial. He needs to understand that their core values are different from his. Your sales pro will get extra points if they can connect on a personal level about social causes, hobbies, or other interests.

18. Engage, engage, engage. Your team must work harder to keep the Millennial audience engaged during this presentation, or they will soon check their emails or work on other projects since Millennials are natural multi-taskers. This is a good thing to practice in those role-playing exercises we discussed earlier.

19. Take your cues from the client when dressing for a meeting. Your sales pro should not over-dress for meetings. Millennials are more comfortable with casual clothes in the workplace. Clothes should give you confidence and be tasteful and neat in appearance.

20. Be prepared. Assume that the buyers have thoroughly vetted your sales pro and your company using social media and may have questions about any (negative) reviews. If there have been any previous adverse incidents, your sales pro must be prepared to address them. Your sales pro can also then refer them to positive postings on your website or explain the work that has been done to address any negative responses.

How Your Sales Pro Can Be Great Without Being "Salesy"

I was an accounting manager for a large hotel chain without formal sales training before entering sales. Prospects and customers often told me they appreciated my sales style because I was not "salesy." Being salesy was a pejorative term, probably derived from the style and actions of pushy sales pros that most of us have encountered when buying automobiles. It refers to people who use "hard" or trick closing techniques and don't take "no" for an answer, which I never used. They are offensive, insulting, often patronizing, and almost always unproductive. I am very uncomfortable trying to persuade someone to buy something that may not be of value to them, especially by being manipulative. When somebody uses hard closes on me to buy something, I am offended and immediately end the conversation and move on.

So, it all goes back to earning the trust of the buyer. According to sales market research data, "A total of 79% of business buyers claim that it is of the utmost importance to interact with a salesperson who is a trusted advisor," who can add value to their business, instead of sales reps who are only there to sell products and services.[75]

The best way for your sales pros to earn buyers' trust is always to be ethical, never lie, be respectful, be on time for all meetings, follow up on all commitments, and avoid selling them something they don't need or won't bring them substantial benefits. This conduct needs to be continually reinforced to sales pros, especially those who are more aggressive and do not want to let sales cycles take their normal time to close. Less-than-ethical sales pros will miss out on any future business from the customer, which is usually around 50 percent of my total sales each year. Word about a customer's bad experience will undoubtedly become known. In my experience, a single bad experience will eliminate a thousand good or excellent experiences. Maintaining ethical standards is the right thing to do, but it's also important to note that being unethical can be a financial disaster for your company and your sales pros.

Understanding how to best sell to Millennials and adapting your sales pitches to them is essential now because members of this generation have become prominent buyers at corporations. It is widely acknowledged that the Millennial generation is very different from prior generations, and the sales tactics and strategies that worked well in the past with previous generations will likely be unsuccessful with Millennial buyers. Sales pros must be challenged to adapt to the values and needs of this generation, which will be taking over most purchasing decisions in forthcoming years. Using this knowledge will give your sales pros an edge if their competitors aren't aware of differences in sales styles and pitches. Doing the same sales pitches to Millennials that have been done to other generations in the past is sales malpractice.

CHAPTER 9

Supporting Sales Pros to Close Sales

How often do sales managers meet with their sales pros individually to discuss their overall performance? This is not an account review but one in which they can each discuss whether they are meeting the other's expectations. Unfortunately, in my experience, this rarely happens. Typically, all the employees in the company receive a minimum of an annual review. So why are sales pros excluded? Should sales pros only be evaluated based on sales performance? I don't think so.

Account reviews exist to discuss the status of each opportunity in the pipeline. The takeaways from the account review should be the suggested tactics, strategies, and next steps the sales pro needs to take to close each of their opportunities. In addition, any resources the sales pro needs to assist in closing the deals should be discussed and agreed upon.

Takeaway 20 – It Is Important for Sales Managers to Have "One-on-One" Conversations with Sales Pros

The purpose of the one-on-ones with sales pros is to discuss their overall performance and career goals, not their sales performance and current pipeline. Sales pros should receive periodic formal reviews like all other employees because they need constructive feedback outside their sales activities. It is also an opportunity for sales pros to discuss their concerns or any issues that may be bothering or hindering them. The performance feedback meeting goals are to discuss the sales pro's performance since the last review, agree on any necessary corrections that may be needed in the future, and agree on a remedial plan, if required. The discussion should include short and long-term career development aspirations and clarification of expectations. And the dialogue must be two ways—with each contributing their viewpoints. Sales managers must also evaluate whether the sales pros are good corporate citizens. What do the sales professionals see themselves doing in two, five, or ten years? This should be openly discussed, and plans should be implemented to help the sales professional achieve her aspirations.

In many organizations, sales pros are exempted from this standard human resource practice, which must be corrected. Sales pros are employees and should be treated similarly to others in this respect. Unacceptable or undesirable behavior by a sales pro, such as mistreating others or violating company rules, must be addressed. Conducting performance reviews should also result in greater retention of sales pros. It will also force the sales manager to address and remove non-performers needed to optimize sales performance, something often neglected by many sales managers. Some think retaining a misbehaving or underperforming sales professional is better than having no sales professional. It is not.

The effect on the morale of others is too great to allow. Sometimes, you must practice "addition through subtraction." Make the tough decision and do it now!

Simply put, the sales manager's job is to achieve the sales results that management expects. The key is how you do that. I suggest focusing on hiring the best sales pros, making sure they are appropriately trained and equipped (the onboarding process), and receiving the proper amount of support from pre-sales, technical staff, legal, and marketing staff, going out on sales calls with them, especially when they first join the company, coaching them on their sales situations on a very regular basis (always be available) and assisting them in contract negotiations.

Being a good sales manager is not just rescuing sales pros from situations where they are losing and then trying to turn them around when it appears the decision is going the other way. Those are often hopeless cases and show that the sales pro needed to be made aware of what happened during the sales process. (Remember—if you are not winning, you are losing.) I have had to try to rescue some situations like this several times when requested and was successful a few times, but it is not a productive use of my time or abilities. And it told me that the sales pro, sometimes a top performer, was not "plugged in" to this sales opportunity.

In the best-selling book *One Minute Manager*, authors Blanchard and Johnson wrote about "catching them (employees) doing something right" and helping them "reach their full potential."[76] I subscribe to this theory. The best place to make this happen is to accompany the sales pros on sales calls and observe the sales pros in action. The sales manager must have a minor role, at best, on the sales call and let the sales pro drive the call. The sales pros will learn more by conducting the meeting than by observing the sales manager. It will also enhance the sales pro's credibility with the buyer, who will not be looking to the sales manager to answer each question.

The Value of Call Debriefs

When attending a sales meeting with a sales pro, the manager should take notes during the meeting, observing what various people said, their areas of interest, and their questions, and note which items or comments require follow-up. The sales manager should provide constructive feedback by reviewing the specific notes with the sales pro shortly after the meeting, usually one-on-one. The sales manager should explain to the sales pro how the call went, and the sales pro should not be insulted or yelled at if the meeting fails to accomplish its goals. I preferred to find a nearby coffee shop with a relaxed atmosphere where we could replay the entire meeting. At least thirty minutes should be allowed for this meeting; this is a learning opportunity for the sales pro, and it has great value.

Three key questions that I always asked the sales pro during the debrief were:

- What do you think went well on the sales call and why? (Cite specific points in the meeting.)
- What did not go well and why? (How did the sales pro know this?)
- What did the sales pro learn from the meeting, and what would they do differently at the next similar meeting? If there was such a thing as a "do-over", which

there is not, what would you do or say, now that the meeting is over, and you have more knowledge? This is where the most significant value of the debrief is, and the sales pro will need to be reminded of this from time to time.

Most sales pros can recognize what went right and wrong in the meeting and try to avoid making the same mistakes twice—and most will admit it to you. The sales pro will perform better next time, as immediate, constructive feedback is most beneficial while everything is fresh in their minds. The discussion is held in a non-threatening manner, and the sales pro knows she will not lose her job because of the meeting or the conversation. The sales pro feels better about herself and is eager to move on to the next time and prove that she can handle the sales call much better. It is all about communication and the willingness to improve oneself.

If a sales pro could not recognize her errors and were unwilling to work on correcting them, I would typically work less with that person, as it is a waste of my valuable time that could be spent with more receptive individuals. In most cases, those unwilling to improve their skills after such a meeting with the sales manager would be terminated from the company in the next three to six months due to performance issues. It is challenging to encourage somebody to recognize what they can do better and expect them to act on the suggestions if they are uninterested. Therefore, I usually focused on the new hires and those sales pros who had yet to reach over-quota performance but were willing to receive and respond to constructive coaching. In addition to going out on sales calls with these individuals and providing feedback, I would review their opportunity summary: what is working? What is not? Where are they stuck or blocked? Who are the people they are meeting with—or not meeting with? Do they need internal resources?

As the sales manager, I would also discuss any contract negotiation issues and perhaps inform my superiors of the situation and whether I may need assistance or more flexibility with my sales pros. This is where I could "move the needle" and improve the team's sales performance.

The debrief with feedback after a client meeting should be more comprehensive than calls with new hires during their formal onboarding. I utilized this practice with every sales pro I went out on sales calls with throughout my career as a sales manager, no matter how experienced or accomplished they were. I sought similar feedback when I reverted to the individual contributor role at the end of my career. Every sales pro can always get better!

Takeaway 21 – A Debrief Is Essential After Every Prospect Meeting

The Difficulty of a Sales Pro Letting Go of a Sales Opportunity

Have your sales pros ever called on a prospect that indicated they had genuine interest, provided access to decision-makers, stated they had the budget to proceed, and promptly returned your calls—but yet they did not purchase from your company? They passed all the markers of a "qualified prospect" on your sales pro's checklist form. Perhaps they were even a match to your company's "ideal customer profile."

But the prospect still didn't buy from your sales pro (or anyone else.) When your sales pro called, they told him they were still considering your proposal, so your sales pro kept the prospect on his pipeline and noted another follow-up date.

They did not provide any objections to the sales pro, such as your company's price being too high or outside their budget. But you're anxious and wonder when or if this opportunity will ever close.

Early in my career, I called on a manufacturing company in the Midwest that was in the market for fixed asset accounting software. They were worried about the financial effect of making a change and gave me sample data for a test. When I presented the test reports to the Tax Manager, Joe, he compared his calculations to my test report, and miraculously, they matched to the exact cent. I was elated. I had proved to Joe that our product was a good fit and that it would not cause a significant change in depreciation expense. I asked Joe if they were ready to purchase, and he said he thought they were. But weeks and then months went by. They still did not purchase. I tried to understand how and why this had happened. Bottom line: Joe didn't have the power and authority to make the purchase, and the company's executives determined that the cost of doing nothing was preferable to purchasing our solution.

I learned three valuable lessons from this experience, and I used these to train my sales teams in the future:

1. The qualification process needs to be foolproof. Even if a company passes your tests, they must still be ready to purchase. Also, even though they were qualified or prepared initially, they will still need to requalify

throughout the process. What is causing them to make the change? If they can't explain to your satisfaction, maybe it will not change. What is the real "why?" Perhaps something may have taken a higher priority during the sales cycle than this project. Sales pros must continually assess the prospect's willingness to buy, even after you have jointly built a compelling value proposition. And that includes validating their interest with the ultimate decision-maker or economic buyer several times.

2. The prospect was reluctant to deliver bad news to me, and I was too optimistic that I would eventually close the sale because of the perfect test results. I was over-confident.

3. I determined that the buyer's interest in fixing the problem and concluding a sale declined drastically each month, so the likelihood of purchase was unrecoverable. I later developed my "Theory of Diminishing Interest" based on such experiences. A simple explanation is that the buyer's interest in concluding the sale is the highest the day they formally recommend buying your product. Each day afterward, the level of interest in concluding the sale decreases at an increasing rate.

Takeaway 22 – Do a Hard Qualification to Avoid Opportunities That Don't Close

It is emotionally tough for a sales pro to let go of an opportunity he has invested so much time and resources in and thought he was close to closing. However, the sales pro must accept that, as time goes by, there is a lesser chance that the stalled opportunity will ever close. And the sooner your sales pro decides not to fret over sunk costs, the quicker he will close his next sale and achieve his sales goal.

Is it difficult for a sales pro to leave a deal where he has invested so much time? Absolutely. I have often had difficulty with this during my sales career, especially because I was very emotionally invested in that prospect. But there is no consolation prize in sales or commissions on activity, only on results. Maximizing time spent on prospects that can close is a much more prudent choice than continuing to chase deals that have become nonresponsive or show no indications of buying, despite all the sales activities that have occurred to this date.

I assume your sales pro has tried different strategies and tactics, and none has successfully moved the opportunity to a close. Now your sales pro needs to break free of the impulse to continue to call on the prospect and move on to others, occasionally checking with the prospect when there is some extra time. Still, the sales pro must recognize that the additional resources or calls made to the prospect will not cause the opportunity to close or move it along in the pipeline. Perhaps it is like trying to get a reluctant toddler to eat broccoli. You can keep trying, but it's unlikely you will be successful in getting the toddler to change his mind.

The prospect may be stuck on their "do nothing" current solution, may not have executive support, the expenditure may not be in their current budget, may have already decided to go with a competitor, or just may not see the value in your solution. If you cannot fix these issues within a month or two, there is very little likelihood the prospect will wake up one morning and say "yes." So, your sales pro needs to recognize the futility of continued efforts and invest his time in developing other qualified prospects.

Remember, the goal is for your sales pros to reach their sales goals, not to continue to chase reticent prospects. Spending time on sales that probably will not close could be the difference between achieving sales goals or not.

In summary, you can add a lot of value to your sales pros by providing consistent individual "one on one" coaching to them. Discuss the entire sales call, from beginning to end, preferably in a very informal setting outside your office. Discuss the areas that need improvement, including the next steps required and changes necessary to the account and opportunity sales plan.

I have found letting go of an opportunity to be one of the most difficult steps I have had to take as a sales pro, and it is the sales manager's responsibility to ensure that your sales pros are not investing excessive time on "lost causes." They need to realize that their selling time is precious, and it is time to move on to others or develop new pipeline opportunities.

CHAPTER 10

50 Tips for Negotiating a Favorable Contract

Your sales pro is now at the point where the buyer has informed her that the buying team has chosen your company to be their solution. Some sales pros think they are at the finish line. But you are not even close—at best, you're at the ¾ pole in the race. A lot of work still needs to be done to *seal the deal*.

This is the point in the sales cycle where the buyer's procurement person, contracts administrator, or attorney often enters the sales cycle if they have not already been involved. And this is also the point where the cordial relationship with the buying team can turn contentious. The business executive or your sales pro's contact may have now handed the negotiations with your company to a professional negotiator, generally from the legal department or procurement. Your sales pro's contact or coach is now on the sidelines. There may now be pushback on the price and other issues which may not have been previously discussed. It would be best if your sales pro did not take this personally. Remember, your sales pro is often dealing with a professional negotiator. It is their job to get the "best deal" for their company and their success in doing so is how their performance is evaluated. This often means presenting an unacceptable set of terms and prices to your company. If you have done an excellent job of establishing the value of your solution, the price should be acceptable, at least for business executives. If not, they will view your solution as a commodity and look only for the best price, and not consider the value they might derive from it. Or perhaps the negotiator must be made aware of the value the company buyer has placed on your solution.

I am assuming that the sales pro will lead the contract negotiation. If it is the sales manager and not the sales pro, then incorporate the following advice into your own process:

1. The goal of the contract negotiation and the new customer relationship, if none previously existed, is that purchasing your product or service results in better outcomes for the buyer. As a result, both parties will benefit and gain value. Keep that goal in mind.

2. Review the contracting process with the buyer's team early on to set expectations on both sides. Do not allow your sales pro to wait until the very end. The sales pro should schedule this meeting immediately after the buyer has selected your company. The review should include a discussion of which people will be involved, the roles and responsibilities of each person, where and when the meetings will be held, who will author the contract, how proposed changes will be handled, any rules that are important to each side, and the expected or desired timetable for completion. The sales pro should diarize the schedule and include who (on each side) is responsible for each task or event, realistic goals, benchmarks, and estimated deadlines. As the sales manager, it might be

helpful if you provide your team a checklist to help them navigate this list.

Takeaway 23 – The Sales Pro Needs to Prepare a Formal Contract Negotiation Timetable with the Buyer

3. The negotiation cannot be scripted, but preparation is essential. Your sales pro does not know what the buyer's contract attorney will focus on. Still, preparation will include anticipating various possible changes and different dynamics in the closing scenario.

4. Buyers are much better prepared now and have become better negotiators. They are much better informed, know more about alternatives, have built business cases that include forecasted return on investment for the project and will use this information to their advantage. There is also much more information available to them on the Internet. The buyers will be preparing for the negotiation, and your sales pro must also do so. Start by preparing answers to questions and objections you will likely receive. Before your sales pro undertakes the negotiation, she must prepare a list of the critical issues for your company and be prepared to defend them. Thoroughly discuss with your CEO, CRO or VP of Sales what the best case, worst case, and acceptable terms and price are ahead of time. You and your sales pro must be prepared for any eventual change—because there are often unanticipated requests. The sales pro should also prepare questions to ask her primary contacts and the

negotiator or procurement person. You and your sales pro cannot over-prepare for the negotiation.

5. There is no need to panic if the buyer's company brings in a professional negotiator, even if it happens at the end of the sales cycle. Remember, you are both invested in the purchase.

Takeaway 24 – The Sales Pro Should Always Know Who You Are Negotiating With—and What Their Authority Is

6. Always clarify the buyer's negotiator's authority before the negotiation begins. Please feel free to ask the person assigned to negotiate to describe how they are empowered to make proposals and commitments and agree to changes and decisions in the contract negotiation. Although they may inform you that they are fully authorized, you might find out later that it is untrue. Or, the negotiator may believe they have the authority, but they do not. For example, the legal counsel or procurement person will rarely have complete authority, but they might say they do. Usually, the economic buyer, or executive business sponsor, has the authority over all business and some legal issues. The negotiator will likely ask your sales pro the same question, so she must be prepared to respond.

7. Your sales pro should have anticipated that a protracted negotiation could happen in your sales cycle planning and have prepared for it. Negotiations will often extend the anticipated closing or contract date beyond your sales pro's and management's expectations. The buyer's negotiator

understands that time is usually to the buyer's advantage and a lever they can use to extract additional concessions. Still, it may be to the seller's advantage if there is a sense of urgency due to a hard deadline from management or regulatory mandates. When your sales pro enters the negotiation, they must understand the value of time in this buying decision and act accordingly.

8. The procurement or strategic-sourcing person's full-time job is negotiating contracts with vendors or suppliers. They are usually very competent at what they do. They are "pros," just like your sales pro is at selling. The buyer's negotiator is working in the company's best interests to get the deal done. They are interested in something other than achieving a win/win result. They want to win and your company to lose. It is not personal. They do not hate your sales pro or your company. The negotiator is often measured by the outcome of the negotiation, which is usually the savings they can secure.

9. Listening skills are critical. Be sure your sales pro understands what the contract negotiator is saying and writing and, if not, ask them to explain it. Always clarify terminology and assumptions. Never assume anything. I have seen many complex negotiations reach standstills resulting from one or both sides failing to understand what the other has requested.

10. Your sales pro should not let her ego or eagerness to get the deal done influence the negotiation. If it happens, your company will end up with an undesirable contract that your executive management may reject for economic or legal reasons.

11. Your company should never agree to the first draft the buyer sends your sales pro. Even if it looks agreeable, find something objectionable because the buyer will likely do so later, and your sales pro will need something to trade with them. Understand that the first revisions your sales pro receives of your contract from the buyer or their "redlines" is their initial offer. It is not their final offer and not the last version—even if they say it is.

12. Your sales pro should always request that your company's attorney author the contract, not the buyer's. Some buyers' negotiators will vigorously resist this, especially if they are in the technology field. My experience is that having your own company accept a customer's contract is more challenging than the reverse. The buyer expects to receive the seller's contract and to propose changes to it by exchanging redlines.

13. It is essential to present the buyer with a standard contract containing reasonable language or terms, as the buyer's lawyers may sometimes approve it with minor changes. But if the buyer's lawyers see unreasonable terms, they will usually change everything they do not like in the contract; the more acceptable the standard agreement is, the more likely it will be quickly accepted with minimal changes.

Takeaway 25 – The Sales Pro Should Not Negotiate Via Emails

14. Meeting in person is the most productive way to finalize a deal, instead of endlessly sending "redlines" back and forth, which I term "contract tennis." The second-best option is

via telephone or teleconference. Finally, the least desirable and most often used is via email. My experience is that solely using email can extend the negotiation by weeks or even months because it is easier to misunderstand what is being written or to take the information out of context. Instead, try to schedule a telephone or video call to resolve open issues.

Recently, there was a song in the play "Hamilton" called "The Room Where It Happens." It refers to the historic meeting between the nation's founders when Thomas Jefferson, Alexander Hamilton, and James Madison met together in 1790 to work out a compromise to move the nation's capital to the Potomac River (currently Washington, DC) in exchange for support of Hamilton's national banking plan. Could that have been accomplished if they had email at that time? I doubt it. Meeting in person is optimal.

I negotiated with a Fortune 500 company located in the Chicago area. After exchanging multiple versions of the contract changes via email, I suggested that we meet in a conference room at their location, order lunch and dinner, if necessary, lock the door, store our smartphones, and not leave until we reached an agreement. We negotiated until about 8:00 p.m. and left with a license that we then executed.

15. When your sales pro receives the buyer's list of proposed contract changes or redlines, acknowledge that you have received them and will give them immediate, serious

consideration. Then, your sales pro should review the requested changes with you and, if possible, your executive management and legal team, and then examine the requested changes with the buyer to understand their objectives. The sales pro needs to let the buyer know that she and her sales manager need to understand the reasons for the buyer's proposed changes to advocate on the buyer's behalf to their company. Teach your sales pro to understand your buyer's point of view who may want legal assurances or protections to minimize their risks. For example, are they asking for an additional two years of warranty because they will not deploy the solution for fifteen months and need more time for testing? Can you and your sales pro work together to address those issues before the contract negotiation? If so, do not wait.

16. The sales pro should rank the buyers "redlines" by priority, from most to least important for you and your company, and conversely, what you believe are the most and least important that your sales pro thinks the buyer wants. This is why it's so important for your sales pro to connect with the buyer and think like them. Whatever you do, do *not* provide your priority list to the buyer's procurement person!

Takeaway 26 – The Sales Pro Should Negotiate the Entire Contract at One Time, Not Bit-by-Bit

17. Always negotiate the entire contract or purchase order, not by individual items. Inform your counterpart that you will review all their proposed changes simultaneously. In

other words, acceptance of one item by you is conditional on acceptance of the entire document. It is sub-optimal to review each item and give in on some, then get stuck on others. If you do so you will lose bargaining power. For example, let's say their first five items are easy gives, but the last five are not. Only give them the first five initially after receiving something in return. Even the "easy ones" have value to them. That way, you can start with the last five and try to reach an agreement using the first five as negotiating tools and leverage to complete the deal. Also, your sales pro should inform them that your company must review all prior agreements or concessions if they ask for additional changes later (very common). For example, after you have already agreed on all fifteen points they brought up and have assumed that the legal negotiation has been completed, they come back with additional changes. Some negotiators use this ploy to get further concessions after you have already reached an agreement.

18. Similarly, your sales pro needs to be wary of what I call the "*Columbo*-style" negotiation method some attorneys or procurement people use. (It is okay for you to utilize it!) Some might remember the 1970s – 1980s television show *Columbo*. Peter Falk was the actor who played the frumpy, often bumbling, and socially inept police detective who would solve murders by asking very innocuous and sometimes distracting questions that eventually yielded the truth. Usually, after turning to walk away, Columbo would turn around just as he was about to go out the door, asking the perpetrator a simple question by saying, "Just one more thing . . . ," and then asking about an inconsistency that nobody noticed except Columbo.

Here is an example of a *Columbo*-style dialogue in a contract negotiation:

A few days after a negotiation is concluded (in your mind), when you believe the final contract is ready to be drafted, the negotiator introduces another issue or objection that must be met to proceed. You and your sales manager feel you are close to concluding the deal, and you both are "blind-sided." Here is how the dialogue may occur:

You: *We have agreed on the last three areas that were open. I will summarize them. They were:*

- *Number 1: We will agree to hold this price for ninety days.*
- *Number 2: You have agreed to pay us 50 percent down and the remaining 50 percent within thirty days of delivery; and*
- *Number 3: We will provide you with an extended warranty of sixteen months rather than the usual twelve months. You have agreed to execute the contract by Friday of next week. Is that correct?*

Customer: *Yes.*

You: *Are these all the open items?*

Customer: *Yes.*

You: *I will speak with our attorneys and have a new contract sent to you by tomorrow morning. Should I send a copy to Ms. Jones as well?*

Customer: *Yes, that is a good idea. She will be the signer.*

You: *Thank you for your time today. You will have the new
contract shortly.*
Pause
Customer: *Oh, just one more thing.*
You: *Yes?*
Customer: *We would also like to receive a 10 percent discount
on the second shipment*
You: *I thought we had agreed on all the open items.*
Customer: *Yes, but we would like this discount as well.*

Your company is now in the position of either giving in
and granting the additional discount, killing the deal, or
renegotiating the contract, all of which are undesirable.
Since you probably do not want to kill the sale at this
late stage, you will add a 10 percent discount on the
second shipment, which could put you over the allotted
discount amount. However, if you allow it, they have
an even better deal than what you previously agreed
on. Is this a dirty trick on the part of the procurement
person or a sharp negotiating skill? It depends on which
side you are on, but I can assure you that this happens
frequently and puts you in a difficult place. To avoid it,
ask if you have received all the changes, then ask again
to confirm it. When they "Oh, just one more thing,"
your response is, "You just confirmed that we received
all the changes; apparently, that was not the case, so we
need to review this request in the context of the entire
contract." Or, you can add your "just one more thing."

Consider the whole list of items they are asking for, and then decide what you want to give on your part. I advise agreeing to their points only when getting something of value in return. It could be that they will sign the agreement by next Thursday, agree to write a case study for you, or be a reference for a certain number of prospect calls (assuming a successful purchase.)

I recently negotiated a large contract with a leading technology firm where they assured me they had asked for their last contract change. Then, after we agreed, they came up with additional change requests three or four more times. When you are that far into a negotiation and believe a deal is imminent, it is tough to walk away or restart it by stating, "If I give in on this, then I want this other point back that we gave in on." However, if it does happen, you should not feel obligated to give in without getting something else. It could be large or small, depending on their last ask. You should also ask them if this is their final item or if more are coming. If they say there could be more, it is suggested that these be handled at one time, not one at a time, which always favors the buyer, as I previously noted. The buyer will often have a better outcome than if everything was considered at one time.

19. Often, when the buyer asks for unanticipated items, there is a "hidden agenda," and the sales pro must find out what that is for a successful sales closure. For example, their hidden agenda may be that they want you to agree to a

much lower professional services rate or throw in a few extra days of services or training at no cost.

20. There often are differences in terminology between the seller and buyer. For example, "guarantee" and "warranty" can have different meanings for each side. I recall several instances where we argued over changes and found that we were thinking of different ideas. If that happens, be sure your sales pro asks them to clarify what they are looking for to be sure you have understood.

21. Payment terms are always important for both sides. The buyer may want to tie payments to deliverables. Whether your company agrees to this should be a matter of your company policy or the executive business sponsor's approval. If your company agrees, add a "no later than" date. And there should be an agreed-upon specific criteria for acceptance. It should not be based only on the buyer's opinion. For example, "25% of the payment for services shall be paid upon the acceptance of the deliverables, defined as the customer using the solution in a production environment, but in no event later than October 31, 2025."

22. Your sales pro will not have any insight into what is going on once you have submitted your response to their contract "redlines" back to the buyer and passed them on to their legal department. Often, the buyer's contact needs insight, too. This is an uncomfortable position. Sometimes, several weeks or months may go by, and you still have not heard back. Do not panic. It means that resolving the contract is a low priority for them. Other higher-priority agreements may be in the way. I suggest contacting the business

executive in charge of the purchase to see if she has insight or if she can call the legal department to find out what is happening. Resist the urge to offer an additional price discount or more "goodies" to move it along. The deal is already sold. This could cause it to go back to the procurement person for re-negotiation if they sense that you have yet to offer your best value. And, indeed, they may ask for more concessions.

23. Sometimes, the person you are negotiating with says she must receive approval from a higher-level person as a negotiating tactic—even if she assured you at the beginning that she is completely empowered. This way, they receive a concession from you right now and another when the higher-level person provides input. For example, your price is $10,000. The buyer wants to pay $6,000. After much negotiation, you agree to a compromise of $8,000. Then, it goes to the higher authority, and she wants $7,000. A solution is that you can say that you also need to go to a higher authority, and they pushed back and want $7,850. It is best to involve a higher-level person in the negotiation as soon as possible.

24. Making the case that you need to book the deal at the end of the calendar or fiscal year has more credibility. I have had some buyers make miracles happen to help me, or my sales pros, reach goal at the end of the year. Once, they even contacted an executive skiing in Utah and brought him off the slopes to sign the contract via fax on December 31.

25. Your sales pro must know when to leave a negotiation. I have told buyers that we cannot accept their proposed terms. They had "deal killers" in their changes. In each case, we could resume negotiations and successfully conclude a contract. However, they need to know your company will walk away rather than negotiate a "bad deal" and the reasons why.

26. Your sales pro may receive a "take it or leave it, give me your answer right now" ultimatum from a buyer. Do not overreact to it. Treat it like any other offer, not as a final offer from the buyer. It will remain, regardless of whether the contract is acceptable. The sales pro should let the buyer know your company will consider the request and get back to them. She can still make a counteroffer if their offer is unacceptable, even though they told you it was their final offer. She could tell them you are willing to achieve a compromise. If they reject it, they are unreasonable, and you may not want them as a customer. You can also withdraw your previous proposal if the buyer is unreasonable. This should only be done in rare circumstances, as it will probably antagonize the buyer. However, it is a strategy that can be used if they provide you with an offer that is far from acceptable. It lets them know that you must return to the negotiation's beginning.

27. There is value in the buyer's commitment to future additional purchases, which allows your company to agree to a concession providing the buyer purchases "x by y date." Another way to handle this is to include an option in the contract: "The buyer may purchase a new ice machine, SKU #123456, from the company at the cost of $1,995 by December 31, 2025."

28. Be aware that including a contingency, or even an acceptance clause, could result in the contract's value not being recognizable as revenue in the current period by the company, which usually results in a postponement of a commission. This is due to Generally Accepted Accounting Principle (GAAP) rules on revenue recognition, not your Controller or CFO being upset with you.

29. Sometimes, the buyer will want to include your company's response to their Request for Proposal (RFP) in the contract. Avoid doing this, as the RFP responses have often yet to be reviewed by the legal department. The RFP document may be lengthy, and it may take your legal a lot of time to examine and evaluate it. However, if the buyer insists on including the RFP, you must decide at that time and carefully review the responses for accuracy and downstream ramifications.

30. Your sales pro should communicate and work closely with the sales manager, VP of Sales, CRO, or CEO to ensure they agree to the negotiated terms. A worst-case scenario is that a negotiation is completed and then rejected by your company.

31. The sales pro needs to have complete control of her emotions. Under any circumstances, the sales pro should not lose her temper in a meeting with the prospect—even if they are insulting, or ask for ridiculous terms.

32. As mentioned earlier, let your sales pro use you, the sales manager, as the "bad cop" in the contract negotiation. For example, the sales pro can tell the buyer she sympathizes with them but that the sales manager will never approve their request.

33. The sales manager may also need to help the sales pro manage the company's attorneys to ensure they are not unreasonable. I have had this happen many times. Understand that many attorneys are often over-protective and are "deal killers."

34. The sales pro must avoid arguing with the buyer, especially over facts, such as their recent experiences with your company. She should repeat what she thought she heard them say to ensure she understood it correctly, such as, "Carl, did you just say that you are unwilling to pay for any services? If so, why is that?" The sales pro should never raise her voice and should always be respectful to the person you are negotiating with. One of the best negotiators I know, Scott, never raises his voice, no matter how angry or upset he might be. He keeps his poise and lets the other person make a fool of themselves by shouting or losing their composure. Hugh Jones, the CEO of RX, lowers his voice during negotiations so that others must strain to hear what he is saying. That is far more effective than increasing your voice volume. That forces the other party to focus more on listening to what he is saying.

35. A buyer sometimes sends a purchase order (PO) or letter of intent (LOI) to assure the seller they are going through with the purchase and may want access to the product or service, but the transaction is not final. In some industries or companies, a PO is a firm commitment. Some sellers can book a PO as a sale and a firm commitment, while others will not. If your sales pro receives a PO or LOI, it must be discussed with sales management and the legal department. If only an executed contract seals the deal, the buyer should be thanked for the PO or LOI and told that your company can only ship with an executed contract.

Your sales pro's contact or the project team may have informed her that your company's proposal (including the price) was acceptable, but the procurement person can and will often override them. Nonetheless, the likelihood is over ninety percent that you can still get the deal done once the terms are agreed on and legal issues are satisfied.

36. Your attorney must be on any call their attorney attends so ask if one is present. Conversely, if their attorney is not on the call, your attorney should not be on the call. Attorneys are very aware of this and believe contact with the other side without one attorney being present is unethical.

37. The sales pro should avoid filling in silences with unnecessary conversation during a negotiation meeting. Be mindful that silence is not a negative.

38. The sales pro should clarify to the buyer the ramifications of some of the proposed issues. For example, I negotiated a multi-million-dollar, multi-year life policy management implementation with a large life insurance organization. One of their proposed contract changes was that they wanted to be able to approve all the services personnel assigned to their project and only have them reassigned during the life of the project with their prior approval. (That is a common request.) I explained to the person that if we wanted to assign our most qualified people to the project, we needed the flexibility to reassign people if there was an unusual, unplanned circumstance in the future, such as another client emergency. I also explained that if we agreed to his condition, which we would if they insisted, we would assign our most junior people to his project, knowing that we could not move them in an unusual future circumstance. After the explanation, he better understood the ramifications of his request and dropped it.

39. Avoid involving multi-party negotiations, for example, with a customer and another supplier. It is best to work on each separately.

40. There might be occasions where you need to go directly to the buyer's executive management to tell them you cannot finalize the deal with the procurement person or attorney because they have asked for terms your company cannot agree to. I have done this several times, and each time, the buyer's executive management has overruled their procurement person or the attorney to get the deal done. However, this is a one-time "silver bullet" and cannot be used lightly, as it will often poison the relationship with the procurement person or attorney. Executive management must also be very motivated to get the deal done to override the procurement person, or they must view their company's position as unreasonable to succeed. You need

to know which is likely. It is recommended that this alternative only be chosen as a last resort. And this assumes that you have had prior contact and a good relationship with the executive.

41. If both parties reach an impasse in the negotiations, primarily due to legal issues when both legal departments are stubborn on one or more concerns, a non-interested thirty party can be brought in to help resolve the problem. However, both parties must want to conclude a deal, so a third party or another attorney may be necessary to break the impasse. A mediator may also solve a situation where there is a lack of trust between the buyer and sellers—but they still want to conclude a negotiated agreement. Another strategy is to ask for additional negotiators, or substitutes, from your buyer. They may wish to do the same. Often an impasse is the result of a misunderstanding or unclear assumptions. If that happens, it is best to reiterate your understanding of their position for clarification.

42. How does the buyer conduct their own business and contracting? It is essential to understand how the targeted prospective customer does business or how they earn profits. Questions include how they handle legal issues such as intellectual property; who are their customers; what are their strategic goals; who is their competition? This will often lead to a better understanding of how to approach them with a value proposition and, later, when discussing contract terms, to structure a more mutually beneficial agreement. Your sales pro should remind them that you cannot agree to business terms they also would not agree

to when they do business with their customers. I once had a request from a large software company that they would have never accepted from one of their buyers. When I reminded them of that, it was dropped. Research the company by visiting its website, reading its annual reports and S.E.C. 10-K filings, checking out its LinkedIn.com site, and even looking at comments on Glassdoor.

43. I have had several procurement managers tell me that they wanted my company to be a "partner" of theirs as opposed to being just a vendor or supplier. When I inquired as to what they meant, I found out that "partnership" was a euphemism, or code word, for their request/demand for either 1) a substantial price reduction to ostensibly help them meet their cost reduction goals or 2) share the risk. Be aware of this language. They do not want a genuine partnership that benefits both parties; they want a significantly reduced price and term it a "partnership."

Here is an edited version of a letter that a company received from one of its customers:

We remain interested in partnering with vendors who assist you in reducing cost and/or maximizing the value in our existing investments. We believe that moving forward requires a spirit of partnership which is not reflected in the most recent offer. The costs are heading in the wrong direction. From a pricing perspective, our goal is to be in alignment with our standard contract framework. According to benchmarking information:

- *We look forward to discounts in a range between 20 – 40 percent off list pricing.*
- *We are interested in pricing options for a one year and a three year term.*
- *There should be no increase in prices during renewal term(s).*

The vendor should represent and warrant that all prices, benefits, and warranties will be no less favorable to us than currently being offered (or will be offered by your firm) to any of its similarly suited customers.

Thank you in advance for your interest in helping us reach our goals.

        M. Smith, Procurement

They also use "partnership" to indicate that we need to meet their needs and their aggressive "request." The customer also has requested a "most favored nations" clause, which many sellers' attorneys find problematic but is very common when dealing with federal and state governments. So, do they want a partner? Or do they want a significant price reduction? It is often more the latter.

44. Contract management software can be very helpful in tracking the progress of contracts, both internally and externally, and in cataloging specific language or paragraphs that have been accepted for sales pros to use in contracts and licenses.

45. Understand how leverage can affect contract negotiations. "In negotiation, leverage is the power that one side of a negotiation has to influence the other side to move closer

to their negotiating position"[77] Or, it can be understood as which party needs to have the contract signed relative to the other. The other party would then have the advantage or leverage in this negotiation. Is there a compelling reason why the buyer needs to make a purchase now? It is important to know the "real why." For example, is there a federal sanction, OSHA, or OFAC violation that needs to be remediated by the buyer? If so, then the supplier has leverage. Are there many comparable products on the market, each of which will solve the customer's problem? If so, the buyer has leverage. Is your product or solution strategic to the buyer? Does it have anything to do with helping them move into new markets, as the CEO might have noted in a recent press release or annual report? If the buyer has been fined or received unfavorable publicity due to an event and needs your solution to mitigate the problem, then the seller has leverage. I read about a bank that could not complete a desired merger with a multi-billion-dollar bank because its anti-money laundering system was deemed inadequate. Do you think that the bank is not motivated to fix that, and that the seller of an anti-money laundering solution will have some leverage? This is important to know as you enter negotiations. Leverage allows one to hold out longer for concessions, but your sales pro should be careful not to brag if she thinks your company has leverage over the buyer. Be happy but be silent about it.

46. I have heard that the best outcome of a negotiation is a compromise that both parties are dissatisfied with, as each had to make concessions they would otherwise not have made.[78] I am unsure if this is true because many view negotiations as a contest where one side wins and the other loses. Although a win/win is desirable, the final negotiated contract is rarely considered as such by both parties.

47. Your sales pro should never embarrass your counterpart in front of others in their company, especially with derogatory comments. That will cause the negotiator or your contact to turn on your sales pro and could cost your company the sale. Also, the sales pro should not try to back your counterpart into a corner as it could backfire. Always be professional.

48. If the negotiation is taking place with a company that does not utilize English as their native language, be sure to hire a recommended, trusted business translator, a person who generally assists in corporate negotiations, not just a person who is multi-lingual, as they may not be familiar with the terminology or business customs that are important in the talks. Sales managers should keep a list of good translators for their team. Here is an example of the importance of hiring the proper translator.

Our CEO flew to Beijing to negotiate a joint-venture arrangement with a Chinese technology firm. The prior discussions had been conducted via email in both English and Mandarin. Coincidently, one of our customer support representatives, Dawai, planned a personal trip to visit his grandparents, who lived near Beijing, and he offered to aid the CEO. Dawai was born in China but raised in the US and is bilingual. The negotiations between the CEO and the Chinese company became bogged down. Dawai attended the negotiations from the start and listened as the hired translator explained what the Chinese firm wanted. However, Dawai was not satisfied with the translation that the CEO received from the hired translator and asked to speak with the CEO in the hallway. He then asked the CEO if he could clarify the issues directly with the Chinese firm. The CEO agreed. When the meeting resumed, Dawai determined that the previous translation needed more clarification. There was a misunderstanding due to a misalignment in why the joint-venture partner's deals were not closing with the Chinese banks because they did not fully understand the practices and requirements of anti-money laundering. Dawai's assistance successfully concluded the negotiation to both sides' satisfaction. This is how he described it to me:

"I think what made the negotiations ultimately successful were that the willingness to work with each other transcended the language barrier. Both sides knew that there was a genuine intent to embark on the journey together. That authenticity which later helped forge trust was the biggest takeaway on both sides. Cross-cultural negotiations are never easy and especially so if the subject matter is not widely known or challenging to convey. What you'll need then in finding success is to make sure you have those universal bonds; in this case that was mutual intent and converged interests to work together." Later, Dawai was promoted to higher positions within the company and now has a management position in the Singapore office where he can capitalize on his business acumen and language skills.

49. Try role-playing the negotiation, especially in preparation for negotiations and presentations. If you anticipate a tough negotiation, a best practice is to role-play the negotiation internally, like how you would prepare for a debate or a mock trial. This will give you an idea of some of the objections you may face beforehand. And it should lower your anxiety.

50. Understand your "BATNA" or best alternative to a negotiated agreement. It is your best outcome if you cannot reach a negotiated agreement. It is your next best option. "It is not your ideal or desired outcome, but your fallback or backup plan."[79] Identifying your BATNA should be part of your negotiation planning process. You can have a strong or weak BATNA, depending on the circumstances. And you can improve or weaken their BATNA through actions.

"The better your BATNA, the greater your power. People think negotiating power is determined by resources like wealth, political connections, physical strength, friends, and military might. The relative negotiating power of two parties depends primarily upon how attractive to each is the option of not reaching an agreement." In economics, that is called the "opportunity cost."

In 1981, IBM wanted QDOS (which became PC-DOS and MS-DOS) from Microsoft as its operating system for its personal computers. Bill Gates initially desired a lump sum license amount. His BATNA was to receive a dollar amount per computer shipped. This was a much more favorable financial outcome for Microsoft and resulted in Gates becoming one of the wealthiest people in the world.

I recently saw the movie *Air*, which was about the negotiations between Nike and Michael Jordan when he went from North Carolina University to the Chicago Bulls and into the NBA. He also signed a contract that gave him a royalty payment for every Air Jordan shoe sold in addition to the initial payment. This has been worth millions of dollars to him.

What does your sales pro think the buyer's BATNA is? How bad do they want to get a deal done? How much power does their procurement/legal team have over the final agreement? They need to assess this before the negotiation begins.

If the buyer does not accept the proposal, what is your team's fallback or next best deal? What is the minimum needed by your company to reach an agreement? What is the walk-away point? The Harvard Law School Program on Negotiation recommends these steps to determine your BATNA:

- "List your alternatives. Consider all the alternatives available to you if the current negotiation ends in an impasse. What are your no-deal options?

- "Evaluate your alternatives. Examine each option and calculate the value of pursuing each one.
- "You can package different options together. For example, if you give on price, they give on payment terms plus delivery date. If you give on service daily/ rates, they give on flexibility to reassign consultants. Try to pre-determine what the buyers value most.
- "Establish your BATNA. Choose a course of action that would have the highest expected value for you. This is your BATNA—the course you should pursue if the current negotiation fails.
- "Calculate your reservation value. Now that you know your BATNA, calculate your reservation value—the lowest-valued deal you are willing to accept. If the value of the deal proposed to you is lower than your reservation value, you'll be better off rejecting the offer and pursuing your BATNA. If the final offer is higher than your reservation value, you should accept it."[80]

Takeaway 27 – The Sales Pro Needs to be Prepared to Negotiate with a Professional

I've dealt with many complex negotiations. One negotiation, which was the largest sale in the company's history, was not going well. Every negotiation meeting ended in a stalemate. I was very discouraged, but then I had an idea for a possible breakthrough. I called the person in charge of the contract negotiation directly and asked him if he was genuinely interested in getting a deal done. He said he was. I suggested we meet in his office, just the two of us, with no lawyers or others in attendance. So, nobody could report to others that he had given in to us. He quickly agreed. Once in his office, we sat down, and I told him that we would never agree to expand the scope of the proposed license to include the company's customers for the same license fee amount. Still, we could work out a separate schedule for any customers who subsequently elected to license our systems. He was agreeable. After drawing up a schedule of fees for the customers that we both agreed on, we put the terms on a flipchart, and the attorneys divided the work and started drafting.

After the long, acrimonious negotiation, I mentioned to the prospect's contract lead that I had doubts that we would reach an agreement. He responded, "I knew we would." When I acted surprised, he looked at me and said, "Steve, I do this for a living every day, and I am very good at it." I knew then that I had negotiated with a real pro, and we were playing his game—on his terms, not ours. Lesson learned: Know who you are dealing with, determine your walkaway position—and stick to it. Also, many conflicts can be resolved by removing most of the audience and resolving the issues in a "one-on-one" conversation, where both participants are honest about their motives and goals. Often, people feel they need to take a strong position to not "lose face" in front of their managers, peers, or, even more importantly, their subordinates.

These are some of the lessons that I took away that day. I, and later my sales pro team, found them very useful for future negotiations.

- Know with whom you are negotiating and their authority level.
- Make sure you have the proper legal representation if the buyer brings in professional negotiators.
- The scope of the agreement is important; if it changes significantly, then you have a right to renegotiate your fee.
- Be aware of the negotiating trick almost to complete the negotiation and then bring in a completely different negotiating team.
- Do not be intimidated by the people you are negotiating with.
- Be aware of breaches in privacy by an unscrupulous or unethical negotiator.
- Be patient and confident when you negotiate.
- Be prepared to walk away from a bad deal.

It is always essential to act ethically in the negotiation, as in the sales cycle. Trust is important. Once it is lost, it can never be regained. There is an old saying that it takes a lot of time, perhaps months, to establish trust, but only seconds to destroy it.

Contract negotiation is an art, not a science. It is also a skill like archery or pocket billiards. One can get better at it only by studying and a lot of practice. The best negotiators are those who are extremely well prepared before the negotiation begins, and it is best done by teams of people working together because sometimes the best solutions are not always obvious.

SECTION 3

How Sales Management
Can Optimize Their Sales Forces

Up until this point, we have discussed many topics relating to how to best sell to prospects, with a special focus on managing sales pros. This section will examine how your company can best organize your sales force to achieve optimum results. The structure of your sales force can positively or adversely affect your desired results. This includes the definition of responsibilities for each of the sales and sales-related functions. I have determined that the optimum design varies from company to company, based on the individual circumstances. The perfect organization that works well for one company could result in a complete failure in another, even if they sold similar products in the same geographical area. A lot depends on the company's goals, culture, management style, products, maturity, pricing strategy, and desire to utilize third parties or agents.

When choosing and designing the desired organization, you need to consider the effect on current as well as future sales because you do not want to damage the company so much in the interim that it is beyond recovery. The best practice to accomplish this is to map out the desired end solution, then the steps that you take and the estimated timeframe to get there.

Like many things in life, the change in a sales organization does not have to be revolutionary but can be evolutionary. Your company can design the desired organization and take months or years to achieve it incrementally. Or you can change course along the way and choose another desired solution. I believe in adapting to changes in circumstances. The organization set up five years ago, which has worked well, may not be optimized for the digital, post-pandemic marketplace.

CHAPTER 11

Staffing Your Sales Force to Success

Hiring the Best Qualified Candidates Is Critical

I have often been asked what the most critical action a sales manager must take to achieve his sales goals for this year. I have thought about this quite a bit, and the answer may seem obvious to many, but I can relate that it is rarely the top priority for sales managers. Most sales managers will focus on closing deals far along in the pipeline, perhaps conducting detailed account reviews with their sales pros. But the most important action you must take is to ensure that your team is at full staff and that you have filled it with the best possible candidates. You can close the deals that are in the pipeline, but you still may miss your overall target, as I will demonstrate with examples below. Hiring and firing are preeminent over anything else. That means you need to invest the proper time to screen and interview candidates and then properly onboard those you select, even if your manager is pressing you to close sales.

Your Priority Is to Build a High-Performing Sales Team

The sales manager's first responsibility is to build a high-performing sales team. The first step to accomplishing this goal is to evaluate each current sales professional's performance. If the sales manager doesn't believe they can achieve their annual quota, she must take remedial action, including termination if necessary. Unfilled positions need to be filled with qualified new hires, so staffing is a higher priority than deal management. Staffing must be evaluated at least ninety days before the beginning of the sales year so that new hires are in place when the new sales year begins.

Takeaway 28 – The Sales Manager Must Give Priority to Staffing Sales Positions

A study by Gallup found that "Companies fail to choose the candidate with the right talent for the job 82% of the time."[81] That level of hiring failure is shocking and must be avoided to succeed as a sales manager. Imagine if 82 percent of surgeons at a hospital or commercial airplane pilots were not right for the job!

The sales pros on the team do not need to like each other or socialize, but they must work in a congenial atmosphere of mutual trust, respect, and teamwork. They must work collaboratively and assist each other when necessary, such as substituting for one of their teammates if there is an illness or they are temporarily unavailable. The sales manager must ensure that this level of cooperation is in effect.

Suppose your team is geographically disbursed or working remotely (which is now the norm). In that case, it is desirable to bring the team together several times each year for training, company and product updates, team building, and socializing, especially in the evenings. Once I met people, my impressions of them often became more positive. Of course, some companies want to avoid incurring this cost, but I can assure you that it is usually worth the expense.

Effect of Employee Turnover on Sales Goals

It's dramatic! There were years when I achieved my team goals because all the sales positions were staffed throughout the year, and at least one time when all the sales pros on my team exceeded their sales quotas, but because there were open positions during the year, the team didn't achieve its annual sales target. And my earnings suffered as a result.

Let's look at an example of three sales teams: A, B, and C, to understand the effect of turnover, or open position, on the overall team revenue goal. In this example, each sales pro has a quota of $1,000,000, and the sales manager's sales quota is the sum of five sales pros, or $5,000,000.

SALES RESULTS

Person	Team A	Team B	Team C
Person A	$1,000,000	$1,000,000	$1,000,000
Person B	$1,110,000	$1,000,000	$1,000,000
Person C	$1,500,000	$1,250,000	$1,250,000
Person D	$1,110,000	$1,500,000	$750,000
Person E	0 (open all year)	0 (person hired 9/1)	$250,000 person hired 7/1)
Total	$4,720,000	$4,750,000	$4,250,000

Team A had four people who achieved or exceeded their annual sales quota, but the fifth position was left unfilled all year. So, the sales manager did not reach her quota of $5,000,000 and will not receive her bonus—even though her four team members did very well, and the sales manager kept very busy assisting the team members in closing deals.

Team B also had four individuals who achieved or exceeded their goals. The manager filled the open position on September 1, but the new hire did not close a sale during the calendar year because it took several months to become productive. This manager also failed to reach her team quota, even though she helped close sales and interviewed several candidates before selecting one.

Team C had three individuals who achieved or exceeded their sales goal. Person D on the team was there all year but did not achieve his quota. Person E was hired on July 1 and closed $250,000 in sales in the calendar year. Nevertheless, the sales manager did not reach her annual sales quota of $5,000,000.

These examples illustrate the cost to a sales manager of having a sales position open for all or part of the calendar year. It will severely negatively impact the likelihood of reaching the team sales goal. Ideally, the sales manager should be interviewing sales candidates starting in the July/August timeframe, with the aim of hiring a qualified sales pro and beginning onboarding by November 1. In addition, sales managers should over-allocate their quota to the sales pros. In this example, they would assign $5,250,000 to the sales pros, which provides an allowance or cushion of $250,000.

My experience is that many sales managers are so immersed in working with their sales pros on active deals, especially those that may close in the next thirty to sixty days, that they neglect their staffing needs. And there are rarely enough active deals to close to compensate for the lost time of leaving a territory open. Also, many sales managers, myself included, do not enjoy interviewing new sales pros. We enjoy the pursuits of new sales far more than sourcing, meeting, and evaluating potential new hires. Recruiting and hiring can be very tedious and difficult. Let's look at the costs associated with sales pro turnover and what you can do to fix the problem.

- The cost to replace a sales pro can be $100,000, or more, covering the cost of a recruiter, the opportunity cost of the interviewers' time, lost productivity of territory being unstaffed for months, and the ramp-up time for the new sales pro. I found that turnover invariably made reaching my annual team sales quota almost impossible. To combat this, you should incentivize all high-performing sales pros to stay with the company—beyond the commission plans—with a year-end sales pro retention bonus of:
  - $X for each year of employment, or
  - $X for each year of quota achievement
- Ideally, new hires should not be put on a quota immediately. Take at least ninety days to train and acquaint them with the company, its culture, management, and territory. Consider this data: "The average new hire is fully productive in 5.3 months. While 24% are ready in one to three months, 16% take longer than seven months."[82]

Some sales pros will push you to put them on quota as soon as possible because they are eager to earn commissions. Resist.

Hiring and Firing Sales Pros: Best Practices

It is essential that you hire the best possible sales pros you can find. Yet some sales managers would rather have a tooth extracted than interview applicants. It's true that the process can often be tedious and difficult, but it is essential. And going without someone in the position at all can be far more costly than spending the time to hire the right one in the first place.

Your first step is to write a description of the characteristics you desire in your ideal sales pro. For example, it could look like this:

Our ideal new sales pro has these characteristics:
- A person with five to ten years in sales experience
- Knowledge of your industry and competitors
- Someone who has a history of achieving their sales quota
- Located in the following locations (Los Angeles, Denver, Chicago, New York, or Atlanta)
- Is willing to travel up to fifty percent of the time
- Has a bachelor's degree
- Friendly, outgoing personality
- A recommendation by a current sales pro is a plus

You should follow all applicable laws concerning bias: do not consider age, race, color, sex, religion, national origin, disability, or genetic information. Not only is this illegal, but having a diverse team with unique perspectives will strengthen your team.

Once this list is completed, send it to the human resources department or an outside recruiter. They will use it to source candidates for you. Once you receive applicants, you can screen them against these criteria. You may want to give each a weight. For example, the sales experience may have a higher weight than the university degree or location. Then, you can score each applicant and decide which you want to interview personally. I would normally interview four to six candidates for each position. If none are acceptable, I would ask for another batch of candidates or go to the next four to six highest-ranking candidates from the existing list.

An interviewing practice that Jay Ryan, my sensei, employed was to ask each candidate to do a ten-to-fifteen-minute sales role-play of a sales pitch with which they were familiar. The audience would ask serious questions. These were often very informative and revealing. We found that some we thought were good candidates struggled while others excelled.

You may also occasionally have internal candidates come forward for an open position. I've found that there is always a bias against the internal candidates because we know their strengths, especially their faults, whereas we evaluate outside candidates at their best. It is important to consider this when there are internal candidates under consideration. When you evaluate what you know of their strengths and weaknesses, also evaluate how well you think they can learn to overcome those weaknesses. And keep in mind that because you know them from the beginning, you can address them right away, whereas the faults of external candidates are unknown.

In *Above Quota Performance*, I discussed thirty characteristics a sales manager should look for when hiring a high-performing sales pro. Of those thirty, the top ten are:

1. High character and integrity
2. Passionate about their work and self-motivated
3. Intelligent
4. Achievement-oriented
5. Sales acumen
6. Empathy
7. Emotional intelligence (EQ)
8. Self-confident
9. Communication
10. Persuasion skills

Many sales managers try to hire sales pros who seem to have personalities and backgrounds like their own. I initially did this, too. I looked for sales pros with accounting or financial experience before they went into sales (which is what I did) and then abandoned the practice after about one year. It was a mistake. I found that high-performing sales pros have diverse characteristics. In fact, I found very little commonality between the highest performers.

It is essential that you, as the sales manager, invest enough time to make them successful. New hires must participate in a formal onboarding program to familiarize them with the company, the organization, and its products. But at the same time, they should be hired with a probationary period, so they can easily be terminated if they do not work out. Finding the right fit for your team is essential. The effect of having a high turnover rate on your team can severely impede your ability to meet your team sales goals and will cost you in the long run.

Can You Afford to Keep a "Cowboy?"

What should a sales manager do when confronted with a high-producing sales pro who cannot follow company sales practices? This is not one of the common causes for termination, as it has nothing to do with specific bad behaviors or for lack of sales or lack of an acceptable sales pipeline. I call these sales pros "Cowboys" (can be male or female) because of their desire to operate like they were in the American Wild West, without rules or much supervision. They are often egotistical, narcissistic persons. As a sales manager, I often had to defend keeping these rebels on the sales force to top management because they often didn't follow defined company procedures or upset their co-workers. At some point, the cost and time spent fixing the collateral damage they create may offset the benefit of keeping them on board. One obvious issue is that the sales revenue they bring in is not easily replaced, not by others in the sales force, and not through a new hire.

> ### Takeaway 29 – Cowboys Are Challenging to Manage and Sometimes Wear Out Their Welcome

Cowboys are usually very self-motivated. They are not the sales pros that show up late at the office, spend too much time at the coffee machine, or gossip.

In a recent *Inc.* magazine article the founder and CEO of a medium-sized national business, A1 Garage Door Service, said he fired his top salesman and his profits soared. His COO told him: "Tommy, he's disrespectful. He's not compassionate. He only cares about himself. He does not care about you; he doesn't care about our customers; he doesn't care about great reviews. He's in there to make a dollar and he's not playing the long game."[83]

The CEO, Tommy Mello, said, "Letting go of that sales person set standards for everyone else's behavior. It changed the culture in a very positive way. Everyone tried to do their best every day, and we became even more profitable."[84] The top sales pro was a producer, but also a poor corporate citizen, and he crossed the line between being worth all the disruptions compared to the sales he brought into the company. Others in the company cheered his departure. He was a cowboy who did not fit the corporate culture.

I have had the fortune and misfortune of having several cowboys work for me. They were all ultra-competitive, high-producing sales pros; some were the top producers. I had to determine if their superior performance was due to misbehaving, for example, misrepresenting the product's capabilities, but that was rarely the case. They were successful in sales because they flourished with the job's greater autonomy. They often felt rules were for others, not them, and would deliberately flout them. Their nonconformist behavior was usually the byproduct of their high energy level and extreme eagerness to close business in the shortest amount of time, which, when done by following the rules, brings praise, not scorn. These individuals were often charismatic and fun to be around. But sometimes, their strengths, including operating independently, became weaknesses.

Perhaps the cowboy decided to cut a corner and not receive pre-approval to offer a discount or provide a resource at no cost. They may have scheduled another person's time without checking with them first. Or, they may have aggressively pursued their prospect to the point where they annoyed them. Maybe they did not receive a prompt enough response from one of the internal product, marketing, or legal staff people, and the sales pro insulted them. The cowboy often operated with the philosophy of asking for forgiveness afterward rather than permission earlier. Worried that not receiving approval would hurt their likelihood of closing the sale, they went ahead without consent and believed that their productivity would absolve them of most of their "sins." And that was usually the case.

When deciding how I needed to handle cowboys, I classified their conduct into three categories:

1. Were the problems the result of impatience, over-eagerness, or rule-bending?
2. Did they lie or misrepresent something to either the prospect or to sales management?
3. Was there a mental health issue, such as drug or alcohol addiction, PTSD, or a personality disorder?

If it was the first category, I reminded them that their conduct annoyed others and was not acceptable. The result of this conversation was sometimes successful with egregious issues corrected. They were often unaware of the severity and repercussions of their conduct and had not considered the impact that it had on others.

If it was the second category, I would give the person one warning and terminate them the second time it happened. I had a zero-tolerance policy for lying, misrepresentation, or a lack of business ethics.

If it was the third category, I would get the human resources department involved to assure that we considered the person's condition and followed the company policy. These people were often able to close sales, but often were unreliable and had absence issues. It is possible that professional counseling may help them.

I tried to be as tolerant as possible to keep the high-producing sales pros on my team because of their disproportionate contributions to the company's sales revenue. Unfortunately, the reality is that many will eventually wear out their welcome and move on regardless; it is best to try to contain their bad habits while trying to backfill with other sales pros who will be better than average producers in the long run.

This is one of the most difficult challenges a sales manager must handle. Is the revenue from high-performing sales pros offset by the trouble they cause while selling? No sales manager wants to let a high performer go, so you often need extreme tolerance and patience. Don't enable the cowboy, which will become very time-consuming and put you on a collision path with your manager. Top management pressures you to close sales, but they do not like rule breakers or people who cause internal morale problems. Understanding cowboy behavior and handling it according to the three categories can help you be successful in your sales management career. Sometimes, there is even "addition by subtraction" because other people will become more productive when a cowboy is let go.

Promoting a Sales Pro to Sales Manager

Let's look at a hypothetical example. "Jennifer" is among the best-performing sales pros on your team. She has let you know that she wants to be considered for your sales manager opening. You had not previously considered Jennifer for this role. Perhaps she has only worked for you for a short time and may be too inexperienced. Yet she has exceeded her sales quota in the last two years, one of only two who accomplished that. What should you consider when deciding whether to promote Jennifer?

The best practice is for companies to establish defined growth tracks so that the paths to management are established and well-known. Candidates are identified and nurtured along the path by periodic reviews and training.

Does Jennifer Fit the Sales Manager Skill and Competencies Set?

The skill set of a sales manager is vastly different from that of a sales pro. It is not a senior sales pro position either. An exceptional sales manager must be able to transfer their knowledge to their team members. They must devote adequate time to training and coaching, emphasizing new and failing sales pros. In addition, they need to manage the sales pipeline, hire and fire sales pros, accurately forecast sales, and manage upward.

Returning to our example of Jennifer, is she respected and well-liked by the other team members? Will her former peers see her as their manager or their friend? Often, there is respect because they know that Jennifer has achieved the sales quotas. But sometimes friendships interfere with the new roles Jennifer and her friends will have. If some despise her because of her achievements or aggressiveness, the situation will be exacerbated when she becomes the manager. If Jennifer is promoted, she will need coaching on how to work with her former peers. And her friends should also receive coaching on how to interact with her.

I always asked, "Would we hire Jennifer for this position if she was an outside candidate?" If not, let's pause and consider the risks.

What are the Known Risk Factors of Promoting Jennifer?

Many star sales pros fail as sales managers because of the difference in skills needed for each position. Successful sales pros are usually "lone wolves." They like to work independently and dislike managers who try to control them. Successful managers must be the ultimate team players. They must be constantly engaged and communicating with their team. A good example is that many high-performing professional athletes have failed as managers, while some of the greatest coaches and managers were below average as players. It's a different skill set.

Another consideration is Jennifer's ability to drive the team to success. Does she have the capability, drive, and energy to direct others, not just herself? She will need the courage to push her former teammates to achieve the team sales quota. Can she recognize it and take corrective actions if they are not achieving success? Can she terminate a non-performer? If the answer to these three questions is negative, you must consider somebody else.

What If You Don't Promote Jennifer to Sales Manager?

The greatest risk of not promoting Jennifer is that she may leave for a sales manager opportunity at another company if that is her ambition and you don't promote her now. This is especially concerning if her peers know she has applied for the position. It is also impossible to return Jennifer to your sales force if she is unsuccessful as a sales manager because that is too big an ego hit. Your competitors and other companies are always searching for outstanding sales pros and already know about her.

Secondly, but equally important, taking a top seller out of the sales force and making her a manager reduces the probability of your team reaching quota. Who will make up for the lost above-quota sales revenue? A new hire? Not likely. Of course, depending on her motives for wanting the promotion, you may lose here regardless.

The Ultimate Outcome

What message will you send to the company if you hire Jennifer? Or, if you don't? If Jennifer is promoted, it sends a message that you will promote from within, which is a positive signal, assuming she is qualified. If she isn't qualified, it may send the message that she was promoted because she was favored. It also may be considered a reward for Jennifer's outstanding performance.

Takeaway 30 – Promoting a Top Sales Producer Has Both Positive and Negative Risks

Suppose you do not promote Jennifer to sales manager and hire someone from outside the company. In that case, it may send the message that the company isn't confident in Jennifer, or perhaps of their employees and training in general. Or it may send the message that the company prefers to hire from outside, which can result in morale issues.

Having faced this situation on many occasions, I advise careful decision-making. I suggest interviewing people from the outside and others on the inside and comparing all candidates to a specific standard. Sometimes companies feel the need for "new blood" but then choose the best candidate with the best skills for the new job opening.

However, it may be worth hiring her if Jennifer seems to have the necessary skills and ambition. You could be gaining a new outstanding sales manager—or creating a disaster in which you lose a sales pro and the sales manager by resignation or termination. Then, you will need to deal with the disruption of replacing the sales manager and a productive sales pro. Whatever the decision, you must provide increased coaching on leadership, team-building skills, and assistance in learning on how to do proper pipeline management of their team, as they usually did not pay much attention to this as a sales pro.

Companies Should Have Career Paths for Sales Pros

If you don't promote your top sales pro to sales manager, you need to have an honest discussion of the reasons for your decision, what skills she needs to be promoted in the future, and your willingness to help her obtain those skills. This must be done promptly, not waiting until the next formal performance review, and I suggest you request the assistance of a human resources person in planning the discussion.

Perhaps this situation could have been avoided by regularly scheduled honest career discussions with Jennifer in which you emphasized both your delight about her sales performance but also your concerns about her ambitions to be promoted to sales manager. Also, you should specify which skills Jennifer is missing and possible actions she could take to acquire them. The more you disclose and clarify, the better it will be for all.

It should also be emphasized that she does not have to move to a sales management position to be appreciated and recognized for her significant contributions to the company. Sometimes, they are just seeking recognition of their value, not necessarily a promotion, and this can be easily provided.

Always remember that your objective is to try to promote the best person for the position to ensure their success, your success, and the company's success.

What Are Causes for Sales Pro Terminations?

While turnover should be avoided when possible—you want to hold on to your talented sales pros—sometimes there is no choice but to fire someone. As I mentioned, I have terminated sales pros who have lied to me, regardless of their sales performance. I insist that sales pros tell me the truth, especially about the status of their sales opportunities. I also always insist they conduct themselves professionally and be good corporate citizens. Other behaviors that will result in either a strong formal warning or are cause for termination are:

1. Misrepresentation or lying to a prospect or customer
2. Dishonesty

3. Theft (of Company property, intellectual property, or another team member's property)
4. Not following company policy by blatantly breaking rules, including violations of a company Code of Conduct policy
5. Cybersecurity violations, including stalking
6. Violating company confidentiality policies
7. Sexual harassment of other company employees
8. Unexcused absences, tardiness, or repeatedly not showing up for work
9. Illegal activity
10. Refusal to complete company requested internal training or compliance courses
11. Repeated or deliberately incorrect sales forecasts
12. Not being willing to be coached
13. Deliberately closing unprofitable sales
14. Creating internal conflicts
15. Not taking responsibility for their own actions— or inactions
16. Unwillingness to prospect for new business
17. Use of drugs and illegal substances
18. Being rude to prospects, customers, and other team members
19. Lack of respect or insubordination
20. Working for another company at the same time, or going into business for himself

I have had experience with some sales pros that exhibited some of the unacceptable behaviors listed above and, in most cases, terminated the person from employment. You may have noticed that I did not list "not being a good team player," as I have found that many high-performing sales pros are not team players. And they might not get along well with others on their team, or in the company. That is acceptable (but not desirable) to me, if they are not disruptive, don't negatively affect the team morale to an objectionable extent, and they don't violate the twenty behaviors listed above. I call these people "Reggie Jacksons" after the famous major league baseball player that was notorious for having a very high ego and strained relationships with many of his teammates, but usually performed at the highest level himself. His teammates only liked Reggie after they cashed their World Series winning paycheck.

Not achieving quota or having an inadequate pipeline will often result in the sales pro being placed on a performance plan. It is up to sales management to coach sales pros to achieve an acceptable level of sales production within that defined probationary period. Failure to achieve agreed upon metrics even while on a performance plan can result in termination of employment. A negative attitude is not grounds for termination, in my opinion, but it deserves a warning that it needs correction within that same period.

The Importance of Operating in the Best Interests of Your Customers

The sales profession has had a bad reputation historically because there have been sales pros that would lie or stretch the truth, obfuscate, and cheat. This has especially been widespread in some businesses, such as the sales of vehicles, land, home improvements, and houses, as well as door-to-door sales of products such as vacuum cleaners and home health care.

I strongly reject those practices and the negative characterizations of sales pros, both individuals and sales managers. All sales pros should conduct themselves using the highest standards of business ethics and morality. It is not enough to operate within legal bounds; one must incorporate the highest ethics, integrity, trustworthiness, respect, loyalty, and social responsibility in all personal and business dealings.

I have a few rules that were paramount for myself and every sales team I have ever managed. First, sales pros should always operate with the best interests of the customer or prospect in mind. Second, sales pros must be completely honest with the customer or prospect in all respects. That includes being truthful about product limitations, delivery issues, or any news that might possibly hurt the likelihood of closing the sale. Third, the sales pro must represent the interests of the prospect or customer to the management of his company and similarly represent the interests of his company to the prospect or customer. And last, the sales pro must be completely honest with his sales manager and not be afraid to report bad news.

Takeaway 31 – The Sales Pro Must Always Be Truthful and Disclose All Relevant Issues to Buyers

Lying or misrepresentation are never acceptable under any circumstance and are causes for immediate termination. I have fired sales managers and sales pros for lying in sales reports to customers, me, and the company. I wanted the company staff I worked with to treat all prospects and customers like their parents. I would not lie or cheat my parents, and I would not do that to a prospect or customer. And anyone who would cheat their parents, I didn't want to work for me. Ever.

To summarize, this chapter has covered many aspects of managing sales pros. First, I have emphasized the importance of promptly filling all open sales positions with qualified sales pros. I have seen many sales managers not reach their annual sales targets because of open sales positions due to a budgeted new hire or turnover, even though the remaining sales pros may have exceeded their sales quotas. I have provided three numerical examples that show how this can happen.

One of a sales manager's most difficult, if not the most difficult, responsibilities is hiring and firing sales pros. It can be very time-consuming, and many need to develop better skills in this area. Some managers don't devote enough time to this responsibility and hire one of the first candidates they interview. This may turn out to be a costly mistake. I have provided some tips that should help identify the best sales candidates. Most companies have particular hiring and termination practices that must be followed.

Many VPs of Sales and sales managers often encounter a conundrum: whether to promote a high-performing sales pro to a sales management role, often at their request. These individuals may be high-performing salespeople but not capable sales managers. Some have intuitive sales skills and cannot transfer that knowledge to others. I have discussed many risks and opportunities to evaluate when considering such a move. It could be a win/win or a lose/lose. I have seen instances where the former high-performing sales pro left the company after failing as a sales manager, often because it was not a good fit, and his ego would not allow him to return to his sales pro position. They then go to another company as a sales professional.

Another challenge for the sales manager is what to do with a Cowboy in the salesforce. These sales pros are often very high performers but are also very high maintenance. They ignore their managers and feel they can get away with doing so because of their outstanding sales performance. They do not follow instructions and sometimes openly disregard them. Readers who are sports fans have seen these types of individuals for many years. Exceptionally talented, they excel at their team position but are "prima donnas" and so difficult to manage that they cause disruptions and morale problems. They are often traded, and each new team thinks they can tame the Cowboy, but at some point, management does a cost/benefit analysis and decides that the team is better without them than with them. Then, they move on to excel and disrupt another team or company. So, when you are confronted with a similar situation, you need to decide whether you are better off with or without such sales pros, and then act accordingly.

CHAPTER 12
Other Important Sales Organization Considerations

Sales Compensation

There has been a lot written about designing ideal sales compensation plans. I prefer a highly leveraged plan, where the base salary is lower than the market, with increasing commission percentages based on sales achievement against quota. Once the sales pro has achieved the annual (or monthly or semi-annual) target the commission percentages continue to increase—with no limit on how much a sales pro can earn. Like many other things in life, the 80/20 rule, or Pareto Principle, applies in sales. Typically, 20 percent of the total salesforce will produce 80 percent of the total new sales. I believe in rewarding the high producers—the top 20 percent—and prefer this commission plan because it encourages and rewards high sales performance. Sales pros with less confidence in their ability to exceed quotas, or some new hires without experience with selling the company's products, will want a higher base salary and lower, graduated-commission rates.

However, it may not be easy to recruit and retain highly competent sales pros with a lower-than-market base salary, even though the expected earnings, if one achieves or surpasses quota, can be much better than the industry average. Thus, a plan should be designed to attract the best sales pros and reward significant contributors. One way to do this is to guarantee earnings for a short period for a new hire, typically three to six months.

Takeaway 32 – The Quota Should Be Achievable for at Least 60 Percent of Sales Pros

My caution here is that a quota should always be an achievable, realistic, and easily measurable goal, not a "pie in the sky" number or metric that only a few exceptional sales pros reach. If it isn't, it is very demotivating, and one can expect a high sales pro turnover. At least 60 percent of the sales force should be able to reach their quotas, on average annually, excluding new hires. I have seen as low as 10 percent achieve their annual quota, which is more representative of what should be an exceptional or "President's Club" performance. Monthly or quarterly quotas are also an option instead of an annual goal. I have also seen quotas work on a rolling twelve-month program, which tends to smooth out performances.

Deming and Commissions

I enjoyed attending a W. Edwards Deming workshop on "Management Today & Tomorrow: How It Must Change" in 1993. Dr. Deming was ninety-three at the time and passed away later that year. Even in his advanced age, he seemed to be very sharp mentally. Deming was one of the most influential promoters of the total quality management movement. He was trained in statistical quality control, and his quality concepts are based on his theory that continual improvement of processes can help increase quality while decreasing costs. His theory is that fixing the process, rather than the individual, produces a greater impact on the output quality. Deming is primarily credited with helping the Japanese automobile makers improve their quality in the post-World War II period. Later in his career, US automobile companies accepted and embraced his concepts.

Deming's quality theories are based on his "14 Points," which are explained in his book *Out of the Crisis*, and he strongly believed that all fourteen points must be embraced and completely adopted, not chosen a la carte.

In his eleventh point, Dr. Deming stated he did not believe in paying sales pros commissions. His thinking was that "paying sales commissions to staff introduced distortions into the organization that damaged overall performance," and he believed that "the problems with sales commissions touch on all four areas of the management system."[85] Those are:

1. **Systems thinking** – he felt that commissions led to organizations that are not customer focused and to decisions that are not in the customer's best interests.
2. **Understanding variation** – he felt bonus systems could reward statistically valid variations, rather than normal causes.
3. **Understanding psychology** – he felt that some employees were being rewarded based on one metric and that commissions devalued teamwork.

4. **Theory of knowledge** – he felt that commissions caused people to ignore management theories.[86]

I respectfully disagree with Dr. Deming's theory about paying sales commissions. Commissions incentivize and reward sales pros for closing sales and do not create customer problems. Properly governed companies have management and legal review of contracts before they are signed to ensure that the sales professional is not selling something that cannot be delivered or puts the company at risk. In addition, the sales pros that close the most sales will earn the most commissions—and income—which rewards exceptional performance. Not paying commissions rewards mediocrity.

Your company should offer a commission plan because it is needed to attract top sales talent. There is a large pool of sales pros in the global workforce, and some of these sales pros, perhaps 10 to 20 percent, are exceptional and will be in high demand by many companies in the marketplace. Indeed, many are quite eager to move to other companies where they can increase their earnings. They will usually choose a company where they believe they will prosper economically, which includes compensation but also other considerations, such as stock, personal advancement, culture, products or services, and compatibility with the sales manager. That would leave the companies that do not pay commissions with mediocre (or worse) sales pros unless their salaries are comparable to what a top-performing sales pro would normally earn. Ben Horowitz, a co-founder and general partner at venture capital firm Andreessen Horowitz, explains:

"Imagine that you are a great sales person who knows you

can sell $10M worth of product in a year. Company A pays commissions and, if you do what you know you can do, you will earn $1M/year. Company B refuses to pay commissions for "cultural reasons" and offers $200K/year. Which job would you take? Now imagine that you are a horrible sales person who would be lucky to sell anything and will get fired in a performance-based commission culture, but may survive in a low-pressure, non-commission culture. Which job would you take?"[87]

Business executives want to reach their company's growth and profitability goals. Their compensation and bonuses are often tied to an earnings metric. Do they want to trust that hiring and retaining mediocre (or worse) sales pros will result in meeting their goals? I would not. If a sales pro told me she would rather receive a salary than a compensation plan consisting of a base salary plus uncapped commissions, I would question her motivations. I would probably not hire her for a sales pro position, perhaps, for pre-sales or an account manager position.

I taught economics at the graduate university level and studied behavioral economics. I know that incentives, monetary or otherwise, matter. They may be either positive (bonuses, commissions, rewards) or negative (penalties or fines) and will affect people's choices and behaviors. People change their actions because of incentives, whether buying a house or car, or sometimes even getting married. Incentives also matter in the workplace. Most people do not perform better for the altruistic good of the company; some do, but they are rare—or they are the owners. People like to be rewarded, whether it is by a bonus, commission, or recognition ("top sales pro of the month.") I have seen some sales pros close challenging sales in an unusually tight timeframe to earn President's Club honors or quarterly bonuses with recognition and compensation that went along with the achievement. And the most talented would probably choose a highly leveraged plan (lower base salary plus possibility to earn higher commissions).

Hiring exceptional sales pros is critical to the success and culture of your organization. It would not be wise to try to find an exceptional sales pro and offer her a salary-only compensation plan. If you successfully found such a person, this person would likely soon be approached by recruiters who offer a better compensation plan and be enticed to leave the company.

Takeaway 33 – Commissioned Sales Pros Are Essential for the Growth of the Company

Years ago, my brother asked me if I was looking for an exceptional sales pro. Since I have never worked for a company with enough talented sales pros I said yes and asked for the details. The company my brother was working for was going to let one of their best sales pros go because he "earned too much money," and they could no longer afford to keep him. This seemed a foolish move for the company because for each commission the sales pro received, the company received incremental revenue of at least 80 percent, while he was paid perhaps as much as 20 percent. However, the company was focused on his total earnings and did not want to have a sales pro earning what they considered to be excessive commissions. This sales pro did not have much trouble finding another high-paying sales position, though not with our company, and his former company ended up going out of business a few years later despite having a market-leading product at one time.

When I was a software company president, I told the owners that I wanted to hire five additional sales pros, and I projected that each would cost us about $100,000 in salary, fringe benefits, technology support, and space. Still, each would bring in $1 million to the company. My projected investment of $500,000 would result in revenues of $5 million or a net increase in EBITDA (or Earnings Before Interest, Tax, Depreciation, and Amortization) of $4.5 million.

Unfortunately, the owners rejected my request and suggested that the existing sales pros, averaging about $1 million each in annual sales, could each be encouraged to add another $250,000 in sales. But most of them were already exceeding their quotas so additional work would be a burden.

Smart businesspeople understand that their company will usually receive more than 80 percent of the incremental revenue, after paying commissions, from each additional new sale, and that adding new accounts is often the organization's lifeblood. They will also understand that the greater the earnings of the commissioned sales pros, the easier it will be to attract high-performing sales talent. And sales growth will fuel the company's overall growth and profitability. I can't ever recall a CEO who explained their company's poor financial performance to shareholders or analysts on "excessive commissions." But they are often called on to explain poor sales performance, regardless of the cause.

How Many Sales Pros Should Report to a Sales Manager?

This question has vexed management for many years and is difficult to answer because some sales managers can handle more sales pros than others. One also must consider the impact on the amount of time the manager can devote to each sales pro by increasing the span of control. But the ideal number is five to seven sales pros, and never more than twelve. Suppose the sales manager is required to manage more than eight. In that case, it will normally result in less time available for each sales pro—and often the needy sales pros receive most of the attention, which is not always the best allocation of the sales manager's time and resources.

I have managed as many as twelve or fourteen sales pros at once and found it difficult to give each sales pro the proper attention they needed or deserved. Sales managers face the paradox of deciding whether to devote their time to failing sales pros—or to the high producers that will help the team achieve its goals. Companies may think they are saving money by having one person manage large sales pro teams, but that sub-optimizes a sales manager's ability to close more sales opportunities. If a sales organization consists of one VP of Sales and more than twelve sales pros they should be broken into teams and managed by district sales managers or team leaders.

Can an Introvert Succeed in Sales?

I think so, but . . .

I recently conducted an informal poll on the Sales Central Group on LinkedIn.com, and the results were that the respondents, all sales pros, overwhelmingly believe that introverts can be successful sales pros.

Perhaps the issue for some is the stereotypical perceptions of introverts and extroverts and the typical sales pro. For example, when you think of extroverts, do you think of somebody gregarious, engaging, and outgoing? When you think of introverts, do you think of most shy people who do not seem to like attention and are not outgoing? But do these stereotypes apply to success in the sales profession today?

Succeeding in Sales

Success in sales requires sales pros to engage in tasks and use skills that are usually very uncomfortable for people with introverted personalities. These include:

- Prospecting for new business, often including cold-calling
- Asking the buyer to attend calls and meetings
- Leading presentations and discussions, often by standing in front of an audience
- Persuasion skills
- Seeking objections buyers might have
- Asking the prospect for the order and closing the sale

These tasks are more easily handled by extroverts, who enjoy being the center of attention, are not reluctant to speak up, thrive on interaction, and love socializing, especially with large groups. Indeed, they seek conversations with others (the "gift of gab") and are unhappy working alone. In addition, extroverts are usually very open to new experiences.

On the other hand, introverts are content when working alone or with a small group of like-minded individuals. They prefer familiarity and disdain conflict, are usually careful and not impulsive, and are often excellent listeners and deep thinkers. Introverts tend to refrain from delegating and instead take on tasks alone, mainly because they do not want to ask for assistance or manage another person. Introverts seek solitude, whereas extroverts thrive on interacting with others in a group. Solitary confinement is torture to an extrovert. To an introvert, it is a party of one!

Introvert's Sales Skills

But what about other vital skills that high-performing sales pros must have? Skills like:

- Participation as a team player
- Subject matter expertise
- Following up on questions and issues and promptly responding to a prospect
- Identifying and solving problems
- Strong, careful, observational proficiencies (for example, reading people's emotions)
- Researching potential solutions
- Challenging the prospect or pushing for more information
- Handling transition and implementation issues

Many introverts excel at these valuable skills. But can that compensate for not wanting to interact with large groups and initiate conversations with people they don't know? When placed in a position that requires extroverted qualities, such as public speaking or social action, some introverts are more adaptable to those tasks and can thrive, whereas others are not.

Takeaway 34 – Introverts Can Be Successful in Sales!

Looking at Sales from Both Sides Now

Let's contrast the pitches that an introvert or an extrovert would use to sell a product to the same people. After spending a lot of time researching, reflecting, and thinking about how to approach the prospect, introverts craft a pitch based on thoughtful logic, their analysis, and their impressions of the audience. The pitch would emphasize the advantages of buying the product in a very subtle, soft-sell manner.

After arriving in the room or introducing herself or himself on the video conference, the extrovert, who may have sourced the lead from cold-calling, would begin the meeting by discussing the weather, the local professional team, or noting the university the decision maker graduated from. He would then jump in and explain why the prospect should purchase the product without getting into much detail. He would be careful not to offend the buyer they want to have as a friend.

And the Winner Is . . .

According to research published by the *Applied Psychology Journal* and cited in an article by Melissa Dittman Tracey, there is almost zero correlation in sales performance between extroversion and introversion sales performance, and the most successful sales pros tend to be a hybrid who falls in between the introvert or extrovert classifications, what are termed "ambiverts."[88] They are more flexible, may have traits that are the best of both worlds and often have very successful sales careers.

My experience has been that all personality types can be successful in sales. Extroverts have the advantage of being socially comfortable meeting and interacting with new groups of people. They are also less intimidated by the prospects and have no problem asking for the order. Introverts can likewise be effective in sales by leveraging their strengths.

In over thirty years of sales management experience, I saw many (but not most) introverts exceed their sales quotas. Introverts were exceptionally successful when the product or subject matter was complicated, such as life insurance policy management or electronic medical records. Introverts may be reluctant to engage with buyers initially, but once the sales cycle is underway, they become more comfortable and can manage the accounts.

Takeaway 35 – Building Trust Is a Skill that an Introvert Can Master

The critical skills to successful selling now are building trust and solving the buyer's problems. Introverts can do this equally as well as extroverts. An ideal scenario would be to set up a separate business development function to find and pass on qualified leads to introverted and extroverted sales pros. That would alleviate any anxieties over making initial contact, and possibly any social awkwardness sales pros may have, especially for introverts.

Mirroring this idea, some companies have broken their sales

forces into "hunters," often extroverts, and "farmers," often intro-verts. The hunters find and develop new accounts. The farmers call on existing customers and try to upsell them on additional products and services. In addition, I have found that many sales pros like hunting, not farming, and the reverse is also true. Some of the best cross-sellers that I have worked with are introverts who worked solely on existing customer accounts. They developed long-lasting relationships with the executives and staff in their accounts. And the customers trusted their advice and efforts to solve their problems. Hunters, on the contrary, usually have no interest in solving billing or shipping issues, for example. An organization of hunters and farmers makes sense because it matches personalities and skill sets with the tasks that need to be performed. It is a good idea to compensate each for the successes of the other to ensure greater cooperation. For example, give a bonus or percent to the hunter that turns a lead over to the farmer, and vice versa.

In summary, introverts can succeed in sales in circumstances that favor their personality strengths: research, listening and observing, planning, and reacting. Management needs to recog-nize the differences in personality types and design the structure of the sales force accordingly.

Should You Specialize Your Sales Force?

Derek Gatehouse, author of *The Perfect Salesforce* believes, as I do, that most top sales pros are natural, not made. (I have pos-tulated that 80 percent of the high-performing sales pros are natural-born, and 20 percent are trained.) He also recognizes that most sales pros have specific strengths and weaknesses and proposes that each should be utilized in a way that utilizes their strengths. They should not be expected to do tasks they do not care about or that others may do better. His "perfect sales force" may have different sales pros for each stage. For example, some people may source and manage leads or set appointments. Some people perform product demonstrations. The sales pros do the "selling" and closing.[89]

I have worked with several sales organizations that were organized in this manner: There were different types of sales pros with specific roles: marketing assistants or inside sales pros who conducted marketing programs and called prospects to try to obtain an appointment, which was then turned over to the sales pro. When needed, a subject matter expert or a pre-sales pro who was highly trained would perform mostly scripted demonstrations. This process usually worked well. I found it worked even better when I kept the marketing, inside sales, and pre-sales pros engaged in the success of the sales cycle of an opportunity by including them in strategy meetings and perhaps by adding a bonus component to their compensation. Also, in many cases I was able to *grow* sales pros from the other internal roles. This would not normally be the case in the Gatehouse model.

Gatehouse takes this a step further, by assigning each sales pro to the tasks that they like and do well. For example, some could do demonstrations and answer questions, but not close sales. Others would only qualify leads, and some would only service clients. This also means that some sales pros will sell certain product and not others, which is often the case and consistent with my beliefs. All are specialists, like American professional football players. It works well in football: there are kick return-ers, pass rushers, punters, and running backs; why would it not work with sales? Gatehouse further noted, "It is easier to find top performers when you require them to perform fewer sales stages. It is easier to manage and to grow such a structure."[90] This arrangement may make it easier to attract and hire top performers for each sales stage. By handling fewer responsibilities, a sales pro should focus completely on the tasks they are charged with, which should increase sales results.

However, I'm afraid I disagree with Gatehouse's idea that his specialized sales force would be easier to manage without some level of uniformity of roles. I agree that most sales pros would be happier and perhaps more productive doing only what they like. According to Gatehouse, this should reduce the costly turnover of sales pros. However, imagine a situation where a sales team needs to be staffed so that Jeff Jones, for example, who only closes, comes in at the end of the sales cycle, Mary Smith can only perform demonstrations, and Alan Ellis can qualify leads, conduct presentation, answer product questions, build *statements of work,* and close the sale. Although this leverages each person's strengths, it seems very complicated and cumbersome to me. This concept is very idealistic, probably impractical, and could be very inefficient. It becomes difficult to scale up because there are so many special-role sales pros. There are also greater possibilities for communication issues, missed follow-ups or awkward hand-offs due to a lack of clarity in roles. They must be clearly defined and properly managed—all differently.

Takeaway 36 – The Salesforce Needs to be Organized to Best Fit the Buyer's Needs, Not the Sellers'

Most importantly, we must look at organizing the sales force from the buyer's viewpoint. Do they want different people from the seller shuffling in and out of the account? I would also wonder about the impact of switching sales pros on the prospects and customers. I know that most prefer a single, constant point of contact because it provides the continuity of one person handling all aspects of communication with the buyer. The buyer may need to repeat information they already provided to different people, which will annoy them. Don't tell me it will be documented in the customer relationship management (CRM) because, from experience, we all know that is not likely to happen.

How can an equitable compensation plan be designed that properly rewards sales pros fairly based on their real contribution? In terms of managing, on a day-to-day basis, I would think that this could be a compensation application nightmare. It appears that we are changing the organization to fit the tastes of the sales pros, instead of the other way around. Would you design a sales organization in this manner from the ground up, or is it an accommodation to the skills and desires of the top sales pros? Is this an ideal arrangement?

I do agree with Gatehouse that the productivity of the top sales pros could increase if they focus only on the activities they prefer to handle. He has worked with clients where their results have increased with this approach. Certainly, if people do only what they do well and enjoy, they will out-perform others. Specialists will always do better than generalists in their area. For example, a carpenter will always do carpentry better than a plumber, and vice versa. However, if a handyman company wanted generalists that do carpentry, plumbing, electrical work, fix appliances, and repair windows, they would hire people with those skills rather than specialists. Still, we all would prefer to have an operation performed by a highly experienced brain surgeon for a brain aneurism, not a general surgeon.

Specialization of the sales force can be based on products, markets, customer segments, or activities, such as calling on existing customers versus new prospects.[91] As discussed earlier, many companies deploy a "hunter" versus "farmer" approach. Using this type of organization is akin to the prehistoric early human practice of some men functioning as hunter-gatherers and others tending to livestock, gardens, and shelters.

In the sales model, the hunter sales pros go after new business, and the farmers call on the existing customer base to try to upsell and cross-sell. Usually, the hunters will receive greater compensation due to the difficulty of finding and closing new business sales. This division of responsibilities aims to maximize each group's skills to its fullest extent. There would also be managers for each group to ensure proper training and to handle hiring and firing new sales pros. Another advantage to the farmer model is that it should create greater "stickiness" in your customer base when someone is tending to their needs. Maintaining your customer base is especially important in the subscription or SAAS (software as a service) model. And having a dedicated resource for upselling and cross-selling additional products and services is often essential. It is much easier to have a specialized sales force when you are operating in a start-up mode. Usually, there are fewer highly qualified opportunities from early-stage buyers, where subject matter expertise is greatly valued. Coverage and scalability are not issues at that point. As product lines expand, it becomes more difficult to manage sales opportunities and territories. Many companies will also employ indirect sales forces and agents, especially in foreign markets. This gives the company the advantage of added coverage in markets they cannot cover at a very cost-efficient rate. On the other side, there are training and control issues. And indirect sales forces and agents will act in their best interests, not yours.

In the early years of McCormack and Dodge, the company used a different sales pro to sell each product in a defined geographical territory. These individuals handled both the sales and pre-sales roles, as they had product expertise. Some could even perform post-sales user training. Initially, only two products were sold, and this arrangement worked well. When the company reached eight product lines, it became impractical if a prospect considered all products. I spoke with a prospect in Connecticut who informed me that the messaging from several sales pros contradicted each other. The sales pros of the newest products emphasized that they had the latest and greatest features and easy user interfaces. The sales pros with the more mature products emphasized how their products had been in the market for many years, were proven, and were less likely to have any bugs in them. Plus, sending up to eight sales pros to visit a prospect at their office became costly. And some of the sales pros became anxious or bored while the others were doing the selling. At that point, I reorganized the sales force so that each sales pro managed all the products in a territory, and each had access to pre-sales subject matter experts. This was admittedly disruptive—people left established accounts, and we lost the expertise advantage we had on single product sales. Only one sales pro, who would not go along with the change, left the company (out of twenty), but, in the end, buyer's satisfaction and company revenues increased.

Most sales pros do not like to make cold calls. In fact, I am not sure I ever met one who did. I have seen some reasonably competent doing them, but most did not want to do so. It is difficult to reach people, and the rejection rate is very high. Most sales pros considered it a necessary evil, a tedious task with low payback and part of their job that they had to do but did not want to do. I have seen sales pros do every possible task they could to avoid making cold calls, even cleaning their desktops with anti-bacterial soap. Does that mean that you should never ask them to do so? Certainly, their productivity suffers when tasked with doing an activity they dislike. But cold-calling is a part of selling, and sometimes sales pros need to do things they dislike. It may not be fun, and it's sometimes boring, but as with many jobs, some unpleasant tasks must be done. To reduce the boredom, I set daily call goals to reach.

Another consideration is how account leads are assigned to sales pros. I have seen many different methods: geographical (assigned states or zip codes), named or assigned accounts, alphabetical, by vertical industry, or sequentially. My preference is to use geographical or assigned accounts. The weakness of the geographical approach is that some sales pros will not contact some accounts that others who are not as busy would be able to call on.

My sensei, Jay Ryan, preferred the assigned account method and would check to see which accounts were being called. If the assigned sales pro was not contacting them, he would assign them to another sales pro on a trial basis and check back in sixty days to see if they were contacted. If not, he would assign them to someone else. This incentivizes each sales pro to call on each of their assigned accounts or risk losing them. The weakness of assigned accounts is that the company could have two or more sales pros going to the same city or state, rather than taking advantage of sales pros already calling in that city.

The Perfect Sales Force Organization

What is the organization of the perfect sales force? There is no one-size-fits-all solution. It depends on many factors: whether the company is a start-up or established; the current success or lack of it by the existing sales force; the market; the barriers to entry; the complexity of the items being sold; the existing sales resources; the ability to hire additional resources; the company's budget; the training and on-onboarding program; the management style; the culture; and the geography covered. Do not be afraid to experiment or try new ideas occasionally, preferably with a small sample size. Some will work, and some will not. This is especially true in specific vertical markets. Companies may want to hire or supplement their sales force with indirect sales pros for various reasons, as discussed in the next chapter.

Takeaway 37 – The Hybrid Sales Model Is Preferred

According to McKinsey & Co, "winning companies deploy hybrid sales teams . . . which are comprised of roles with a mix of both in-person and remote time with customers, are deployed by 57% of winning companies, compared with 40 percent of those that lost market share. The adoption of larger hybrid teams is correlated with greater market share gains, especially in TMT [my note: Technology, media, and entertainment, and telecommunications]; finance, banking, and insurance; and travel, transportation, and logistics. The benefits from hybrid sales models are not exclusive to large companies: respondents from small to midsize companies with larger hybrid adoption rates reported seeing greater share gains."[92] Hybrid sales teams also incorporate digital (including social media) and third-party channel or partner strategies, including e-commerce.

The hybrid sales model is also my preference. In this model, there will be inside sales pros, sales pros, pre-sales pros, technical advisors, product managers or specialists, and a professional services person that can provide implementation estimates or statements of work. Sometimes there may be a need for an outside or third-party specialist depending on the buyer's needs. I have successfully worked with this model for many years. The sales pro's role is like that of an orchestra conductor. She is responsible for organizing the team, setting the strategy, and bringing in each team member as needed. The sales territories, for example, may be organized geographically, by named accounts, alphabetically, sequentially (leads assigned to sales pros in order), or by industry.

Can a Trained Monkey Sell for Your Company?

I worked for a CEO who told me he didn't understand why he employed a highly compensated sales force. Instead, he sarcastically said all he needed was a team of "trained monkeys" to sell for him.

He was half-serious. He certainly had a negative viewpoint of the value of sales pros to his company. His attitude was that sales pros were overpaid and were less valuable than other contributors, such as developers and technical support, and his anti-sales attitude permeated the culture of the company. As a result, sales pros were not treated with much respect in the company, and it was sometimes challenging to get cooperation from others. This made it much more difficult to close sales. And, of course, there was little recognition (even when we did close sales)—which all sales pros crave. It is challenging to maintain a positive attitude when you work for someone that does not appreciate your work, and it is also difficult not to carry that attitude into your calls on prospects, which will affect your sales close rate.

The CEO knew he could not hire an organ-grinder and send monkeys out on the road to call on executives at his target market, large and mid-sized corporations. However, he believed that the product he helped design was so rich in features and functionality that it could "sell itself." The CEO had accompanied sales pros on calls; buyers were usually pleased with the product and impressed that the CEO was calling on them, and since the sales closed, he thought selling his product was easy.

I dismissed the CEO's comment as demonstrating his pervasive negativity towards sales pros. But he repeated the derogatory comment to me on several occasions. The reality is that now, more than ever, most companies need highly skilled sales pros. The need is more significant than it was a few years ago, and sales pros need to improve their skills to succeed in today's highly competitive and complex digital, post-pandemic marketplace.

Today's sales landscape consists of knowledgeable buyers who have done hours of research before sellers arrive and are armed with more information than ever. They limit the amount of face time sellers receive, going from several face-to-face meetings to, more typically, just a few shorter meetings over videoconference. Competition, including the "do-nothing" decision, is fiercer than ever. In addition, many companies now have included procurement or strategic sourcing experts in their most rigorous selection process, especially in contract negotiation, to assure themselves of supplier due diligence and better contract terms.

Takeaway 38 – Companies Need Highly Skilled Sales Pros to Succeed Today

Among other capabilities, sales pros selling complex products and services now need to:

- Know how to prospect and develop new business leads.
- Build trusted relationships with buyers.
- Demonstrate expertise in your company's products and industry and be able to inform buyers of industry trends and the latest developments.
- Gain an understanding of the problems the buyers wish to fix through both open and closed-end questions.
- Succinctly articulate your company's value proposition—what is in it for the buyers?
- Be viewed as a trusted partner by buyers, not an obtrusive sales pro, by demonstrating empathy throughout the sales cycle.
- Be current on digital marketing technology.

- Must excel at qualifying buyers to eliminate those who will not buy now or are not in the product's "sweet spot" and will likely be a waste of time.
- Have business acumen and an exceptional understanding of business terminology.
- Be agile and adept. The sales cycle will rarely go as planned. Your time with buyers will be more limited than previously.
- Be able to close sales at the proper time in the sales cycle.

These superior sales skills typically take years, not months or days, to develop. Therefore, executive and sales management must consider top-quality, skilled, and higher-achieving sales pros as valuable assets. Their job performance is critical for the company to achieve its growth goals. Conversely, employing lower-paid and barely competent sales pros is usually doomed to failure. Such companies typically have high turnover and are always in a hiring and training mode.

Selling today is no longer a "smile and a shoeshine" job. Executives who believe otherwise are mistaken. Sales is a skilled position, just like other specialized employees who are employed by a company, whether they are in IT, security, inventory control, website development, or product design. Sometimes management takes sales pros for granted. In that case, it is up the VP of Sales to have a serious discussion with the CEO or other managers to explain the contributions that the sales force has made to the company, both in terms of results, as well other areas of contribution. This should not be left without a proper response.

Trained monkeys may be able to do routine tasks, but trained monkeys selling for your company? No way!

CHAPTER 13

Sales Enablement Tools and AI Will Make Sales Forces More Productive

The sales enablement function has received much recent attention, and according to a CSO Insights poll, 53 percent of companies surveyed have staffed and increased their budgets for it.[93] Forbes magazine noted that sales enablement solutions are currently the top technology investment chosen to improve sales productivity.[94]

Gartner Inc. defines the sales enablement function as follows:

> *"Sales enablement is designed to make it easier for sellers to sell. The sales enablement function is designed to evolve new seller skills, provide content that directly enables buyers and teach sellers how to connect customers to the best tools and resources to assist in the completion of their critical buying tasks."[95]*

Sales enablement's goals, according to Gartner, are to increase pipeline conversion rates, optimize the overall sales process, increase the size of the pipeline, increase the quantity of new customers acquired, improve seller skills and competencies and "reduce time-to-full productivity for new reps."[96] An effective sales enablement solution should also increase the speed and efficiency of "go-to-market" plans by providing all necessary marketing and sales components. Sales enablement tools should positively change the sales pros' selling behaviors by providing them with more information on their prospects, products, and company messages.

For example, the tool may provide the sales pro with current information on the prospective company (including real-time stock quotes), updated digital sales content and collateral, a prepared email message that links to an updated customized video, access to a library of use cases and testimonials, and a tracking tool that informs the sales pro when the last message was sent and when it was opened, how many times, and if it was forwarded. Such data and functionality, readily available on their smartphone, should positively impact the sales performances of all sales pros.

In 2023, I have seen greater interest in investing in sales enablement solutions by companies, and articles about the benefits. The Gartner Inc. research group predicts that corporate spending on sales enablement tools will increase by 50 percent by 2027 "as a way to address shifting buyer preferences, boost seller effectiveness and drive revenue growth"[97] According to Shayne Jackson, Sr. Director Analyst in the Gartner for Sales Leaders Practice, "Sales enablement is the most critical function for navigating sales teams through the constant change that surrounds them, from economic headwinds to evolving seller roles."[98] Forbes and Brainshark have noted that 59% of top-performing companies have a defined sales enablement role, as do 72% of all companies that report revenues more than 25% above plan.[99]

Takeaway 39 – Sales Enablement Needs Management Support to Add Value

Many sales technology initiatives failed because they needed greater managerial support. Since deploying a sales enablement solution is a significant change in sales operations, it will not be successful without the complete and active "buy-in" and participation by the company's management, in addition to the sales force. Sales management must be actively engaged and committed to the change and be invested in its success—it is not a "hands-off" environment.

Before investing in sales enablement, you must optimize your CRM system and eliminate anything hindering or interfering with the new functionality. I have seen very few CRM systems that are currently easy to use and updated by the sales pros. I recommend cleaning the CRM first and then adding sales enablement capabilities. It is best not to put them in place on top of a dysfunctional CRM system, which is like putting a turbocharged engine into a barely operational jalopy. Imperfect data is worse than useless. It saps the sales pro's selling time, may be misleading, and causes users to mistrust the CRM data. There are excellent software tools that will help improve the quality of your CRM data.

Here are some of the benefits of deploying a sales enablement function:

- More than 50 percent of sales pros should achieve or surpass their annual sales quotas.

- It should fill the gaps between the development of a sales strategy and the execution of the design and tasks by defining how to achieve the chosen strategy.
- It should result in a closer relationship between the marketing and sales functions since the proper deployment of a sales enablement solution requires greater cooperation and a symbiotic relationship.
- It will identify gaps between the desired marketing and digital content with the current situation, leading to a reduction or removal of the gap.
- The competitive win rate will almost certainly increase because of implementing the new tools and data. According to CSO Insights, there was an increase of 27 percent in the win rate, which resulted in happier sales pros earning higher commissions and helped attract sales pros from competitors.[100]
- The increase in the competitive win rate will result in new (name or logo) customers.
- The sales pros should experience more selling time and shorter sales cycles.
- A deployed robust sales enablement solution that contains training and tools will make the company more attractive for hiring top sales talent and reduce the attrition of current sales pros.
- Sales pros are now better equipped with tools and resources to aid them and can focus more of their time on chasing and closing deals.
- It will facilitate the success of remote selling which is here to stay.

Some may think the sales enablement solution is hype by some software companies; perhaps it is the "trick of the month/year," or a new "toy," as some sales solutions have been touted in prior years. But I don't think so. Instead, it is a serious effort to improve sales performance and address the high 50 percent sales pro quota failure rate.

Best practice sales enablement solutions typically include the following tools and data:

- **Profile** – A sales hiring profile that defines what behaviors, skills, or competencies the ideal sales pro needs to succeed at your company.
- **Buyer personas** – What are the titles and characteristics of the target buyers? What are their typical "hot buttons" or interests? What industry associations do they usually belong to? What messages should you use/not use when contacting them?
- **Onboarding tools and content** – To improve the process of welcoming and efficiently training new hires. The respondents to the Seismic survey noted that "83% say that their company's onboarding process doesn't train new hires quickly enough to prevent workflow disruptions."[101] The sales enablement solution must be able to handle remote onboarding, as well as continued coaching after the onboarding.
- **Sales engagement tools** – Using integration with sales communication channels and devices, management of messaging, and automation of messages using artificial intelligence such as conversation intelligence. Customer intelligence solutions "can record practice

and live customer calls, provide call transcriptions, recommend content based on call topics and analyze improvement areas for reps."[102] In a LinkedIn.com article, it was noted that "Sales enablement recognizes that effective selling requires identifying key moments in the buyer's journey and building a strategy to reach the consumer with the right content at the right time. A best-in-class enablement solution helps organizations achieve this via targeted content with personalized sales messages."[103]

The following are video platforms that are usually included in sales enablement solutions:

- **Video-based sales coaching** – enables the capture of best practices for training purposes.

- **Digital sales content automation and management for content creation** – this allows you to proactively recommend content and makes it easier for sales pros to gather up-to-date, marketing-approved content. A recent Seismic survey found that respondents spend ten hours per week (two hours per day) searching for content.[104] In my experience, that amount seems a little low. But that amount is 25 percent of the standard forty-hour work week, a substantial amount. Often the content found by sales pros may be out of date or not applicable to that prospect. A well-maintained sales library should include case studies and customer stories, reference lists, price lists, product catalogs and information, slide decks (best if highly customizable by industry), videos of demos and prior trainings, blog posts, white papers, webinars, and competitive intelligence. The content management system must provide flexibility to present the content to prospects differently.

- **Sales intelligence tools –** such as tracking of content usage (clicks) by email recipients, prospects, customers, and product data to help with cross-sell and upsell as well as customer retention. Some applications provide the capability to strengthen introductions to potential buyers.
- **Use cases and customer testimonials –** there always needs to be more of these. Sometimes sales pros must be encouraged to contribute or obtain testimonials directly from customers.
- **Mobility capabilities –** the solution must be accessible through smartphones and by laptop.
- The solution should be completely integrated with a CRM system that ties enablement to pipeline growth and surfacing content in the flow of work.
- Ideally, the sales enablement solution should be personalized for each sales pro.
- The tools, and content must provide qualitative and quantitative data to guide sales management in making real-time corrections. The outcomes must be tracked to prove the return on investment of the sales enablement expenditures.

Implement the various sales enablement components with realistic first, second, and third-year goals. Failure to dedicate adequate resources to the implementation, as well as have complete buy-in from all affected parties (including executive and sales management, the sales force including sales support and operations, marketing, channel partners, and legal) will leave your company marginally better off than you were previously, or perhaps even worse since management will expect improvements in sales results because of their investment.

Track Your Results!

Many metrics or key performance indicators (KPIs) tracked by the sales enablement function are those of current performance and efficiency and the pipeline's health. Most of these metrics should be reported for this period, compared to this period last year and last month. Some of these are:

- Total sales or net revenue
- Average revenue generated per sales pro
- Sales pro sales performance (quota attainment)
- Average purchase amount (deal size)
- The quantity of sales pros attaining quota
- Year-over-year sales or revenue growth
- The number of new customers (new logos) added (customer acquisition)
- Percentage of revenue from existing customers (cross-selling, up-selling)
- Lead to customer conversion ratios
- Competitive win/loss ratios (by sales pro, by manager, and total)
- Competitive win rate versus top 3 competitors, plus "no decision"

- Average length of the sales cycle
- Amount in sales pipeline, by stage
- Age of opportunities in pipeline (under thirty days, thirty to sixty days, sixty to ninety days, over ninety days)
- Time for new sales hires to program completion and productivity
- Sales enablement training class achievement measurements
- Sales pro turnover rate
- New hire satisfaction
- Comparison of accuracy of monthly close-date sales forecasts (by sales pro, by manager, and total)
- Customer retention percentage (by sales pro, by manager, and total)
- Customer churn rate, or a measurement of lost customers
- Customer satisfaction measurement
- Amount of marketing content added or updated to the library

A valuable sales enablement measurement to focus on is the quality of leads or lead conversion rate (listed above,) especially those sourced by the marketing department, the company website, or in-house or outsourced, outbound marketing. Is the company wasting time and resources finding leads that create unproductive activity? How likely will the leads turn into qualified leads and sales opportunities? Examine the source and question the quality of the mailing list you deployed and the content of your messages if the percentage is too low. Re-evaluate your vendor if you are utilizing outbound marketing for prospecting. What is your email or telephone call response rate? Is it higher or lower than you expected? How can it be improved?

Takeaway 40 – Sales Pros Spend Too Much Time on Non-selling Activities!

I suggest tracking the time sales pros spend on non-selling activities (those where the sales pro is not actively prospecting, calling on, or following up on sales opportunities or closing sales) using a daily log. As I mentioned earlier in the Overview of Section 2, many sales pros spend a lot of their prime selling time (9:00 a.m. – 6:00 p.m.) checking and replying to prospect and personal emails, checking social media, handling customer relationship issues, tending to administrative details, entering data into an often cumbersome CRM system, searching for existing contracts or agreements or marketing collateral, completing RFPs, completing sales forecasts, begging the legal department to prepare a contract or license promptly, and attending internal meetings, including sales meetings and conference calls, all of which are non-sales activities. According to a *Forbes* article, the amount of time spent by the typical sales pros on non-selling activities is an astonishing 64.8 percent.[105] (Travel time to and from customers counts as sales time.) It is excessive when the non-selling time approaches or exceeds 40 percent of the sales pro's time which can devastate productivity and calls for intervention by the sales manager to reorder priorities. I have seen this amount reach as much as 50 percent of the sales pros available time. Think of the impact on sales results and profitability if these times were significantly reduced.

The non-selling time is normally spent on sales pros prospecting, qualifying, following up, and closing opportunities. But how can we expect sales pros to achieve their sales quota with only 60 percent of their time available for selling? It is like trying to walk across a busy street with a two-second green light!

Many sales enablement solutions are oriented toward the learning methodologies Millennials and Gen Zers utilize. The methodologies are online, primarily through self-paced rather than in-person classroom instruction. Since most workforces will be comprised mainly of these generations soon, it is much more suitable for them.

It is important to consider "opportunity costs" (or the potential value from a missed opportunity—the result of choosing one alternative and foregoing another.) For example, a value derived from sales enablement is that it should result in sales managers being able to devote more of their time to their team members' training, coaching, and pipeline management.

Investing in sales enablement, whether as a function or in the various available products, is not the panacea or "silver bullet" that will solve many of your company's sales performance issues. (For example, improved hiring and more "one-on-one" coaching will likely have a more significant impact.) But sales enablement is not a fad. It is a worthwhile investment that can be scaled and introduced in phases. There will always be benefits to having a centralized deposit of content and the tools most packaged sales enablement solutions provide. I also see an excellent return on investment for organizations in improving their sales onboarding process. "In addition to driving efficiency, enablement bridges the knowledge gap that new employees face—setting them up for successful conversations with customers and reducing time to ramp into new roles."[106]

Deploying Artificial Intelligence (AI) to Improve Your Sales Operations

Artificial intelligence (AI) applications are all the rage now. But, unlike other recent "breakthrough" technologies, such as virtual reality, blockchain, neural networks, autonomous driving cars, digital identity, IBM's" Jeopardy" playing Watson, and eliminating cash payments (and cashiers) at checkouts, AI is genuinely transformative and will change all our lives in 2024 and beyond, perhaps even more than television, air travel, and the internet, all of which were significant developments in human history. Accenture has noted that "artificial intelligence is fundamentally transforming the way the world lives, works and plays."[107] It is trendy amongst the Millennial and Gen X generations in the US.

So, what is AI and why does it matter to people in sales? AI may be described as a newly emerging field of computer science where machines are programmed to use their memory or learning experiences to react to stored information to make decisions like human beings. It is "machine-displayed intelligence that simulates human behavior or thinking and can be trained to solve specific problems. It is a combination of Machine Learning techniques and Deep Learning Types of artificial intelligence models trained using vast volumes of data and can make intelligent decisions."[108] By imitating human thinking, the complex decisions made by computers will more approximate those made by a normal human brain. One may think of C3PO and R2D2 from "Star Wars." They are droids or robots that were designed to operate like humans.

The business applications of AI are unlimited and are already in widespread usage for e-commerce, life sciences and health care, banking and financial services, education, media and telecom, security and privacy, navigation, manufacturing, robotics, agriculture, data analytics, military and government usage, and sales and marketing. AI applications have "the potential to add contextual awareness and human-like decision-making to enterprise workflows and could radically change how we do business."[109]

In addition, AI is very affordable and does not require huge investments. It may also be deployed project-by-project, not requiring the enterprise-wide commitment of implementing large enterprise resource planning (ERP) systems.

Some are concerned that AI may take over the critical thinking functions necessary to make good decisions, and I agree. AI must be deployed when decisions are very routine and not consequential. Microsoft co-founder "Bill Gates said he believes artificial intelligence is the most revolutionary technology he has seen in decades, on par with computers, cellphones and the internet."[110]

"The development of AI is as fundamental as the creation of the microprocessor, the personal computer, the internet, and the mobile phone . . . Entire industries will reorient around it. Businesses will distinguish themselves by how well they use it."[111]

Is AI Hype or a Giant Leap Forward?

It is the latter. It is the next step from using Apple's Siri or Amazon's Alexa, which we may consider "pouring the foundation." Microsoft has also released a similar AI chatbot application called

Bing Chat, and Google has released Gemini. I expect Apple and many others will follow.

In a recent report on AI, Deloitte stated, "Ultimately, Generative AI could create a more profound relationship between humans and technology, even more than the cloud, the smartphone, and the internet did before."[112] We have already reached the "tipping point" and there is no going back to the pre-AI technology world. There are new applications of AI introduced every day, so I do not believe that the recent publicity is over-hyped.

Technologist and venture capitalist Marc Andreesen, a co-creator of the popular Mosaic internet web browser and Netscape believes that artificial intelligence is not just hype but is a real breakthrough because there are well-defined tests to measure its capabilities and the use of large language model (LLM) functionality, which has been developed over many years.[113] Andreesen notes, "LLMs are basically very fancy autocompletes across a paragraph."[114] Any of us who use Google or smartphones are very familiar with this standard functionality that reads what you have written, fixes your spelling, and anticipates the remainder of the sentence for you. AI applications also include self-driving automobiles and trucks. You may have heard or read examples of how ChatGPT, a free AI application, generates text. It was developed by a start-up, OpenAI, and released in November 2022.

Michael Neiberg, Professor of History at the US Army War College, stated "I have spent the past few weeks learning as much as I can about AI and its application to learning and teaching. My conclusion is that this is the single most powerful tool to emerge at least in my lifetime, quite possibly ever in human history . . . In short, you can think of AI as the enemy or as something to avoid until retirement, but if you do you are missing this incredible tool . . . We have a responsibility to be a voice in this discussion. If we don't use our voice then we are begging to be labelled as irrelevant in the 21st century or we will cede the ground to people who will do our jobs badly, thus distorting what AI 'learns.'"[115]

ChatGPT generates text from a simple query interface based on the data it has gathered, stored, and processed from the available text on the internet (which may be true or not) using complex algorithmic models. Contrary to what the alarmists are saying, ChatGPT, or other AI apps, will not put many people out of work, nor will it take over the writing of authors and analysts. It can aid in providing conversational texts and in creating messages.

Below is how ChatGPT explains itself:

> *"ChatGPT is an AI-powered chatbot that uses a deep learning language model called GPT (Generative Pre-trained Transformer) to generate human-like responses to user inputs. It was developed by OpenAI, a research organization dedicated to advancing AI safely and beneficially.*
>
> *"The GPT model used in ChatGPT has been trained on massive amounts of text data to be able to generate text that is coherent and contextually relevant. When a user interacts with ChatGPT by typing a message, the model generates a response based on the patterns and relationships it has learned from the text it has been trained on.*
>
> *"ChatGPT is designed to be a conversational agent that can understand and respond to a wide range of topics and questions. Its responses can vary in tone and style*

depending on the context and user preferences. ChatGPT can be used for a variety of purposes, such as customer service, personal assistants, and language learning tools. [116]

A breakthrough artificial intelligence application called DALL-E2, from Open AI, can create realistic images and art from a natural language (written) description.

Takeaway 41 - AI Can Help Optimize Sales and Marketing Processes

AI has a role in helping optimize sales and marketing processes and solving simple data crunching. AI will be beneficial for creating content, quickly sifting through and analyzing large volumes of data, designing and editing marketing material (see Simplified), routine messaging such as handling inbound information requests, developing and executing email campaigns, completing portions of Request for Proposals (RFPs), marketing intelligence, collecting data on potential prospects, creating presentations, and for predictive lead scoring. Lead scoring is an application that utilizes AI to analyze the characteristics and history of prospects to determine which leads are in the company's "Sweet Spot" and are the highest priority, and to provide information on those accounts to the CRM system and the sales pro. There is now technology on the market that can work with naturalized human voices (think Siri), email, and WhatsApp to qualify leads that come in through the company website. AI can also be used to distribute the leads to various sales pros depending on specific criteria, such as territory, history of prior relationships, or the success rate of the sales pro with those types of accounts.

The software company Salesforce.com surveyed in 2023 over 1,000 full time sales pros on generative AI in partnership with YouGov. They found that about one-third of all sales pros are currently utilizing generative AI:

- "58% of sales pros agree generative AI helps or will help them increase productivity. They estimate it saves or could save them 4.5 hours a week.
- 56% say it helps or will help them increase sales.
- 61% say it helps or will help them better serve customers." [117]

I am wary of relying on AI for written communications between sales pros and their prospects without human oversight. Your messages must be carefully crafted and customized for each instance and not created by computer software that does not have the contextual knowledge of the circumstances or the person receiving it. I am also wary of using AI for preparing sales forecasts based on the data inputted in the CRM by sales pros, as I found that the data submitted by sales pros were often overly optimistic. (I used to divide the forecasts submitted by the sales pros by two, and it was often too high.)

There are also currently hundreds (and will eventually be thousands) of apps that plug into ChatGPT to extend its value for many purposes, like the network of apps built for the Apple iPhone and Android phones. For example, some apps assist in providing medical information. I am sure many more apps are currently being developed for sales operations. The possibilities are endless. Many excellent AI applications exist for various sales functions, as shown in the chart below by Cem Dilmegani of

AIMultiple. Sales managers need to put together a training workshop to familiarize their sales pros with AI and then another to determine which AI applications the company should consider in order of priority.[118]

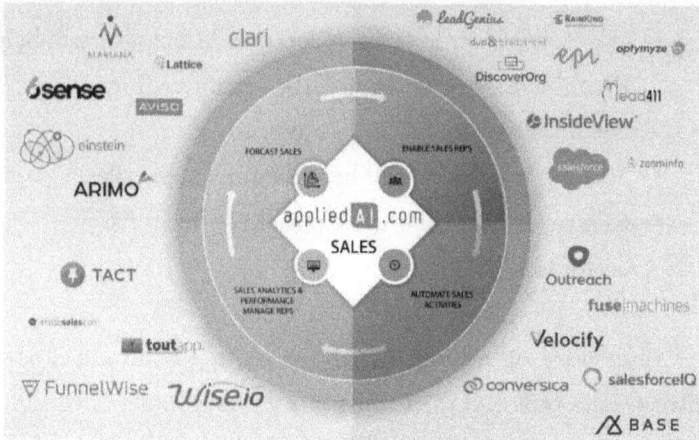

Since technology, especially AI technology, changes daily, keeping up with the latest developments is essential to determine which applications can positively impact your sales results—"move the needle." (Perhaps this is an excellent assignment for a Gen Z person interested in the latest technologies.) When there is something that you think might be useful, I recommend testing it with a small pilot rather than committing to a complete conversion. The pilot should provide you with most of the information you need to determine whether to go forward and the benefits and limitations of the application.

Takeaway 42 – Pausing AI Development Is Not Feasible

Pope Francis "issued a warning against artificial intelligence . . . , saying in a statement it should be used in 'service of humanity' and warning to be vigilant of the 'rapidly increasing impact' the technology is having on society."[119] In a statement from the Vatican, the pope "called for 'an open dialogue on the meaning of these new technologies, endowed with disruptive possibilities and ambivalent effects' and said there is an 'urgent need to orient" the use of AI in a responsible way so as to avoid 'conflicts and antagonism.' He said in the statement that AI must be used ethically in the specific fields of education and law, and that the development of the technology shouldn't come 'at the expense of the most fragile and excluded.'"[120]

Tesla and X (formerly Twitter) CEO Elon Musk, Apple co-founder Steve Wozniak, entrepreneur and former presidential candidate Andrew Yang, and over 1800 technologists have recently asked AI developers to slow down and take a six-month pause. Musk said, "governments should step in and institute a moratorium."[121] Machine Intelligence Research Institute co-founder Eliazer Yudlowsky said a "'pause' is insufficient. We need to shut it all down."[122] The skeptics are concerned that AI tools present "profound risks to society and humanity" because of uncontrolled, unrestrained advances with unknown ramifications. They want to "give the industry time to set safety standards for AI design and head off potential harms."[123] Their foremost concern is the effect of AI on existing jobs and the environment. Their document cautioned that "Advanced AI could represent a profound change in the history of life on Earth and should be planned for and managed with commensurate care and resources."[124]

Artificial intelligence and neural networks pioneer Geoffrey Hinton quit a key position at Google "so he can warn the world about the dangers of AI without having to watch his words."[125] Perhaps we should listen more to David Meerman Scott, who noted that AI is "just data plus math."[126] The reality is that AI is a technological innovation, which, like many in the past, will make some jobs obsolete, but will also create many more for people who become proficient in this burgeoning field. A Wall Street Journal columnist, Peggy Noonan, argues that a six-month moratorium is insufficient. She said, "Pause it for a few years. Call in the world's counsel, and get everybody in. Heck, hold a World Congress."[127] I think some people are over-dramatic. It also seems that many people calling for a pause are those working for companies that are in the lead now—and they want to maintain that lead by having everybody else freeze their efforts to catch up or go ahead. And nobody seems to be protesting the number of cashier jobs displaced by self-checking in supermarkets, Walmart, and Target. Far more (lower wage) cashiers have been replaced by AI than any workers so far.

This is a paradox to me. Why would we want to suspend development in something many tech leaders acknowledge to be a significant breakthrough technology? A mutually agreed upon pause by developers is futile, impractical, and unnecessary, as each company wants to develop breakthrough technologies ahead of its competition and will likely continue its efforts regardless. You cannot put the "genie back in the bottle." We did not suspend the development of space technology (and other breakthrough technologies) so that all the social consequences were considered. Developers are eager to move forward with new technologies, but this does not preclude developers and scientists, including social scientists, from considering all aspects, positive and negative, of each new application.

Ronald Bailey, in *Reason* magazine, noted that many recent alarmists made apocalyptic forecasts that turned out to be failed prophesies. This included philosopher Bertrand Russell forecasting the danger of human survival and biologist Paul Ehrlich warning us about human overpopulation and starvation. So perhaps we should be wary of the doomsayers.[128] There will not be a cataclysm on a war or natural disaster scale. But we have passed the "point of no return," and there is no turning back.

Resistance to new technologies did not stop the development of the automobile, crop biotechnology, robotics, nanotechnology, the birth control pill, and advances in artificial insemination, and they will not stop the new development of AI. And who will oversee whether or not the AI developments will be harmful to humanity? A tribunal? A tribunal accused Galileo of religious heresy, and he was imprisoned for the remainder of his life.[129] We have seen several examples of politicizing controversial new technologies, and I do not trust there can be a genuinely non-partisan scientific study. There is always disruption due to new technologies: the horse and buggy whip manufacturers were put out of business by the creation of automobiles (my grandfather was in the horse-trading business in the early 1900s, and his company went bankrupt due to hoof and mouth disease and the proliferation of the automobile); elevator operators were retired due to push button controls in the elevators; telephone switchboard operators, 35mm film processors, cinema projector operators, Blockbuster video store employees, travel agents; and grocery cashiers are being displaced by self-checkout. Millions of people will not lose their jobs due to AI, as some alarmists are warning, but they will probably change jobs. Look at the number of new jobs added to the economy due to the introduction of personal computers and smartphones in recent years.

I am reminded of an economic game theory called "the prisoner's dilemma," in which individual decision-makers can choose a solution that is best for the group but is sacrificial for themselves. Usually, the individual's self-interest prevails and the group result is less than optimal. I think similar results will happen if there is a mandated pause in development. Also, technologists and other scientists can observe and recommend changes to correct any negative consequences to society while AI application development continues.

Sales managers should eagerly adopt the possible productivity improvements that AI can bring while keeping watch for any issues that may arise from the adoption of new technologies. At the least, new technologies will result in additional training of sales pros and support staff. "Technology innovation is no longer a 'nice to have' but a strategic imperative that is a vital part of decisions being made today. With the right approach, companies can use innovative technologies to create rapid response today, shape the journey to the future, and set tomorrow's standard."[130]

The bottom line is that AI is a breakthrough technology that has been in development for many years, and it is not here to replace but rather to help sales pros. Like all prior technological leaps, including the introduction of the personal computer, the internet, and the smartphone, you should embrace it. Learn how to leverage it in your company and add mastery to your skill set.

In summary, the introduction of commercial sales enablement tools into the marketplace has been very helpful to sales managers and sales pros. They can be valuable additions that will increase the productivity of your salesforce. Initially, they will substantially assist in the onboarding of new sales pros. They also reduce many of the often-tedious tasks that sales pros have had to do before making sales calls, such as assembling and customizing the proper sales collateral and presentation materials. They promote the collaboration of the sales and marketing teams. In addition, many companies have staffed a sales enablement function, which can contribute to sales productivity and efficiency.

It is almost impossible to read a newspaper or watch a television news program without seeing a news story about artificial intelligence (AI) or the effects of it on people and the economy. AI will surely cause significant changes in our lives, but just like previous technological leaps, there will be more positive changes than negative ones. My advice is to consider the context of the warnings and how they will affect you and others, but do not let them cause you to become too traumatized.

CHAPTER 14

Supporting a Sales Pro's Mental Health and Wellbeing

I have been asked by several people, inside and outside the sales vocation, how I have dealt with the rejection that sales pros typically encounter when calling on or trying to close prospects. The truth is that I did not think much about it except when asked and I never took it personally. Rejection usually occurs when prospecting and sometimes at the end of the sales cycle if the prospect purchases another product or solution. I consider cold-calling a sometimes unpleasant, necessary part of the sales job. I know that the prospects were not rejecting me as a person, as they usually didn't personally know me, but rather that they were not interested in my product or listening to my sales pitch. And if they are genuinely not interested in buying, I am not interested in wasting the time it takes to convert them into a qualified prospect.

> ### Takeaway 43 – Sales Pros Should Not Take Rejection Personally

Understand the mathematics of the sales funnel (explained in *Above Quota Performance*)—that you need to prospect many targets, which over time is reduced to a smaller number of qualified prospects, and then eventually to an even smaller number of finalists. Of course, most suspects your sales pro contacts will tell you they do not need what your sales pro is selling, that they are too busy, and some will just hang up the telephone on your sales pros. But a certain number will speak with them, and those are the gems that you want to find amongst the clutter of non-interested people.

For example, your sales pro needs to make one hundred calls to find five suspects and anticipate the standard rejection in advance; and, most importantly, if your sales pro has realistic expectations, most of the people they contact by calling will not want to speak with them. Therefore, the sales pro will not be disappointed with the high rejection rate and become depressed. If the sales pro understands the formula behind obtaining a successful prospect, they may learn to accept the rejection of the business proposal and not believe it to be personal. While rejection and disappointment are a part of life, some employees may struggle in dealing with the frequent rejections experienced in sales. It is a matter of setting proper expectations before beginning daily prospecting calls. When they encounter the expected level of rejections, which can be over 90 percent, they are mentally prepared for it.

Rejection in sales, such as when cold-calling or not closing a deal, is not personal. Rejection in sales is an unpleasant experience that is a normal part of the sales job, just as other people must deal with distasteful tasks in theirs. When a prospect chooses another supplier, sales pros should only hold themselves responsible if the failure was due to a mistake or something they did. In that case, it should become a learning experience that a sales pro should avoid repeating in the future. But the sales pro should not take it personally if it is due to a simple lack of interest by the buyer.

"If you focus on the hurt you will continue to suffer. If you focus on the lesson, you will continue to grow."[131]

Workplace Stress

People who work in the sales profession can lead very stressful lives. Sales pros may be very worried about achieving their monthly, quarterly, or annual quotas, closing specific sales, dealing with noncommunicative prospects or unreasonable bosses, and home and family issues. They may have anxieties because of the lack of progress of some prospects they are trying to close. My experience was that some sales pros divorced because of job stresses caused by pressures to close sales or lack of enough income due to poor sales performance. Others experienced job burnout due to the long hours and travel requirements that sales pros typically must handle. Air travel, especially, has become much more stressful.

Many sales pros may require professional mental health assistance to deal with anxiety disorders, depression, toxic workplaces, negative culture, rejection by prospects, not achieving quotas, demanding sales managers, prospects that are less than truthful to them, and requirements to fulfill non-sales administrative tasks. Sales managers can no longer ignore the mental health needs of their subordinates. Recognition of your sales pros' psychological needs must receive immediate attention and not be buried beneath your need to close sales this month. Mental health issues cannot be willed away, and threats by sales managers to "get your act together" will only exacerbate the problem.

The consequence of not addressing these needs is that sales pros may have a mental health episode, experience burnout, become less productive, or other issues. It may then require a substantial amount of time off and hospitalization, or they will resign.

Sales managers are not experts on handling mental health issues, but they can be more empathetic and try to make the work environment more desirable and less stressful for those who indicate they need help or any who you think might need assistance, including for drug usage. You must refer them to the HR department or a company-sponsored outside employee assistance program (EAP) that handles such issues, as they are much better prepared to handle the situation than the sales manager.

Eliminate Negativity in Your Life and Be More Successful

Negativity is a slow-acting poison. When negativity affects your mind, your body can often show the symptoms. It is toxic and should be addressed as soon as possible. It can destroy you, your marriage, your friendships, and your career if it isn't addressed. It's a burden, like carrying a heavy anchor while trying to swim. It also adds stress to your life. I believe in the power of positive thinking and the energy it brings to your life. This is all easier said than done, but it is important to be aware of it and work to find solutions immediately. We all experience it at one point or another, but what we do next is most important.

Nobody Likes a "Firkrimptor"

Sometimes, the perfect word for something doesn't exist in English. *Firkrimptor* is one such example. It is a Yiddish word that best translates as a sourpuss or a bad-tempered or habitually sullen person.

While I am not a mental health expert, I have found removing as many *firkrimptors* from my life as is possible, even if they are relatives and longtime friends, was enormously helpful, and I recommend both sales managers and sales pros consider doing the same. "Stay away from negative people. They have a problem for every solution."[132] Minimize your contacts and social interactions if you cannot completely disassociate from them. I have found that negativity is a self-sustaining cycle. It feeds on itself and attracts more negativity. Other people's negativity brings you down psychologically, which can affect your attitude about life, relationships with others, and job performance. They also drain your energy and consume a disproportionate amount of your time. John Mark Green says it well: "Toxic people attach themselves like cinder blocks tied to your ankles, and then invite you for a swim in their poisoned waters."[133]

You may not be aware of it, but negative people can unintentionally ruin your day, week, and life. They may not intend to harm you, but it can happen through their actions, speech, and interactions with you. If I had listened to the people who told me the reasons why I shouldn't publish a book, I would not have started the first one. (And I am glad I wrote it.) They never encourage you, especially when you need it, and they will not comfort you when you are hurt. They enjoy damaging your self-esteem. They are "drama kings or queens" and suck you into their dramas, whether you want to be there or not. They will stagnate your growth as a person who contributes to society, your family, and your church or synagogue.

The people that will hurt you the most and cause the most damage to your self-esteem, your life, and your career are more likely to be people you know (not real friends) and relatives. As the Daniel Lang character says to the Erin Carter character in the television series *Who is Erin Carter?* "Oh, Erin, there is nobody that can stab you in the back quite like a friend can."[134] How true. I expect adversaries who do not like me to treat me poorly—and I can prepare for that or respond accordingly. But the hurt from someone that I know and may have previously trusted is permanent.

Dr. Awu Isaac Oben sums it perfectly:

"Just as seasons or ocean waves, friends will come and go, some will make you and some will break you. Some will leave footprints in your life for you to flourish while others leave fingerprints of remarkable scars for you to perish. I guess you are familiar with phrases like 'friends with benefits' or 'fair-weather friends'? Be careful of people who come around, need you, and 'USE' you only to achieve their personal goals without increasing yours. Once they are done exploiting you, they will vehemently neglect you and the chain of victims continues. Be careful else you will forever be prioritizing and supporting people who can't support you. At one point they will start draining you. Remember, a friend to all is a friend to none because they will leave you, develop your dream/vision without you, and surely use your weaknesses against you. Sharing your information, achievements, and problems with fake people can become a lifetime issue to reckon with. Life is far too short to waste time with fake friends or people who pretend to care more than they do."[135]

My attitude, outlook on life, and productivity improved dramatically when I decided to distance myself from certain friends and acquaintances (including a relative, one close friend of more than forty years, and a neighbor that I felt was passive-aggressive and manipulative to my wife) that lived in a negative world: nothing was ever their fault or due to their own decisions; the world was out to get them; they had no control over their circumstances; they hated their jobs, their manager was unfair to them; they woke up sour and stayed that way throughout the day. When they encountered people, they treated them with suspicion, not friendliness. They treat store clerks and restaurant workers like servants.

Minimize your time with those that are toxic and do not help you grow spiritually, intellectually, or emotionally. Instead, invest your time in associating with people who are encouraging, exude positive energy, and are fun to speak with and be with. Some people may not be good friends now but will be later. You will be amazed how this simple alteration will change your life dramatically. You are stuck with your toxic relatives, but you can distance yourself from them as much as possible, even when your siblings or children are close to them or their children. Rather than confronting a close relative or friend, I advise prioritizing your well-being over theirs. You also do not owe them an explanation—and not an apology. You do no need to speak further with them, in person, on the telephone, or via text. Choose to spend time with more positive and supportive relatives and friends. They will appreciate your friendship and will not try to bring you down.

Sales managers may need to help their sales pros remove

negativity from their work lives by assuring them it is in their best long-term interests. And I guarantee it will help increase their sales performance! Legendary investor Warren Buffett advises, "Pick out associates whose behavior is better than yours, and you'll drift in that direction."[136] You will find yourself more energized. And you will learn from these individuals in ways you may not expect.

Sales Pro Be Wary

Negative and pessimistic thoughts are detrimental to our confidence and self-esteem, and they are extremely draining to those who are subjected to them. This lack of positivity puts a damper on everything. If your sales pros do not have self-confidence or are affected by such negativity, their prospects will sense it, and they are unlikely to be successful.

Look at sales results: "Optimistic sales pros outperform pessimists by 57%. That's even true when pessimists have better selling skill sets."[137] You, the sales manager, must remove negativity and pessimism in your team and replace them with positivity and optimism. You can do that by emphasizing the positive outlook for this year and the new products that will be released this year or by conveying your confidence in their abilities and chances to achieve their sales quota this year. After all, who wants to buy from a sourpuss or a negative person?

Let's look at it from the buyer's side: If you were making a purchase decision and two sales pros called on you and you could tell that one was very positive with a great attitude and seemed to be enjoying her job and life and the other was negative and dour and started the conversation by telling you about the flat tire they had this morning, after they accidentally spilled coffee on themselves, and then encountered a rainstorm on the way to your office that caused them to be late, which person would you rather spend time with to discuss your needs?

The Negative MO

You can identify people in your life who seem to go from one misfortune to another, believing the world is out to get them. These negatively-natured people are never satisfied, whether with the food they ordered at the restaurant, the service from the wait staff, or the accommodations at hotels while on vacation. Moreover, they are likely to criticize your personal choices, whether it's your home, your car, your lawn, your vacation trip, or the school you went to. Theirs is always better.

A very negative person will also react to other people's good news with condescension or skepticism that can undermine your confidence and self-esteem. In sales, if you have self-confidence, your prospects will sense it, you will approach your prospects with a calm mindset, and you are more likely to be successful.

To Accentuate the Positive, Eliminate the Negative

A person can do a few things to improve their mental health without the assistance of a mental health professional, and the simplest is to remove the negative people from your life. This includes people who are your relatives or those with whom you may have a long friendship.

Negativity is toxic for many reasons:

1. it destroys your mental health
2. it can actually make you physically sick
3. it just brings the mood down for everyone else around you.

Just as positive thinking can promote a healthy mindset, negative thoughts can do the opposite. When you constantly entertain negativity, you seek experiences and people that reflect your mindset. The quote from Buddha that says "What you think, you become" very much applies here. Everything in life comes down to your mindset and how you approach obstacles. "As they say, it doesn't matter much about your situation. Instead, it's the attitude you have about your circumstances. A positive attitude can help you overcome any challenges. But negativity tends to drain your energy, rendering you powerless and stagnant. Studies have shown that a negative disposition can actually cause some of the world's most common mental illnesses, like anxiety and depression. A U.K. study of more than 30,000 people, the largest of its kind, found that traumatic life events played more of a role in mental illness than even genetics or life circumstances."[138] Enrich your life by getting rid of the negativity in your life. As sales expert Zig Ziglar said "Don't let negative and toxic people rent space in your head. Raise the rent and kick them out."[139] According to *VITAL Worklife*, the Mental Health Foundation defines emotional health as "a positive state of wellbeing which enables an individual to be able to function in society and meet the demands of everyday life."[140] Every achieving triathlete, marathoner, or mountain-climber believes they can complete the difficult physical and mental challenge ahead of them. If they didn't think they could complete the task, would they even start? Do you see how this can translate into your sales pros' selling approach?

Mike Ditka, the Hall of Fame football player and Super Bowl-winning coach, said, "If you have a bad attitude, it's hard to do anything good. If you have a positive attitude and you're willing to pay the price of work and discipline yourself, then you've got a chance."[141]

Your sales pros own their success or failure. It's not somebody else's fault or fate if they are underachieving. The question is, what are the sales pros going to do about it? Their attitude influences how they approach their workday, how they interact with others, and how others perceive them, and as a result, will affect the outcomes of all their sales and management efforts. Optimistic people get out of bed looking forward to the workday. Pessimistic people wake up dreading the day and act accordingly. You will live longer and happier if you have positive social relationships!

Yes, it's true. According to Bill Murphy, Jr. in *Inc.*, "The longest-running longitudinal study in history found that good relationships were the most important factor in a long and happy life. Likewise, this study suggests having good relationships led to a 5% predicted effect on longevity."[142] So, in addition to improving your attitude, it will result in you living a longer and happier life. Your life will become more pleasant, your relationships with others will improve, and your success in sales will improve if you discard negativity and the negative people in your life as soon as possible. They are like a tumor; the cure is removing it to live a better life.

Supporting the Mental Health of Your Team

The importance of your team's mental health has been well documented since the onset of the COVID-19 pandemic. In addition, high-performing athletes, like US Olympians Simone Biles and Michael Phelps, have helped bring attention to mental health issues and how anxieties can affect anybody, including very successful people. As a result, the need for mental health treatments, including alcohol, drug, and gambling interventions, has lost the negative stigma that it once had.

Sales managers need to be especially aware of sales pros' hidden mental health needs. Sales pros can be especially affected by sales pressures, poor results, and simple burnout. Managers need to have open ears and an open mind and engage more often with their team to determine if they are under any non-job-related stresses and encourage immediate help if they are. Appropriate follow-up with team members is necessary to ensure they receive the support they need.

Sales managers must always treat their staff respectfully and with dignity and promote a caring culture—no more of the past's dictatorial, intimidating management style. I like the idea of team-building activities, such as an occasional beer night, an activity such as golf or bowling where everybody can participate, and celebration of birthdays and anniversaries with the company, especially when closing significant sales. Ring the bell! A once-per-year family event like a picnic is also a good idea.

Having a safe workplace that is free from violence, bullying, and intimidation is important for both the mental and physical health of all employees. At the minimum this includes training employees how to handle incidents such as active shooters, unruly employees, bullying, threats, harassment, intimidation, hacking, identity theft, and other disruptive behavior. The company should also emphasize that all such behavior is unacceptable, will not be tolerated, and that all incidents will be reported. A robust workplace violence prevention program must be put in place and unequivocally practiced. Normally handled by the human resources department or by an outside employee assistance program (EAP), the solution is not a simple sign in the refreshment room. The sales manager must take a proactive and professional approach to make sure that the mental health needs of all his direct reports are properly handled. This should come from the top down. If your company doesn't have the training for you as a manager, ask for it!

Special Issues for Women

Women in the workplace, including sales managers and sales pros, typically have special needs due to the everyday stresses of work/life balance and childcare issues. Historically discriminated against in employment, many women feel they must demonstrate superior skills and toughness to receive corporate promotions and to have workplace equality. Even though women often shoulder the responsibilities of caring for children, they often feel like they cannot request special accommodations. UKG, a human capital management (HCM) firm, notes that "recent surveys show women are struggling disproportionately when it comes to many aspects of their work experiences and overall mental health."[143]

Women typically incur stresses including "chronic exhaustion, empathy fatigue, and learned hopelessness."[144] There could also be sexual harassment or discrimination in the workplace. Therefore, executive and sales management must take an active role in assuring that all women (as well as men) are treated with respect and that their mental health needs are met. Use your company's HR policies to determine your sales pros' individual needs and work out arrangements that are satisfactory to everyone. Often, there can be an easy accommodation if the company is flexible with some of its policies, and the result will be your company will end up with a high performer.

What are the Dangers of Overcompensating?

While studies have shown that contented employees are usually more productive, sometimes companies try too hard to make the workplace enjoyable and congenial. They sometimes go out of their way to please everyone and find that they may please no one. They put programs in place to foster team building and improve employee relations. They may try to make everybody a part of the company "family," but your workplace is not your family, and the boundaries must be respected.

Some people on the team will not like others, and they may not want to socialize with each other after hours. Some team members may forego going out for snacks and drinks with the other team members because they prefer to be with their family or friends away from work, or they may not socialize for religious or emotional reasons, or simply because they are introverts and need some time alone to recharge. Employees should never be forced to participate in extra-curricular activities or shamed for choosing not to participate.

Companies must also understand that enforcing policies such as mandatory vacations and illness and health procedures (such as vaccinations) can be an invasion of privacy or counter-productive. For example, one company where I was employed had perfect annual attendance recognized by the CEO. Unfortunately, the result was that people came to work ill and infected others.

Your workplace should be a pleasant and collaborative environment. Companies that cross into a familial environment are crossing the line and potentially will violate the work/life balance. Sales managers will get better results by being fair, transparent, and respectful and by having defined parameters.

If You Need Immediate Assistance with Mental Issues

Mental health is as essential to your team's well-being as any other health issue. We tend to seek immediate help when we have diseases such as influenza or hurt our backs and knees, but we often neglect mental health issues.

Sometimes sales managers and sales pros become overly depressed, overwhelmed, stressed, agitated, angry, or anxious and need immediate help. These conditions have been exacerbated by the COVID pandemic of 2020 – 2021, and the economic recession and workplace adjustments that followed. "It's no secret that employee wellbeing, in a post-pandemic landscape, is suffering: Employees are struggling with stress, burnout, and loneliness like never before. In fact, four in 10 U.S. employees say their job is negatively impacting their mental health. To make matters worse, fewer than one in four employees say their organization cares about their wellbeing – nearly half the number who said the same before COVID-19 rocked the workplace."[145]

The sales pros' mental illnesses could be temporary, acute, or more long-term chronic conditions. It is essential not to let unneeded suffering persist and that the sales pro seek immediate professional help. Consider contacting any of the following organizations for mental or emotional support:

- **Employer**
  - Check if your employer has an employee assistance program (EAP) or obtain a list of providers on your health insurance website. EAP plans typically offer mental health counseling as part of overall wellness. Professionals staff EAP phone lines.
- **National Institute of Mental Health**
  - www.nimh.nih.gov
  - Phone: 1-866-615-6464
- **Substance Abuse and Mental Health Services Administration (SAMHSA) Hotline**
  - Phone: 1-800-662-HELP (4357)
- **National Suicide Prevention Lifeline**
  - www.suicidepreventionlifeline.org
  - Phone: 1-800-273-TALK (8255)
  - Or call or text 988
- **NAMI – National Alliance on Mental Illness**
  - www.nami.org
  - Phone: 1-800-950-NAMI (6264)

- **Mental health professionals can provide you with immediate advice on where to go next for help.** There is no shame in getting the mental or emotional help you need.
  - Call your primary care physician for a referral.

Sales managers must be aware of mental health resources and take positive actions to contribute towards better mental health of their sales pros. Many of your sales pros have had personal and business stresses and issues that would benefit from professional attention. Some of these have been diagnosed, but others have not been. According to statistics from Mental Health America, approximately one out of every five adults experiences a mental health illness, and in about 5 percent of those cases, it is severe.[146] So, if you manage ten to fifteen sales pros, it is likely that two or three of them have some mental illness that shouldn't be ignored. This does not just impact the life of the person affected, but it is also likely to affect their productivity and their co-workers if not properly addressed. We have all heard of incidences of workplace violence, as well as mass murders, that may have been prevented if the perpetrator had received proper mental illness treatment.

CHAPTER 15
Sales Leadership

I am often asked what the keys are to be an outstanding sales leader. It is difficult to answer this question because there isn't a single "one-size fits all" answer. Each sales team situation is very different, and the tasks and responsibilities the sales manager needs to excel vary by company. A company's goals, cultures, and environments can differ greatly from others. Each of these will affect the type of sales leadership the manager must provide, and the exceptional sales leader must adapt to the company and the situation.

The sales landscape has drastically changed in recent years due to the latest developments in digital technology, the effect of the coronavirus pandemic on accessibility and more people working from home, the #metoo movement, and the ascendance of new generations of sales pros replacing retiring Baby Boomers and Greatest Generation sales pros. As a result, the old sales management style in which the manager dictates all sales practices, has complete control over the sales cycles of deals, and micromanages all sales pros who mindlessly follow instructions is obsolete. Included in this list of outdated practices are formerly popular practices such as the "hard close" sales style to close a deal at all costs, pitching products not solutions, and rushing prospects through the sales process. And that is a good thing!

The best sales managers now must lead, motivate, and inspire their teams to success, not command them—as was done in the past. In addition to the leadership characteristics that all managers (sales and non-sales) must provide, the sales managers must also offer continuous coaching, support, and guidance to each of the sales pros on their team.

You must add value to the efforts of your sales team. You are not there just to collect and forward their monthly sales forecasts. A clerk can do that. You need to help your sales team by eliminating roadblocks—both external and internal. Be their internal advocate—go to upper management and the product managers and ask for the changes the sales pros need to be more effective. You will add value by being your sales team's chief problem solver. By solving problems, you will also be earning the trust of your sales pros and moving sales and other actionable tasks forward. And earning your sales pro's trust and respect is essential for you to be an effective leader.

For example, sales managers must also help their sales pros navigate the internal obstacles and politics that many sales pros face, from obtaining necessary company resources to shepherding the contract through the legal process. Sales pros have often told me that they felt their most significant competitors were within their own company, including the legal department, the CRM system, and order processing, as well as other sales pros who interfered with their accounts. Sales managers must also get the sales pros to focus more on revenue-producing activities rather than wasting time on non-productive activities.

Former US Secretary of State and retired General Colin Powell noted in 2021: "Leadership is solving problems. The day people stop bringing you problems is the day that you stop leading them. They either have lost confidence that you can help them or concluded that you do not care. Either case is a failure of leadership."[147] As with other managers in your company, a sales leader must demonstrate personal integrity, be a strong communicator to team members both orally and in writing, hold sales pros accountable, be an advocate for their team to upper management and an advocate for upper management to the sales pro team, understand how to delegate properly, motivate subordinates to improve their performances, demonstrate the courage to do what is best for the company and the sales pro, show gratitude for jobs well-done, continue to try to improve themselves and have empathy for the well-being of each sales pro. The sales leader does not need to be egalitarian and treat everyone equally. In fact, it is best to individualize your management approaches for each sales pro. However, the manager needs to treat all sales pros fairly.

The sales manager must be friendly but not "a friend." You must hold your team accountable for results, which isn't easy if you are their friend. You must be able to critique them when they have not achieved their goals. Yet, you are expected to always act in the company's best interests and be a significant contributor to its profitability. That implies that you must command the respect of your sales team by providing the leadership needed for all to achieve their sales goals. But it would be best if you always were approachable.

Takeaway 44 – Sales Managers Must Invest in "One-on-One" Coaching to be Most Effective

I believe that one-on-one coaching is the most important role of the front-line sales manager. This includes accompanying the sales pro on sales calls (in the field, not behind the desk, sometimes called "ride-alongs") and conducting detailed debriefs following the call. Effective sales coaching includes setting clear priorities and goals for the team and for individual sales pros. Anja Jeftovic of Taskdrive says, "A company can improve win rates by as much as 29% with effective sales coaching."[148] The elite sales manager must also define standard processes for the team and hold each sales pro accountable for achieving their sales quotas, while helping everyone achieve them. "Three-fourths (74%) of top companies cite coaching or mentoring of sales reps as the front-line manager's most important role" according to a survey by Brainshark and Forbes.[149]

The sales manager must have exceptional knowledge of the company's business processes, strategies, industry, and specific products and services, and must also promote a culture of solid business ethical conduct. All sales managers must master the difficult task of translating the sales pros' often overly optimistic pipeline forecasts into realistic sales forecasts that management can use for monthly operational planning purposes and also be masters of the company's pricing algorithms.

Brainshark notes, "Sales coaching is a leadership skill that develops each sales pro's full potential. Sales managers use their domain expertise and social, communication, and questioning skills to facilitate conversations with their team members that allow them to discover areas for improvement and possibilities to break through to new levels of success."[150]

What Style of Sales Manager Are You?

Are you a strategic/tactical deal coach, a strategist, a manager who holds his sales pros accountable, a delegator, or an active participant in deals? Do you empower your sales pros rather than tell them what to do at each step of the sales cycle? Do you communicate your expectations with your sales team and listen to their concerns? Do you cultivate a culture of excellence and high sales performance? Do you ensure your sales pros are properly trained and updated on technology?

You should be all the above and more, including being available to your sales pros for open communication and "emotional first aid." Show them that you can be empathetic when they are having difficulties selling, with the company, or personally. If they have their emotional intelligence in top form, they will be happier and perform at a higher level. And they will get along better with others.

Some sales managers think they are doing an excellent job for their company if they achieve their sales goal for the year. Perhaps they provided advice for their sales pros on managing and closing their opportunities throughout the sales cycle. While this is important, it is only a minor part of what an outstanding sales manager should do when leading a sales team. This is because success can be interrupted or changed due to variations in product demand, technological advances in competitors' products, pandemics, distribution problems, or other issues.

The sales manager must implement repeatable processes,

such as a consistent sales methodology, which will carry over from year to year, increasing the likelihood of continued success. Included is a pipeline forecasting system with defined steps and common terminology to be used by all sales pros.

The best-performing sales managers must also be actively involved in the onboarding process of all new hires. This task is not delegated to the human resources, training, or sales enablement staff. Sales managers must actively participate and show that they are committed to the success of their new hires. It also gives the sales manager a glimpse into some of the strengths and weaknesses of the new hire that will need to be addressed.

When I joined McCormack & Dodge as a sales pro, I was required to recite (up to four hours long) scripted presentations in front of both Jim McCormack and Frank Dodge before they approved that I could present to a prospect. Then they accompanied me on my first six or seven sales calls and discussed what I needed to do to improve after each call. Everything was discussed: the content, my presentation skills, my posture, how I handled and answered questions, and how I made eye contact with the audience. Eventually, I was allowed to call on prospects on my own. That experience was invaluable to me. I tried replicating this beneficial experience with all the new hires when I became a sales manager.

Sales managers are essential intermediaries between the executive manager and the sales team, who must represent and interpret the interests of top management to the sales pros and provide management with information and concerns of the team members. Likewise, the sales manager must represent the concerns of prospects and customers to the company's management.

Motivate Your Sales Pros!

I have always aspired to hire self-motivated sales pros. But the reality is that not all sales pros are self-motivated, even those who need some motivation occasionally. Sales managers must work with each sales pro individually and then with the entire team to help motivate them to achieve their sales goals. Your efforts to motivate each sales pro must be individually tailored to their personality, strengths, and weaknesses. It is a good idea to meet with the entire team after hours for a beer or snack, or for breakfast and lunch, in a very neutral place—not your office—such as a restaurant.

I always enjoyed using attention grabbers to motivate the salesforce at annual sales meetings. Sometimes, I employed gimmicks to make them more memorable. One of the sales pros recently reminded me of two I used at McCormack & Dodge. I once asked my executive assistant, Tammy, to place $1 bills under everybody's chairs. Then, at the appropriate time, I asked everybody to stand up and look under the seat of their chairs. I told them the lesson was that they "needed to get off their ass to earn a buck." Perhaps a little hokey, but it worked!

Another time, I asked the CFO, Peter, to bring a briefcase containing $10,000 in $100 bills to the sales meeting. I asked one of the sales pros to come to the front of the room and count the money. He went through the money and confirmed that the briefcase had $10,000 in cash. I told the sales pros that this was the 10 percent commission on their next sale to spend as they'd like, or it was how much they would not receive if they lost the sale. The room was quiet for at least five minutes while everybody thought about it.

I also held team building events and even a sales-pro-staffed version of the old Johnny Carson *Carnac the Magnificent* routine, where one pro wore a fortune teller's headdress and then gave the answers first and then read the questions, which were company-specific and often quite hilarious.

John Imlay, the CEO of Management Science America, and later Dun & Bradstreet Software, once brought a live tiger into a sales meeting to emphasize that he wanted the sales pros to be hungry like tigers. (He also wrote a book titled *How to be a Tiger in Business*.) "At various company pep rallies, he brought to the stage an eagle, a fox, a lion, a tiger, and even Clint Eastwood's orangutan to wow the crowds. He was a joker. He once dressed as a ringmaster and at another meeting played a Stradivarius—with lousy results—before bringing on a professional violinist."[151]

The bottom line is that you must ascertain what extra steps you need to take to motivate your team—both person by person and as a team. But it must be done.

Sales Advice

Your role as a sales manager requires you to support your sales pros in every aspect of pipeline management, from sourcing leads, qualifying the prospects, handling requests for proposals, presentations, follow-ups, proposals, contract negotiations, and closing the sale. For example, you must ensure that the sales pros are sourcing enough leads to enter their pipeline to enable them to reach their sales quotas.

Sales managers also must coach sales pros on strategy and tactics as they navigate the sales cycle. It is essential to your job, but should not be your sole (or greater than 50 percent) activity.

By observing sales pros in action, the sales manager can provide feedback that will improve the sales pro's skills development. The manager should also include debriefs on every sales call and won or lost opportunity so that the sales pro understands what he did correctly or areas that need further improvement.

Sales managers should also solicit and listen to feedback from their sales team on many issues, including internal roadblocks, new developments in the marketplace, pricing, compensation, and their performance as managers. This should be done continuously, not once per year.

Time Allocation

Sales managers typically have sales pros who exceed quotas and those who need help to achieve theirs. The question then is which the sales manager should devote the most significant amount of their time to. Sales compensation plans often exacerbate the problem. If the sales manager spends more time with successful sales pros, they will typically receive more compensation. However, much time must be spent working with the struggling sales pros and helping them improve their performance by direct observation. This helps the manager assess whether to keep the sales pro on their team and decide to put them on a performance plan or terminate their employment with the company.

Many failing sales pros will not ask for help because they want to stay "under the radar." They falsely believe it is best not to let their manager know they are struggling on an account, or perhaps many accounts. This unwise strategy will often end with the sales pro being dismissed. Indeed, it is the responsibility of the sales manager to identify those sales pros and begin remediation, whether the sales pro wants it or not.

I recommend that the sales manager provide as much assistance as possible to each of their sales pros—those succeeding and those who are struggling.

How to Handle Being a Player/Coach

I was a sales manager with an individual sales quota in my last position. Although I was successful, it was highly stressful, and I am sure I could have assisted my team more than I did had I not devoted about 50 percent of my time to my personal sales opportunities. So, I am opposed to the player/coach model where sales managers have a personal sales quota, in addition to a team sales quota, for the following reasons:

- It creates a conflict of interest for the sales manager. How does the sales manager allocate her time? Should she work on building her own pipeline and sales activities or work with her team? It takes valuable time away from both and hinders the ability of the sales manager to manage appropriately and for her team to excel and achieve the sales quota.
- It is very challenging to be successful in a player/coach role. Finding a balance between working with your team or on your pipeline is very difficult and often results in irritated sales pros who feel neglected.
- The definition of roles to be successful is very different for each position. To succeed as a sales pro, one must zealously work the pipeline from top to bottom and

minimize all other distractions. The top-performing sales pros are often not "team players," as I noted in *Above Quota Performance*. Unlike the sales pro role, sales managers must be utterly concerned with building a productive team and must be generous with their time.

- The sales manager needs to be actively involved in sales activities, but these should be in support of, not instead of, the sales team.
- The sales manager must provide the team with the necessary coaching time to succeed. The sales manager must be available for constant communication with the sales pros and not be busy with their own sales activities.
- The sales pros on your team will resent the time you spend on their own sales activities.
- Compensation issues: The sales manager will often receive higher compensation for their individual sales than their team's sales. So that would lead to a bias for player/coach sales managers to work on their own pipeline.
- If it has already been decided to deploy a player/coach, I advise only utilizing it if the manager has at most five sales pros reporting to her.
- Measurements of achievement of team sales goals can be confusing. For example, should the sales manager's sales count toward the team goal?

Is the player/coach role a current fad? Perhaps. For some, it is a way for companies to eke out more sales revenue. Still, it results in sub-optimization of the sales team, and it will hinder the effectiveness of the group, both short-term and long-term, and possibly result in unnecessary conflicts. Based on my more than ten years of personal experience as a player/coach, I do not recommend deploying it. I tried to break my time allocation into 50 percent devoted to the team and 50 percent to achieving my own sales goals, but I always felt that I could have offered more assistance to the sales pros who reported to me. Though I usually worked fifty to sixty hours per week, so I shorted my team less, there were days and times that I was not available because I was traveling on my own sales calls.

We don't see the player/coach too much, even in sports anymore. I believe the last player/coach in US professional sports was Pete Rose in 1986 in major league baseball. And it is much easier to be a player/coach in baseball than in sales. All company executives, including sales managers, must be available to "pitch in" and help on sales calls as needed. The CEO of my former employer and current RX Global CEO Hugh M. Jones IV states that "everybody sells."

A great sales leader is more than helping your sales pros close deals. You must add value to your sales pros by training, coaching, motivating, and mentoring them. As their sales leader, it is on you to remind them to allocate time each day and week to new business development and not just closing their current deals. These leadership skills may be intuitive, but many must be developed. There are some specialized courses that you can enroll in online or in-person that may help you develop these skills. Leaders are developed, not born.

SUMMARY
And Conclusion

I first became a sales manager many years ago and have seen countless changes over the years. The basics of sales have remained mostly the same—find and fulfill the prospects' needs. But the sales cycle is entirely different, as is the art of properly managing sales pros to consistent successes; it is much more difficult to be successful in sales, and sales management, than it was in the past. I have previously explained many reasons, but the two most impactful are that buyers are much more educated now than ever before, and access to the buying team has become more limited—even before the COVID pandemic.

Micromanagement is out—empowerment is in.

Trust is in, and trick closes are out.

Proper staffing and retention of high-performing sales pros can "make or break" a sales manager's chances of achieving their team sales quota. Conversely, if a territory is left unstaffed or is staffed by a low performer, the team will probably not reach its goals.

Today's successful sales manager must be a strong leader and a master communicator. In addition, sales managers are no longer omnipotent with autocratic control over their teams. They must be skilled in many facets of management and inspirational leaders, a motivator, a deal strategist, a creator of a positive culture of excellence, a counselor, a pricing expert, a delegator, a company politician, able to eliminate internal roadblocks, and a subject-matter expert.

The role of today's sales manager may be analogous to that of a major league baseball manager. The manager must prepare the players on his team for each game and let them know his expectations. He will coach them on his strategies to win against each opponent. He must choose to play the best players for that matchup and ensure that each player does their job to the best of their ability. There will be different levels of talent and competence: some players will need extra coaching, they will not all be treated the same by the coach to optimize their performance, and some people on the team may not like each other. (I have read of very successful baseball teams where some players openly hated each other, like the 1977 New York Yankees, when Reggie Jackson and the manager, Billy Martin, almost had a fistfight.) Still, all must contribute to the goal of winning baseball games. It is not like rowing, where the rowing coach must ensure that everyone is synchronized and rowing simultaneously, or like a symphony conductor who relies on complete mastery and perfect timing from each of the musicians in the orchestra when performing. In baseball and sales, there can be a lot of different individual performances, and there is no need for uniformity of effort or results. But tranquility is desired!

The good news is that it is a great time for you to be a sales manager! You can add a lot of value to your company. Sales can be a very rewarding career, both professionally and financially, and there are a lot of opportunities for you to grow and excel at your company. It is on you to take advantage of them. I hope this book helps you achieve your career and financial goals.

The reader is invited to visit my website to access additional material, read my blog, and opt-in to be added to my email list. Visit www.steveweinbergsales.com. I welcome all comments and inquiries.

BIBLIOGRAPHY

"Adult Data 2022." Mental Health America. Accessed December 4, 2023. https://www.mhanational.org/issues/2022/mental-health-america-adult-data.

"A New Frontier in Artificial Intelligence: Implications of Generative AI for Businesses," Deloitte, accessed December 5, 2023, https://www2.deloitte.com/content/dam/Deloitte/us/Documents/deloitte-analytics/us-ai-institute-ai-dossier-full-report.pdf.

"Artificial Intelligence Experts Call for Development Pause." The Wall Street Journal. Accessed December 22, 2023. https://www.wsj.com/podcasts/google-news-update/artificial-intelligence-experts-call-for-development-pause/c8778e96-b8ba-4115-972c-5f487ae70608?-mod=error_page.

"BATNA Basics: Boost Your Power at the Bargaining Table." Program on Negotiation at Harvard Law School, April 19, 2015. https://www.pon.harvard.edu/freemium/batna-basics-boost-your-power-at-the-bargaining-table/.

"ChatGPT." Accessed December 23, 2023. https://chat.openai.com.

"CSO Insights 5th Annual Sales Enablement Study - 2019 Sales Enablement Report." Accessed December 23, 2023. https://salesenablement.pro/assets/2019/10/CSO-Insights-5th-Annual-Sales-Enablement-Study.pdf

"Forbes Insights: The Power of Enablement." Accessed December 23, 2023. https://www.forbes.com/forbesinsights/brainshark/index.html.

"From 'Thank You' to Thriving: A Deeper Look at How Recognition Amplifies Wellbeing (EMEA)." Workhuman.com, May 18, 2023. https://www.workhuman.com/resources/reports-guides/from-thank-you-to-thriving-workhuman-gallup-report-emea.

"Gartner Expects Sales Enablement Budgets to Increase by 50% by 2027." Gartner, February 15, 2023. Accessed December 22, 2023. https://www.gartner.com/en/newsroom/press-releases/2023-02-15-gartner-expects-sales-enablement-budgets-to-increase-by-50-percent-by-2027.

"Hiring and Keeping Millennials in the Workplace." LBMC Staffing Solutions. Accessed December 22, 2023. https://www.lbmc.com/blog/hiring-keeping-millennials/.

"How Do You Use the BATNA Concept to Strengthen Your Negotiation Position?" June 07, 2023. Accessed December 22, 2023. https://www.linkedin.com/advice/3/how-do-you-use-batna-concept-strengthen-your-negotiation.

"How Millennials Make Purchase Decisions [Infographic]." ADGlow.com. Accessed December 22, 2023. https://www.adglow.com/en-us/blog/how-millennials-make-purchase-decisions-infographic.

"INFP Snapshot." TypeFinder, May 14, 2014. https://www.
typefinder.com/pdf/infp-snapshot.

"Is It Really a Good Compromise When Both Parties Are
Dissatisfied?" Cornell Course Blog, September 20, 2022.
Accessed December 22, 2023. https://blogs.cornell.edu/
info2040/2022/09/20/is-it-really-a-good-compromise-
when-both-parties-are-dissatisfied/.

"Leverage (Finance)." In Wikipedia, September
30, 2023. https://en.wikipedia.org/w/index.
php?title=Leverage_(finance)&oldid=1177878280.

"Millennials: The Me Me Me Generation." Time,
Accessed December 22, 2023. https://time.com/247/
millennials-the-me-me-me-generation/.

"Sales Enablement Analytics Report 2022–2023." Highspot.
Accessed December 4, 2023. https://engage.highspot.com/
viewer/63ebc5b26541a7f979683a6c.

Conversation with Maryann Karinch, co-author of *The Body
Language Handbook: How to Read Everyone's Hidden
Thoughts and Intentions*, Weiser Publishing, 2010.

"State of Sales Enablement 2021." Sales Enablement PRO.
Accessed December 5, 2023. https://salesenablement.pro/
assets/2021/05/2021-State-of-SE-Report_SE-PRO.pdf.

"Unleashing the Full Potential of AI." Accenture. Accessed
December 5, 2023. https://www.accenture.com/content/
dam/accenture/final/capabilities/strategy-and-consulting/
supply-chain---operations/document/Accenture-
Supply-Chain-Generative-AI-New-Tech-New-Jobs-
New-Value.pdf.

"Technology Innovation Services." Accessed December 22, 2023. https://www.accenture.com/ar-es/services/technology-innovation-index.

"Trends in Generative AI for Sales Report." SalesForce. Accessed December 23, 2023. https://www.salesforce.com/ap/form/pdf/trends-in-generative-ai-report/.

"Typies." The Myers-Briggs Company. Accessed December 21, 2023. https://share.themyersbriggs.com/en-US/Typies.

"What Is Sales Enablement? The CSO's Ultimate Guide." Gartner. Accessed December 22, 2023. https://www.gartner.com/en/sales/topics/sales-enablement.

"Who Is Erin Carter? S01e05 - Episode 5 - Transcripts." TV Show Transcripts. Accessed December 3, 2023. https://tvshowtranscripts.ourboard.org/viewtopic.php?t=64947.

"Why Great Managers Are So Rare." Gallup.com, March 25, 2014. https://www.gallup.com/workplace/231593/why-great-managers-rare.aspx.

Adams, Steve Patrick. "How to Advertise to Millennials: Influencing Purchases and Decision Making." Contobox, July 20, 2022. https://www.advertisers.contobox.com/post/how-to-advertise-to-millennials-influencing-purchas-es-and-decision-making.

Bailey, Ronald. "Don't 'Pause' A.I. Research." Reason.com, June 22, 2023. https://reason.com/2023/06/22/dont-pause-a-i-research/.

Beaulieu, Natalie. "The Seismic 2023 Value of Enablement Report Shows Companies Increasing Enablement Tech Investment in Response to Economic Turbulence." Seismic, February 15, 2023. Accessed December 23, 2023. https://seismic.com/newsroom/2023-value-of-enablement-report/.

Berra, Yogi. *The Yogi Book:" I Really Didn't Say Everything I Said"*. Workman Publishing, 2010.

Bigtincan. "What Is Sales Enablement? A Complete Guide for 2023." Accessed December 21, 2023. https://www.bigtincan.com/what-is-sales-enablement/.

Biswal, Avijeet. "Top 18 Artificial Intelligence (AI) Applications in 2024" Simplilearn. Accessed December 22, 2023. https://www.simplilearn.com/tutorials/artificial-intelligence-tutorial/artificial-intelligence-applications.

Blanchard, Kenneth H., and Spencer Johnson. *The One Minute Manager*. New York, NY: William Morrow, 1982.

Bohannon, Molly. "Pope Warns Artificial Intelligence Could 'Fuel Conflicts And Antagonism.'" Forbes. Accessed December 22, 2023. https://www.forbes.com/sites/mollybohannon/2023/08/08/pope-warns-artificial-intelligence-could-fuel-conflicts-and-antagonism/.

Bradford, Vanessa. "MBTI® Facts and Common Criticisms." Myers Briggs, October 02, 2018. Accessed December 21, 2023. https://www.themyersbriggs.com/en-US/Connect-With-Us/Blog/2018/October/MBTI-Facts--Common-Criticisms.

Brown, Lachlan. "8 Signs You're an INFJ, the World's
    Rarest Personality Type." Ideapod, September 4, 2023.
    Accessed December 22, 2023. https://ideapod.com/
    signs-your-infj-worlds-rarest-personality-type/.

Campbell, Rich. "What Did 1985 Chicago Bears Do with Their
    Super Bowl Rings?" Chicago Tribune, January 27, 2020.
    Accessed December 22, 2023. https://www.chicagotribune.
    com/sports/bears/ct-cb-chicago-bears-1985-super-bowl-
    ring-20200127-ir37jedl2zf2nmfqfesu6jjfha-story.html.

Cobb, Daniel. "Epic List of Famous People With INTJ
    Personalities." Personality Club, June 29, 2020. Accessed
    December 22, 2023. https://www.personalityclub.com/
    blog/famous-intj/.

Dews, Fred. "Brookings Data Now: 75 Percent of 2025
    Workforce Will Be Millennials." Brookings, July 17, 2014.
    Accessed December 22, 2023. https://www.brookings.edu/
    articles/brookings-data-now-75-percent-of-2025-work-
    force-will-be-millennials/.

Dilmegani, Cem. "AI in Sales: 15 AI Sales Applications/ Use
    Cases in 2022." May 09, 2023. Accessed December 22,
    2023. https://research.aimultiple.com/sales-ai/.

Dittmann Tracey, Melissa. "Introverts vs. Extroverts:
    Who's Really Better at Sales?" National Association
    of Realtors, December 12, 2018. https://www.nar.
    realtor/magazine/real-estate-news/sales-marketing/
    introverts-vs-extroverts-who-s-really.

Donovan, George. "Council Post: Six Trends Affecting Sales Enablement In 2022." Forbes. Accessed December 22, 2023. https://www.forbes.com/sites/forbesbusinessdevelopmentcouncil/2021/12/16/six-trends-affecting-sales-enablement-in-2022/.

Eberl, Nik. "How Millennials Are Using LinkedIn [InfoGraphic]." May 23, 2016. Accessed December 22, 2023. https://www.linkedin.com/pulse/how-millennials-using-linkedin-infographic-dr-nikolaus.

Eisenhower, Dwight D. "Dwight D. Eisenhower 1957 : Containing the Public Messages, Speeches, and Statements of the President, January 1 to December 31, 1957." HathiTrust. Accessed January 15, 2024. https://babel.hathitrust.org/cgi/pt?id=miua.4728417.1957.001&seq=858.

Ferron, Liz. "Emotional Well Being Definition." Vital Work Life. Accessed December 22, 2023. https://insights.vitalworklife.com/blog/2016/01/02/wheel-of-well-being-emotional-dimension-definition.

Fisher, Roger, William L. Ury, and Bruce Patton. *Getting to Yes: Negotiating Agreement Without Giving In.* Penguin, 2011.

Fry, Kristen Bialik and Richard. "Millennial Life: How Young Adulthood Today Compares with Prior Generations." Pew Research Center's Social & Demographic Trends Project, February 14, 2019. https://www.pewresearch.org/social-trends/2019/02/14/millennial-life-how-young-adulthood-today-compares-with-prior-generations-2/.

Future of Life Institute. "Pause Giant AI Experiments: An Open Letter." March 22, 2023. Accessed December 22, 2023. https://futureoflife.org/open-letter/pause-giant-ai-experiments/.

Gatehouse, Derek. *The Perfect Salesforce: The 6 Best Practices of the World's Best Sales Teams*. New York, NY: Portfolio, 2007.

Goldberg, Jeff. "4 AI Use Cases to Optimize B2B Lead Management." Sales & Marketing Management, April 12, 2023. https://salesandmarketing.com/4-ai-use-cases-to-optimize-b2b-lead-management/.

Hales, Alex. "Stay Away From Negative People - Albert Einstein Quotes," February 13, 2019. https://themindsjournal.com/quotes/stay-away-from-negative-people/.

Hartley, Gregory, and Maryann Karinch. *The Body Language Handbook: How to Read Everyone's Hidden Thoughts and Intentions*. Franklin Lakes, NJ: Career Press, 2010.

Heyman, Beverlie. "Why Sales Coaching Matters, Plus 5 Ways to Get Started." Brainshark, July 5, 2023. https://www.brainshark.com/ideas-blog/top-coaching-tips-for-sales-managers/.

Highspot. "Why You Need a Sales Enablement Platform (EN-GB)." Accessed December 21, 2023. https://www.highspot.com/en-gb/why-you-need-an-enablement-platform/.

Hisaka, Alex. "Why Best in Class Sales Enablement Is a Necessity." LinkedIn, June 06, 2017. Accessed December 23, 2023. https://www.linkedin.com/business/sales/blog/sales-enablement/why-best-in-class-sales-enablement-is-a-necessity.

Hobson, Nick. "3 Signs That Someone Is Interested in Your Pitch Based on Body Language." Inc.com, April 29, 2023. https://www.inc.com/nick-hobson/3-signs-that-someone-is-interested-in-your-pitch-based-on-body-language.html.

Horowitz, Ben. "Why Must You Pay Sales People Commissions?" Andreessen Horowitz, April 16, 2023. https://a16z.com/2017/09/11/sales-commissions/.

Hunter, John. "Eliminate Sales Commissions: Reject Theory X Management and Embrace Systems Thinking." The W. Edwards Deming Institute, November 01, 2012. Accessed December 22, 2023. https://deming.org/eliminate-sales-commissions-reject-theory-x-management-and-embrace-systems-thinking/.

Itzchakov, Guy, and Avraham N. (Avi) Kluger. "The Power of Listening in Helping People Change." Harvard Business Review, May 17, 2018. https://hbr.org/2018/05/the-power-of-listening-in-helping-people-change.

Jeftovic, Anja. "130+ Sales Statistics to Guide You This Year." TaskDrive, January 3, 2020. https://taskdrive.com/sales/sales-statistics/.

Jozwiak, Agnes. "How Introverts and Extroverts Act Differently in Meetings – Webinar Best Practices." ClickMeeting. Accessed December 21, 2023. https://blog.clickmeeting.com/how-introverts-and-extroverts-act-differently-in-meetings.

Kearns, Deborah. "Survey Reveals What's Holding Millennials Back From Homebuying." Bankrate, September 11, 2019. Accessed December 22, 2023. https://www.bankrate.com/surveys/down-payment-survey-september-2019/.

Kleinman, Zoe, and Chris Valance. "AI 'godfather' Geoffrey Hinton Warns of Dangers as He Quits Google." BBC News, May 02, 2023. Accessed December 22, 2023. https://www.bbc.com/news/world-us-canada-65452940.

Kolmar, Chris. "100+ Important Sales Statistics [2023]: Figures, Salaries, and Statistics." Zippia, February 26, 2023, Accessed December 21, 2023. https://www.zippia.com/advice/sales-statistics/.

Korhonen, Veera. "U.S. Population Share by Generation 2022." Statista, August 29, 2023. Accessed December 22, 2023. https://www.statista.com/statistics/296974/us-population-share-by-generation/.

Kroeger, Otto, and Janet M Thuesen. *Type Talk at Work: How the 16 Personality Types Determine Your Success on the Job*. New York, NY: Delacorte Publishing, 1991.

Krogue, Ken. "Why Sales Reps Spend Less Than 36% Of Time Selling (And Less Than 18% In CRM)." Forbes. Accessed December 21, 2023. https://www.forbes.com/sites/kenkrogue/2018/01/10/why-sales-reps-spend-less-than-36-of-time-selling-and-less-than-18-in-crm/.

Leon Elijah, "Future Forecaster - The Millennials," LinkedIn, January 13, 2020, accessed December 22, 2023, https://www.linkedin.com/pulse/future-forecaster-mmillennials-leon-elijah.

Lestraundra, Alfred, "53 Sales Leadership Stats to Know in 2022," November 28, 2022. https://blog.hubspot.com/sales/sales-leadership-stats.

Livio, Mario. "When Galileo Stood Trial for Defending Science." History, May 19, 2020. https://www.history.com/news/galileo-copernicus-earth-sun-heresy-church.

Lukpat, Alyssa. "Bill Gates Says AI Is the Most Revolutionary Technology in Decades. The Wallstreet Journal, March 22, 2023. Accessed December 22, 2023. https://www.wsj.com/articles/bill-gates-says-artificial-intelligence-is-the-most-revolutionary-technology-in-decades-75fb8562.

Main, Douglas. "Millennials: Definition & Characteristics of Generation Y." Live Science, September 09, 2017. Accessed December 22, 2023. https://www.livescience.com/38061-millennials-generation-y.html.

Mangu-Ward, Katharine. "Marc Andreessen On Artificial Intelligence And The Future." Reason, June 2023.

McClatchy, Julia, Candace Lun Plotkin, Karolina Sauer-Sidor, Jennifer Stanley, and Kevin Wei Wang, "The Multiplier Effect: How B2B Winners Grow." McKinsey, April 13, 2023. Accessed December 22, 2023. https://www.mckinsey.com/capabilities/growth-marketing-and-sales/our-insights/the-multiplier-effect-how-b2b-winners-grow.

McDermott, Nicole. "Myers-Briggs Personality Test (MBTI): What You Need To Know," Forbes Health, February 3, 2022. https://www.forbes.com/health/mind/myers-briggs-personality-test/.

Mello, Tommy. "How I Fired My Top Sales Performer and Saw Profits Soar" Inc.com, October 17, 2023. Accessed December 22, 2023. https://www.inc.com/tommy-mello/how-i-fired-my-top-sales-performer-saw-profits-soar.html.

Monesson, Karina. "Why Are Women More Stressed Out Than Men?" UKG, February 14, 2023. https://www.ukg.com/blog/life-work-trends/ why-are-women-more-stressed-out-men.

Murphy, Bill Jr., "Want to Live 20 Years Longer? A Massive New Study of 719,147 People Says Follow These 8 Habits." Inc.com, August 06, 2023. Accessed December 22, 2023. https://www.inc.com/bill-murphy-jr/want-to-live-20-years-longer-a-massive-new-study-of-719147-people-says-follow-these-8-habits.html.

Nakamura, Amy. "'Leadership Is Solving Problems': General Colin Powell's Rules for Leadership and More." USA TODAY. Accessed December 22, 2023. https://www.usatoday.com/story/news/politics/2021/10/18/general-colin-powells-famous-rules-and-quotes-leadership/8512414002/.

Nanji, Ayaz. "B2B Buying Committees: Millennial Buyer Preferences." Accessed December 22, 2023. https://www.marketingprofs.com/charts/2017/32751/the-preferences-of-millennial-b2b-buyers.

Neiberg, Michael. "Michael Neiberg on Linkedin: #AI." LinkedIn, February 17, 2024. https://www.linkedin.com/posts/michaelneiberg_ai-activity-7164632181636599808-jVl1?utm_source=share&utm_medium=member_desktop.

Neufeld, Dorothy. "Demographics: How Many Millennials Are There in the World?" World Economic Forum, November 08, 2021. Accessed December 22, 2023. https://www.weforum.org/agenda/2021/11/millennials-world-regional-breakdown/.

Noonan, Peggy. "A Six-Month AI Pause? No, Longer Is Needed." The Wallstreet Journal, March 30, 2023. Accessed December 22, 2023. https://www.wsj.com/articles/a-six-month-ai-pause-no-longer-is-needed-civilization-danger-chat-gpt-chatbot-internet-big-tech-4b66da6e.

Oben, Issac. "Stabbed by Best Friend." LinkedIn, November 24, 2021. Accessed December 22, 2023. https://www.linkedin.com/pulse/stabbed-best-friend-oben-ai.

Owens, Molly. "All About the ENTP Personality Type." True You Journal. Accessed December 22, 2023. https://www.truity.com/blog/personality-type/entp.

Owens, Molly. "All About the INFP Personality Type." True You Journal. Accessed December 22, 2023. https://www.truity.com/blog/personality-type/infp.

Owens, Molly. "All About the ISFJ Personality Type." True You Journal. Accessed December 22, 2023. https://www.truity.com/blog/personality-type/isfj.

Owens, Molly. "All About the ISTJ Personality Type." True You Journal. Accessed December 21, 2023. https://www.truity.com/blog/personality-type/istj.

Pangilinan, Jessa. "101 Toxic People Quotes to Stay Away From Negativity." Happier Human, September 7, 2023. http://www.happierhuman.com/toxic-people-quotes.

Parker, Richard Fry and Kim. "Early Benchmarks Show 'Post-Millennials' on Track to Be Most Diverse, Best-Educated Generation Yet." Pew Research Center's Social & Demographic Trends Project (blog), November 15, 2018. https://www.pewresearch.org/social-trends/2018/11/15/early-benchmarks-show-post-millennials-on-track-to-be-most-diverse-best-educated-generation-yet/.

Rampton, John. "Different Motivations for Different Generations of Workers: Boomers, Gen-X, Millennials, and Gen-Z." Inc.com, October 17, 2017, accessed December 22, 2023, https://www.inc.com/john-rampton/different-motivations-for-different-generations-of-workers-boomers-gen-x-millennials-gen-z.html. "Different Motivations for Different Generations of Workers: Boomers, Gen-X, Millennials, and Gen-Z." Inc.com. Accessed December 22, 2023. https://www.inc.com/john-rampton/different-motivations-for-different-generations-of-workers-boomers-gen-x-millennials-gen-z.html.

Ryback, Ralph. "From Baby Boomers to Generation Z." Psychology Today, February 22, 2016. Accessed December 22, 2023. https://www.psychologytoday.com/us/blog/the-truisms-wellness/201602/baby-boomers-generation-z.

S, Gilad. "What Do Millennials Care About? It's Not What You Think," Eclincher, November 30, 2022. https://eclincher.com/what-do-millennials-care-about-its-not-what-you-think.

Schakohl, Trevor. "Fact Check: Did Benjamin Franklin Say, 'By Failing to Prepare, You Are Preparing to Fail'?" Check Your Fact, October 17, 2019. https://checkyourfact.com/2019/10/17/fact-check-benjamin-franklin-failing-prepare/.

Schuyler, Michael. "Michael Shuyler." LinkedIn.com. Accessed December 21, 2023. https://uk.linkedin.com/in/schuyler-michael-22471421

Schwantes, Marcel. "Warren Buffett Says He Lives by 3 Leadership Rules for Success." Inc.com, November 20, 2023. https://www.inc.com/marcel-schwantes/warren-buffett-says-he-lives-by-3-leadership-rules-for-success.html.

Scott, David Meerman. "Super Simple Way to Understand Artificial Intelligence." LinkedIn, May 03, 2023. Accessed December 22, 2023. https://www.linkedin.com/pulse/super-simple-way-understand-artificial-intelligence-scott.

Scudder, Sarah. "How Millennials Are Changing the Procurement Landscape." Future of Sourcing, August 08, 2019. Accessed December 22, 2023. https://futureofsourcing.com/how-millennials-are-changing-the-procurement-landscape.

Selig, Jon. "Busting Misconceptions. #1: It's About the Jokes." November 11, 2019. Accessed December 21, 2023. https://www.jonselig.com/busting-misconceptions-about-the-stuff-i-do/.

Sharma, Mukul. "Millennials Stick to One Workplace For Longer Periods than Baby Boomers Did." WION, September 3, 2023. https://www.wionews.com/business-economy/Millennials-stick-to-one-workplace-for-longer-periods-than-baby-boomers-631917.

Srinivasan, Gopal, Rohan Gupta, Nitin Mittal, Rich Nanda, Costi Perricos, and Kellie Nuttal. "Generative Artificial Intelligence." Accessed December 23, 2023. https://www2.deloitte.com/us/en/pages/consulting/articles/generative-artificial-intelligence.html.

Stafford, Leon. "Atlanta Technology Giant John P. Imlay Jr. Dies." The Atlanta Journal-Constitution, March 26, 2015. https://www.ajc.com/business/atlanta-technology-giant-john-imlay-dies/I6PhhVRShdEcSUTUT4y13M.

Sterbenz, Christina. "12 Famous Quotes That Always Get Misattributed." Business Insider. Accessed December 21, 2023. https://www.businessinsider.com/misattributed-quotes-2013-10.

Storm, Susan. "The Fashion Styles of Every Myers-Briggs® Personality Type." Psychology Junkie, July 23, 2020. Accessed December 22, 2023. https://www.psychology-junkie.com/the-clothing-style-of-every-myers-briggs-personality-type/.

Storm, Susan. "The Most to Least Assertive Myers-Briggs® Personality Types, Ranked." Psychology Junkie, August 11, 2023. Accessed December 22, 2023. https://www.psychologyjunkie.com/the-most-to-least-assertive-myers-briggs-personality-types-ranked/.

Storm, Susan. "The Unique Empathy of Each Myers-Briggs® Personality Type." Psychology Junkie (blog), August 23, 2023. https://www.psychologyjunkie.com/the-unique-empathy-of-each-myers-briggs-personality-type/.

Thomas, Bri. "MBTI® of Sex And The City Characters." ScreenRant, April 2, 2019. https://screenrant.com/mbti-myers-briggs-sex-city-satc/.

Vogels, Emily A. "Millennials Stand out for Their Technology Use, but Older Generations Also Embrace Digital Life." Pew Research Center. Accessed December 22, 2023. https://www.pewresearch.org/short-reads/2019/09/09/us-generations-technology-use/.

Ziglar, Zig. Facebook, October 31, 2012. https://www.facebook.com/ZigZiglar/posts/10151226935492863:0.

Zoltners, Andris, Prabhakant Sinha, and Sally Lorimer. "Match Your Sales Force Structure to Your Business Cycle." Harvard Business Review 10 Must Reads on Sales, 2017.

Zuckerman, Arthur. "42 Millennials Statistics: 2020/2021 Data, Trends & Economic Impact." CompareCamp.com (blog), May 18, 2020. https://comparecamp.com/millennial-statistics/.

TAKEAWAYS

Takeaway 1 – Many CEOs, CROs, and VPs of Sales Accept the 50 Percent Failure Rate

Takeaway 2 – Retention of High-Performers is Key to Reducing the Sales Pro Failure Rate

Takeaway 3 – Sales Pros (and Sales Managers, too) Need to Listen, Not Just Hear

Takeaway 4 – Sales Pros Should Ask Open-Ended Questions to Solicit More Feedback from Buyers.

Takeaway 5 – The Marketing/Sales Problem Begins with the Budget

Takeaway 6 – Sales Pros Need to Review The Content of Your Company's Marketing Messages

Takeaway 7 – Sales Pros Must Prepare a Sales Plan for All Key Opportunities

Takeaway 8 – The Sales Plan Must Be Continually Updated by the Sales Pro

Takeaway 9 – Be Sure to Have Your Sales Pros Identify All "Red Flags" for the Opportunity

Takeaway 10 – "By Failing to Prepare, You Are Preparing to Fail"

Takeaway 11 – The Sales Pro Owns Their Success or Failure— Nobody Else. But the Sales Manager Owns the Success or Failure of the Sales Team.

Takeaway 12 – The "Best" Product Does Not Always Win!

Takeaway 13 – The Time Gap That Competitors Announce New (Superior) Features Is Now in Days, Not Months

Takeaway 14 – The Sales Pro Must Always Have a Business Reason When Calling a C-Level Executive

Takeaway 15 – The Sales Pro Must Never Try to Go Around or Mislead the Executive Assistant

Takeaway 16 – It Is Important for the Sales Pro to Tailor Their Message to the Buyer's Personality

Takeaway 17 – There Are 16 Different Myers-Briggs (MBTI) Personality Types

Takeaway 18 - Millennials Now Comprise the Majority of Today's Workforce

Takeaway 19 - Millennials Are More Involved in Purchasing Decisions Now

Takeaway 20 - It Is Important for Sales Managers to Have "One-on-One" Conversations with Sales Pros

Takeaway 21 - A Debrief Is Essential After Every Prospect Meeting

Takeaway 22 - Do a Hard Qualification to Avoid Opportunities That Don't Close

Takeaway 23 - The Sales Pro Needs to Prepare a Formal Contract Negotiation Timetable with the Buyer

Takeaway 24 - The Sales Pro Should Always Know Who You Are Negotiating With—and What Their Authority Is

Takeaway 25 – The Sales Pro Should Not Negotiate Via Emails

Takeaway 26 - The Sales Pro Should Negotiate the Entire Contract at One Time, Not Bit-by-Bit

Takeaway 27 - The Sales Pro Needs to be Prepared to Negotiate with a Professional

Takeaway 28 – The Sales Manager Must Give Priority to Staffing Sales Positions

Takeaway 29 – Cowboys Are Challenging to Manage and Sometimes Wear Out Their Welcome

Takeaway 30 – Promoting a Top Sales Producer Has Both Positive and Negative Risks

Takeaway 31 – The Sales Pro Must Always Be Truthful and Disclose All Relevant Issues to Buyers

Takeaway 32 – The Quota Should Be Achievable for at Least 60 Percent of Sales Pros

Takeaway 33 – Commissioned Sales Pros Are Essential for the Growth of the Company

Takeaway 34 – Introverts Can Be Successful in Sales!

Takeaway 35 – Building Trust is a Skill that an Introvert Can Master

Takeaway 36 – The Salesforce Needs to be Organized to Best Fit the Buyer's Needs, Not the Sellers

Takeaway 37 – The Hybrid Sales Model Is Preferred

Takeaway 38 - Companies Need Highly Skilled Sales Pros to Succeed Today

Takeaway 39 - Sales Enablement Needs Management Support to Add Value

Takeaway 40 - Sales Pros Spend Too Much Time on Non-selling Activities!

Takeaway 41 - AI Can Help Optimize Sales and Marketing Processes

Takeaway 42 - Pausing AI Development Is Not Feasible

Takeaway 43 - Sales Pros Should Not Take Rejection Personally

Takeaway 44 - Sales Managers Must Invest in "One-on-One" Coaching to be Most Effective

THANK YOU

The author would like to thank the following individuals for assisting with the preparation of the content of the manuscript:

Kimberly Peticolas	Robert (Uri) Geller
Joe Arrigo	Anthony Iannarino
Ralph Babusci	Tom Markert
Carmela Ravi	Steve Maul
Dina Berger	Rick Nichols
Avery Diederich-Watts	Lisa Block
Bill Hoffman	Michael Heyes
Jay Izso	Jenifer Patterson
James Alberg	Phil Gerbyshak
Michael Dockery	Warren Weiss
Daniel Dwyer	Frank Cespedes
Jay Ryan	Dick Reck
Amy Bloustine	Frank Cespedes
David Pan	Gerhard Gschwandter

ENDNOTES

1   Lestraundra Alfred, "53 Sales Leadership Stats to Know in 2022," November 28, 2022, https://blog.hubspot.com/sales/sales-leadership-stats.

2   Anja Jeftovic, "130+ Sales Statistics to Guide You This Year | TaskDrive," January 3, 2020, https://taskdrive.com/sales/sales-statistics/.

3   "Forbes Insights: The Power of Enablement," October, 2015. Accessed December 23, 2023, https://www.forbes.com/forbesinsights/brainshark/index.html. Pg. 6.

4   "What Is Sales Enablement? A Complete Guide for 2023," Bigtincan.com, accessed December 21, 2023, https://www.bigtincan.com/what-is-sales-enablement/.

5   Jon Selig, "Busting Misconceptions. #1: It's About the Jokes." JonSelig.com, November 11, 2019, accessed December 21, 2023, https://www.jonselig.com/busting-misconceptions-about-the-stuff-i-do/.

6   Chris Kolmar, "100+ Important Sales Statistics [2023]: Figures, Salaries, and Statistics," Zippia, February 26, 2023, accessed December 21, 2023, https://www.zippia.com/advice/sales-statistics/.

7   Christina Sterbenz, "12 Famous Quotes That Always Get Misattributed," Business Insider, October 8, 2013, accessed December 21, 2023, https://www.businessinsider.com/misattributed-quotes-2013-10.

8   Guy Itzchakov and Avraham N. (Avi) Kluger, "The Power of Listening in Helping People Change," *Harvard Business Review*, May 17, 2018, https://hbr.org/2018/05/the-power-of-listening-in-helping-people-change.

9   "Michael Schuyler," LinkedIn.com, accessed December 21, 2023, https://uk.linkedin.com/in/schuyler-michael-22471421.

10   "Forbes Insights: The Power of Enablement," October, 2015. Accessed December 23, 2023, https://www.forbes.com/forbesin-sights/brainshark/index.html. Pg. 11.

11   Jeff Goldberg, "4 AI Use Cases to Optimize B2B Lead Management," *Sales & Marketing Management* (blog), April 12, 2023, https://salesandmarketing.com/4-ai-use-cases-to-optimize-b2b-lead-management/.

12   "Why You Need a Sales Enablement Platform (EN-GB)," Highspot, accessed December 21, 2023, https://www.highspot.com/en-gb/why-you-need-an-enablement-platform/.

13   Ken Krogue, "Why Sales Reps Spend Less Than 36% Of Time Selling (And Less Than 18% In CRM)," Forbes, January 10, 2018, accessed December 21, 2023, https://www.forbes.com/sites/kenkrogue/2018/01/10/why-sales-reps-spend-less-than-36-of-time-selling-and-less-than-18-in-crm/.

14   Ibid.

15   Ibid.

16   Dwight D Eisenhower, "Dwight D. Eisenhower 1957 :
      Containing the Public Messages, Speeches, and Statements of
      the President, January 1 to December 31, 1957," HathiTrust,
      accessed January 15, 2024, https://babel.hathitrust.org/cgi/
      pt?id=miua.4728417.1957.001&seq=858.

17   Trevor Schakohl, "Fact Check: Did Benjamin Franklin Say, 'By
      Failing to Prepare, You Are Preparing to Fail'?," Check Your
      Fact, October 17, 2019, https://checkyourfact.com/2019/10/17/
      fact-check-benjamin-franklin-failing-prepare/.

18   Ibid.

19   Gregory Hartley and Maryann Karinch, *The Body Language
      Handbook: How to Read Everyone's Hidden Thoughts and Intentions*
      (Franklin Lakes, NJ: Career Press, 2010).

20   Emily Ratay, "People Who Belong to 5 Specific Personality
      Types Aren't Afraid to Speak Their Mind," YourTango,
      August 24, 2023, https://www.yourtango.com/self/
      most-opinionated-mbti-myers-briggs-types.

21   Ibid.

22   Vanessa Bradford, "MBTI® Facts and Common Criticisms,"
      October 2, 2018, accessed December 21, 2023, https://www.
      themyersbriggs.com/en-US/Connect-With-Us/Blog/2018/
      October/MBTI-Facts--Common-Criticisms.

23   Nicole McDermott, "Myers-Briggs Personality Test
      (MBTI): What You Need To Know," Forbes Health,
      February 3, 2022, https://www.forbes.com/health/mind/
      myers-briggs-personality-test/.

24   Yogi Berra, *The Yogi Book:" I Really Didn't Say Everything I Said,"*
      Workman Publishing, (New York, NY 1998), p. 123.

25   Agnes Jozwiak, "How Introverts and Extroverts Act Differently in Meetings – Webinar Best Practices | ClickMeeting Blog," accessed December 21, 2023, https://blog.clickmeeting.com/how-introverts-and-extroverts-act-differently-in-meetings.

26   "Typies." The Myers-Briggs Company. Accessed December 21, 2023, https://share.themyersbriggs.com/en-US/Typies.

27   Molly Owens, "All About the ISTJ Personality Type." True You Journal. Accessed December 21, 2023, https://www.truity.com/blog/personality-type/istj.

28   Susan Storm, "The Unique Empathy of Each Myers-Briggs® Personality Type," *Psychology Junkie* (blog), August 23, 2023, https://www.psychologyjunkie.com/the-unique-empathy-of-each-myers-briggs-personality-type/.

29   Molly Owens, "All About the ISFJ Personality Type." True You Journal. Accessed December 22, 2023, https://www.truity.com/blog/personality-type/isfj.

30   Molly Owens, "All About the INFP Personality Type." True You Journal. Accessed December 22, 2023, https://www.truity.com/blog/personality-type/infp.

31   Storm, "The Unique Empathy of Each Myers-Briggs® Personality Type."

32   Lachlan Brown, "8 Signs You're an INFJ, the World's Rarest Personality Type," September 4, 2023, accessed December 22, 2023, https://ideapod.com/signs-your-infj-worlds-rarest-personality-type/.

33   "INFP Snapshot," TypeFinder, May 14, 2014, https://www.typefinder.com/pdf/infp-snapshot.

34 Daniel Cobb, "Epic List of Famous People With INTJ Person-
    alities." Personality Club, June 29, 2020, accessed December 22,
    2023, https://www.personalityclub.com/blog/famous-intj/.

35 Storm, "The Unique Empathy of Each Myers-Briggs® Person-
    ality Type."

36 Otto Kroeger and Janet M Thuesen, *Type Talk at Work: How the
    16 Personality Types Determine Your Success on the Job* (New York,
    NY: Delacorte Publishing, 1991), 341.

37 Kroeger, Ibid., p. 369

38 Kroeger, Ibid., p. 370.

39 Storm, "The Unique Empathy of Each Myers-Briggs® Person-
    ality Type."

40 Ibid.

41 Bri Thomas, "MBTI® of Sex And The City Characters,"
    ScreenRant, April 2, 2019, https://screenrant.com/
    mbti-myers-briggs-sex-city-satc/.

42 Storm, "The Unique Empathy of Each Myers-Briggs® Person-
    ality Type."

43 Molly Owens, "All About the ENTP Personality Type" True You
    Journal. Accessed December 22, 2023, https://www.truity.com/
    blog/personality-type/entp.

44 Kroeger and Thuesen, *Type Talk at Work.*, p. 363.

45 Susan Storm, "The Most to Least Assertive Myers-Briggs® Per-
    sonality Types, Ranked - Psychology Junkie," August 11, 2023,
    accessed December 22, 2023, https://www.psychologyjunkie.
    com/the-most-to-least-assertive-myers-briggs-personality-
    types-ranked/.

46   Storm, "The Unique Empathy of Each Myers-Briggs® Personality Type."

47   Susan Storm, "The Fashion Styles of Every Myers-Briggs® Personality Type - Psychology Junkie," July 23, 2020, accessed December 22, 2023, https://www.psychologyjunkie.com/the-clothing-style-of-every-myers-briggs-personality-type/.

48   Veera Korhonen, "U.S. Population Share by Generation 2022," August 29, 2023, Statista, accessed December 22, 2023, https://www.statista.com/statistics/296974/us-population-share-by-generation/.

49   Ibid.

50   Ralph Ryback, "From Baby Boomers to Generation Z | Psychology Today," February 22, 2016, accessed December 22, 2023, https://www.psychologytoday.com/us/blog/the-truisms-wellness/201602/baby-boomers-generation-z.

51   Ibid.

52   John Rampton, "Different Motivations for Different Generations of Workers: Boomers, Gen-X, Millennials, and Gen-Z | Inc.com," October 17, 2017, accessed December 22, 2023, https://www.inc.com/john-rampton/different-motivations-for-different-generations-of-workers-boomers-gen-x-millennials-gen-z.html.

53   Arthur Zuckerman, "42 Millennials Statistics: 2020/2021 Data, Trends & Economic Impact," *CompareCamp.com* (blog), May 18, 2020, https://comparecamp.com/millennial-statistics/.

54   Dorothy Neufeld, "Demographics: How Many Millennials Are There in the World? | World Economic Forum," November 8, 2021, accessed December 22, 2023, https://www.weforum.org/agenda/2021/11/millennials-world-regional-breakdown/.

55   Fred Dews, "Brookings Data Now: 75 Percent of 2025
      Workforce Will Be Millennials," Brookings, July 17, 2014,
      accessed December 22, 2023, https://www.brookings.edu/
      articles/brookings-data-now-75-percent-of-2025-work-
      force-will-be-millennials/.2023, https://www.brookings.edu/
      articles/brookings-data-now-75-percent-of-2025-work-
      force-will-be-millennials/.","plainCitation":""Brookings Data
      Now: 75 Percent of 2025 Workforce Will Be Millennials,"
      Brookings, accessed December 22, 2023, https://www.brookings.
      edu/articles/brookings-data-now-75-percent-of-2025-work-
      force-will-be-millennials/.","noteIndex":53},"citationIte
      ms":[{"id":814,"uris":["http://zotero.org/users/5591388/
      items/5IYJT4Q8"],"itemData":{"id":814,"type":"webpage","ab-
      stract":"In this edition of Brookings Data Now: Millennials
      to dominate workforce in future; Tokyo and foreign direct
      investment; Chinese foreign aid to Africa; U.S. greenhouse
      gas emissions are down less than Germany's; additional
      annual investment required in emerging economies.","contain-
      er-title":"Brookings","language":"en-US","title":"Brookings
      Data Now: 75 Percent of 2025 Workforce Will Be Millen-
      nials","title-short":"Brookings Data Now","URL":"https://
      www.brookings.edu/articles/brookings-data-now-75-per-
      cent-of-2025-workforce-will-be-millennials/","accessed":{"dat
      e-parts":[["2023",12,22]]}}}],"schema":"https://github.com/
      citation-style-language/schema/raw/master/csl-citation.json"}

56   Kristen Bialik and Richard Fry, "Millennial Life: How Young
      Adulthood Today Compares with Prior Generations," *Pew
      Research Center's Social & Demographic Trends Project* (blog),
      February 14, 2019, https://www.pewresearch.org/social-
      trends/2019/02/14/millennial-life-how-young-adulthood-to-
      day-compares-with-prior-generations-2/.

57   Ibid.

58   Leon Elijah, "Future Forecaster - The Millennials," January 13,
      2020, accessed December 22, 2023, https://www.linkedin.com/
      pulse/future-forecaster-mmillennials-leon-elijah.

59   Douglas Main, "Millennials: Definition & Characteristics of
      Generation Y | Live Science," September 09, 2017, accessed
      December 22, 2023, https://www.livescience.com/38061-millen-
      nials-generation-y.html.

60   Ralph Ryback, "From Baby Boomers to Generation Z | Psychol-
      ogy Today." February 22, 2016.

61   Emily a Vogels, "Millennials Stand out for Their Technology
      Use, but Older Generations Also Embrace Digital Life,"
      Pew Research Center (blog), accessed December 22, 2023,
      https://www.pewresearch.org/short-reads/2019/09/09/
      us-generations-technology-use/.

62   Deborah Kearns, "Survey Reveals What's Holding Millennials
      Back From Homebuying," Bankrate, September 11, 2019,
      accessed December 22, 2023, https://www.bankrate.com/
      surveys/down-payment-survey-september-2019/.

63   Richard Fry and Kim Parker, "Early Benchmarks Show
      'Post-Millennials' on Track to Be Most Diverse, Best-Educated
      Generation Yet," *Pew Research Center's Social & Demographic
      Trends Project* (blog), November 15, 2018, https://www.
      pewresearch.org/social-trends/2018/11/15/early-benchmarks-
      show-post-millennials-on-track-to-be-most-diverse-best-edu-
      cated-generation-yet/.

64   "Millennials: The Me Me Me Generation | TIME,"
      accessed December 22, 2023, https://time.com/247/
      millennials-the-me-me-me-generation/.

65   Mukul Sharma, "Millennials Stick to One Workplace For Longer Periods than Baby Boomers Did," WION, September 3, 2023, https://www.wionews.com/business-economy/Millennials-stick-to-one-workplace-for-longer-periods-than-baby-boomers-631917.

66   "Millennials: The Me Me Me Generation," Time, May 20, 2013, https://time.com/247/Millennials-the-me-me-me-generation/.

67   LBMC staffing solutions, "Hiring and Keeping Millennials in the Workplace," LBMC, September 18, 2022, accessed December 22, 2023, https://www.lbmc.com/blog/hiring-keeping-millennials/.

68   Gilad S, "What Do Millennials Care About? It's Not What You Think," November 30, 2022, https://eclincher.com/what-do-millennials-care-about-its-not-what-you-think/.

69   Ibid.

70   Nik Eberl, "How Millennials Are Using LinkedIn [InfoGraphic]," May 23, 2016, accessed December 22, 2023, https://www.linkedin.com/pulse/how-millennials-using-linkedin-infographic-dr-nikolaus.

71   Ayaz Nanji, "B2B Buying Committees: Millennial Buyer Preferences | Marketing Study," accessed December 22, 2023, https://www.marketingprofs.com/charts/2017/32751/the-preferences-of-millennial-b2b-buyers.

72   Sarah Scudder, "How Millennials Are Changing the Procurement Landscape | Future of Sourcing," August 08, 2019, accessed December 22, 2023, https://futureofsourcing.com/how-millennials-are-changing-the-procurement-landscape.

73   Steve Patrick Adams, "How to Advertise to Millennials: Influencing Purchases and Decision Making," Bring your ads to life | Contobox, July 20, 2022, https://www.advertisers.contobox. com/post/how-to-advertise-to-millennials-influencing-purchases-and-decision-making.

74   "How Millennials Make Purchase Decisions {Infographic}," accessed December 22, 2023, https://www.adglow.com/en-us/blog/how-millennials-make-purchase-decisions-infographic.

75   Anja Jeftovic, "130+ Sales Statistics to Guide You This Year | TaskDrive," accessed December 22, 2023, https://taskdrive.com/sales/sales-statistics/.

76   Kenneth H. Blanchard and Spencer Johnson, *The One Minute Manager* (New York, NY: William Morrow, 1982), 39-40.

77   "Leverage (Finance)," in *Wikipedia*, September 30, 2023, https://en.wikipedia.org/w/index.php?title=Leverage_(finance)&oldid=1177878280.leverage (or gearing in the United Kingdom and Australia

78   "Is It Really a Good Compromise When Both Parties Are Dissatisfied?" Cornell Course Blog, September 20, 2022. Accessed December 22, 2023, https://blogs.cornell.edu/info2040/2022/09/20/is-it-really-a-good-compromise-when-both-parties-are-dissatisfied/.

79   "How Do You Use the BATNA Concept to Strengthen Your Negotiation Position?," June 07, 2023. accessed December 22, 2023, https://www.linkedin.com/advice/3/how-do-you-use-batna-concept-strengthen-your-negotiation.

80   P. O. N. Staff, "BATNA Basics: Boost Your Power at the Bargaining Table," PON - Program on Negotiation at Harvard Law School, April 19, 2015, https://www.pon.harvard.edu/freemium/batna-basics-boost-your-power-at-the-bargaining-table/.

81   Gallup Inc, "Why Great Managers Are So Rare," Gallup.com, March 25, 2014, https://www.gallup.com/workplace/231593/why-great-managers-rare.aspx.

82   Kolmar, "100+ Important Sales Statistics [2023]: Figures, Salaries, and Statistics."

83   Tommy Mello, "How I Fired My Top Sales Performer and Saw Profits Soar | Inc.com," October 17, 2023, accessed December 22, 2023, https://www.inc.com/tommy-mello/how-i-fired-my-top-sales-performer-saw-profits-soar.html.

84   Ibid.

85   John Hunter, "Eliminate Sales Commissions: Reject Theory X Management and Embrace Systems Thinking - The W. Edwards Deming Institute," November 01,2012, accessed December 22, 2023, https://deming.org/eliminate-sales-commissions-reject-theory-x-management-and-embrace-systems-thinking/.

86   Ibid.

87   Ben Horowitz, "Why Must You Pay Sales People Commissions?" Andreessen Horowitz, April 16, 2023, https://a16z.com/2017/09/11/sales-commissions/.

88   Melissa Dittmann Tracey, "Introverts vs. Extroverts: Who's Really Better at Sales?," www.nar.realtor, December 12, 2018, https://www.nar.realtor/magazine/real-estate-news/sales-marketing/introverts-vs-extroverts-who-s-really.

89   Derek Gatehouse, *The Perfect Salesforce: The 6 Best Practices of the World's Best Sales Teams* (New York, NY: Portfolio, 2007), 57.

90   Ibid., p. 70.

91   Andris A. Zoltners, Prabhakant Sinha and Sally E. Lorimer. "Match Your Sales Force Structure to Your Business Life Cycle," HBR's 10 Must Reads On Sales. 2017, p. 52

92   Julia McClatchy, Candace Lun Plotkin, Karolina Sau-
     er-Sidor, Jennifer Stanley, and Kevin Wei Wang "The Multiplier
     Effect: How B2B Winners Grow | McKinsey," April 13,
     2023, accessed December 22, 2023, https://www.mckinsey.
     com/capabilities/growth-marketing-and-sales/our-insights/
     the-multiplier-effect-how-b2b-winners-grow.

93   "State of Sales Enablement 2021," Sales Enablement PRO,
     accessed December 5, 2023, https://salesenablement.pro/
     assets/2021/05/2021-State-of-SE-Report_SE-PRO.pdf, 9.

94   "Forbes Insights: The Power of Enablement." https://images.
     forbes.com/forbesinsights/StudyPDFs/Brainshark-ThePowero-
     fEnablement-REPORT.pdf

95   "What Is Sales Enablement? The CSO's Ultimate Guide."
     Gartner, accessed December 22, 2023, https://www.gartner.com/
     en/sales/topics/sales-enablement.

96   Ibid.

97   "Gartner Expects Sales Enablement Budgets to Increase by
     50% by 2027," February 15, 2023, Gartner, accessed December
     22, 2023, https://www.gartner.com/en/newsroom/press-releas-
     es/2023-02-15-gartner-expects-sales-enablement-budgets-to-
     increase-by-50-percent-by-2027.

98   Ibid.

99   "Forbes Insights: The Power of Enablement."

100 "CSO Insights 5th Annual Sales Enablement Study - 2019
     Sales Enablement Report," accessed December 23, 2023. https://
     salesenablement.pro/assets/2019/10/CSO-Insights-5th-Annual-
     Sales-Enablement-Study.pdf

101 Natalie Beaulieu, "The Seismic 2023 Value of Enablement Report Shows Companies Increasing Enablement Tech Investment in Response to Economic Turbulence," February 15, 2023, Seismic, accessed December 23, 2023. https://learn.seismic.com/rs/217-LXS-149/images/Seismic-2023-Value-of-Enablement-Report_ENG.pdf

102 George Donovan, "Council Post: Six Trends Affecting Sales Enablement In 2022," Forbes, December 16, 2021, accessed December 22, 2023, https://www.forbes.com/sites/forbesbusinessdevelopmentcouncil/2021/12/16/six-trends-affecting-sales-enablement-in-2022/.

103 Alex Hisaka, "Why Best in Class Sales Enablement Is a Necessity," June 06, 2017, accessed December 23, 2023, https://www.linkedin.com/business/sales/blog/sales-enablement/why-best-in-class-sales-enablement-is-a-necessity.

104 Natalie Beaulieu, "The Seismic 2023 Value of Enablement Report Shows Companies Increasing Enablement Tech Investment in Response to Economic Turbulence."

105 Krogue, "Why Sales Reps Spend Less Than 36% Of Time Selling (And Less Than 18% In CRM)."

106 "Sales Enablement Analytics Report 2022–2023," Highspot, accessed December 4, 2023, https://engage.highspot.com/viewer/63ebc5b26541a7f979683a6c.

107 "Unleashing the Full Potential of AI," Accenture, accessed December 5, 2023, https://www.accenture.com/content/dam/accenture/final/capabilities/strategy-and-consulting/supply-chain---operations/document/Accenture-Supply-Chain-Generative-AI-New-Tech-New-Jobs-New-Value.pdf.

108   Avijeet Biswal, "Top 18 Artificial Intelligence (AI) Applications in 2024." Simplilearn.com, accessed December 22, 2023, https://www.simplilearn.com/tutorials/artificial-intelligence-tutorial/artificial-intelligence-applications.

109   Gopal Srinivasan, Rohan Gupta, Nitin Mittal, Rich Nanda, Costi Perricos, Kellie Nuttal, "Generative Artificial Intelligence," Deloitte United States, accessed December 23, 2023, https://www2.deloitte.com/us/en/pages/consulting/articles/generative-artificial-intelligence.html.

110   Alyssa Lukpat, "Bill Gates Says AI Is the Most Revolutionary Technology in Decades - WSJ," March 22, 2023, accessed December 22, 2023, https://www.wsj.com/articles/bill-gates-says-artificial-intelligence-is-the-most-revolutionary-technology-in-decades-75fb8562.

111   Ibid.

112   "A New Frontier in Artificial Intelligence: Implications of Generative AI for Businesses," Deloitte, accessed December 5, 2023, https://www2.deloitte.com/content/dam/Deloitte/us/Documents/deloitte-analytics/us-ai-institute-ai-dossier-full-report.pdf.

113   Katharine Mangu-Ward, "Marc Andreessen On Artificial Intelligence And The Future," *Reason*, June 2023, 49-50.

114   Ibid, p. 50.

115   Michael Neiberg, "Michael Neiberg on Linkedin: #AI: 14 Comments," LinkedIn, February 17, 2024, https://www.linkedin.com/posts/michaelneiberg_ai-activity-7164632181636599808-jVl1?utm_source=share&utm_medium=member_desktop.

116 "ChatGPT," accessed December 23, 2023, https://chat.openai.com.

117 "Trends in Generative AI for Sales Report," Salesforce, accessed December 23, 2023, https://www.salesforce.com/ap/form/pdf/trends-in-generative-ai-report/.

118 Cem Dilmegani, "AI in Sales: 15 AI Sales Applications/ Use Cases in 2022," May 09, 2023, accessed December 22, 2023, https://research.aimultiple.com/sales-ai/.

119 Molly Bohannon, "Pope Warns Artificial Intelligence Could 'Fuel Conflicts And Antagonism,'" Forbes, August 08, 2023, accessed December 22, 2023, https://www.forbes.com/sites/mollybohannon/2023/08/08/pope-warns-artificial-intelligence-could-fuel-conflicts-and-antagonism/.

120 Ibid.

121 Ronald Bailey, "Don't 'pause' A.I. Research," *Reason.com* (blog), June 22, 2023. https://reason.com/2023/06/22/dont-pause-a-i-research/.

122 Ibid.

123 "Artificial Intelligence Experts Call for Development Pause." The Wall Street Journal, March 30, 2023. Accessed December 22, 2023, https://www.wsj.com/podcasts/google-news-update/artificial-intelligence-experts-call-for-development-pause/c8778e96-b8ba-4115-972c-5f487ae70608?mod=error_page.

124 "Pause Giant AI Experiments: An Open Letter," *Future of Life Institute* (blog), March 22, 2023, accessed December 22, 2023, https://futureoflife.org/open-letter/pause-giant-ai-experiments/.

125 Zoe Kleinman and Chris Valance, "AI 'Godfather' Geoffrey Hinton Warns of Dangers as He Quits Google." BBC News, May 02, 2023, accessed December 22, 2023, https://www.bbc.com/news/world-us-canada-65452940.

126 David Meerman Scott, "Super Simple Way to Under-
     stand Artificial Intelligence," May 03, 2023, accessed
     December 22, 2023, https://www.linkedin.com/pulse/
     super-simple-way-understand-artificial-intelligence-scott.

127 Peggy Noonan, "A Six-Month AI Pause? No, Longer Is
     Needed." The Wall Street Journal, March 30, 2023, accessed
     December 22, 2023, https://www.wsj.com/articles/a-six-month-
     ai-pause-no-longer-is-needed-civilization-danger-chat-gpt-
     chatbot-internet-big-tech-4b66da6e.

128 Bailey, "Don't 'pause' A.I. Research."

129 Mario Livio, "When Galileo Stood Trial for Defending Sci-
     ence," History, May 19, 2020, https://www.history.com/news/
     galileo-copernicus-earth-sun-heresy-church.

130 "Technology Innovation Services," accessed December
     22, 2023, https://www.accenture.com/ar-es/services/
     technology-innovation-index.

131 Attributed to Buddha.

132 Alex Hales, "Stay Away From Negative People - Albert Einstein
     Quotes," February 13, 2019, https://themindsjournal.com/
     quotes/stay-away-from-negative-people/.

133 Jessa Pangilinan, "101 Toxic People Quotes to Stay Away From
     Negativity," Happier Human, September 7, 2023, http://www.
     happierhuman.com/toxic-people-quotes.

134 "Who Is Erin Carter? S01e05 - Episode 5 - Transcripts,"
     TV Show Transcripts, accessed December 3, 2023, https://
     tvshowtranscripts.ourboard.org/viewtopic.php?t=64947.

135 Isaac Oben, "Stabbed by Best Friend," November 24, 2021,
     accessed December 22, 2023, https://www.linkedin.com/pulse/
     stabbed-best-friend-oben-ai.

136 Marcel Schwantes, "Warren Buffett Says He Lives by 3 Leadership Rules for Success," Inc.com, November 20, 2023, https://www.inc.com/marcel-schwantes/warren-buffett-says-he-lives-by-3-leadership-rules-for-success.html.

137 Kolmar, "100+ Important Sales Statistics [2023]: Figures, Salaries, and Statistics."

138 Power of Positivity, "Science Proves That Negativity Is Toxic (and How to Boost Positivity)," *Power of Positivity: Positive Thinking & Attitude* (blog), September 8, 2020, https://www.powerofpositivity.com/negativity-is-toxic-boost-positivity/.

139 Zig Ziglar, Facebook, October 31, 2012, https://www.facebook.com/ZigZiglar/posts/10151226935492863:0.

140 Liz Ferron LICSW MSW, "Emotional Well Being Definition," accessed December 22, 2023, https://insights.vitalworklife.com/blog/2016/01/02/wheel-of-well-being-emotional-dimension-definition.

141 Rich Campbell, "What Did 1985 Chicago Bears Do with Their Super Bowl Rings?," January 27, 2020, accessed December 22, 2023, https://www.chicagotribune.com/sports/bears/ct-cb-chicago-bears-1985-super-bowl-ring-20200127-ir-37jedl2zf2nmfqfesu6jjfha-story.html.

142 Bill Murphy Jr., "Want to Live 20 Years Longer? A Massive New Study of 719,147 People Says Follow These 8 Habits." Inc.com, August 06, 2023. Accessed December 22, 2023, https://www.inc.com/bill-murphy-jr/want-to-live-20-years-longer-a-massive-new-study-of-719147-people-says-follow-these-8-habits.html.

143 Karina Monesson, "Why Are Women More Stressed Out Than Men?" UKG, February 14, 2023, https://www.ukg.com/blog/life-work-trends/why-are-women-more-stressed-out-men. there are five significant steps employers can take to help ease pressures on women with the aim of providing more equity and support for everyone.","language":"en","title":"Why Are Women More Stressed Out Than Men? | UKG","title-short":"Why Are Women More Stressed Out Than Men?","URL":"https://www.ukg.com/blog/life-work-trends/why-are-women-more-stressed-out-men","accessed":{"date-parts":[["2023",12,22]]},"issued":{"date-parts":[["2023",2,14]]}}}],"schema":"https://github.com/citation-style-language/schema/raw/master/csl-citation.json"}

144 Ibid.

145 "From 'Thank You' to Thriving: A Deeper Look at How Recognition Amplifies Wellbeing (EMEA)," Workhuman.com, May 18, 2023, https://www.workhuman.com/resources/reports-guides/from-thank-you-to-thriving-workhuman-gallup-report-emea.

146 "Adult Data 2022," Mental Health America, accessed December 4, 2023, https://www.mhanational.org/issues/2022/mental-health-america-adult-data.

147 Amy Nakamura, "'Leadership Is Solving Problems': General Colin Powell's Rules for Leadership and More," USA TODAY, October 18, 2021, accessed December 22, 2023, https://www.usatoday.com/story/news/politics/2021/10/18/general-colin-powells-famous-rules-and-quotes-leadership/8512414002/.

148 Jeftovic, "130+ Sales Statistics to Guide You This Year."

149 "Forbes Insights: The Power of Enablement," 13.

150   Beverlie Heyman, "Why Sales Coaching Matters, Plus 5 Ways to Get Started," Brainshark, July 5, 2023, https://www.brain-shark.com/ideas-blog/top-coaching-tips-for-sales-managers/.

151   Leon Stafford, "Atlanta Technology Giant John P. Imlay Jr. Dies," The Atlanta Journal-Constitution, March 26, 2015, https://www.ajc.com/business/atlanta-technology-giant-john-imlay-dies/ I6PhhVRShdEcSUTUT4y13M.